D0127949

"The real work begins after a film is made. The
ing potentially tough truths with an encouraging
any 'how to make it in filmmaking' guide, with the added value of such resources
as screening room listings, a comprehensive list of international film festivals and
websites, and commonly used forms."
— *Library Journal*, February 2012

"Finally! A straight-shooting guide to the film festival circuit. Skerbelis' and Edwards'
research pays off in this comprehensive guide to navigating your film through
markets and festivals. Whether you're heading for Sundance or SilverDocs, this is a
must-have for the indie filmmaker."
— Tony Safford, Executive Vice President, World-Wide Acquisitions,
20th Century Fox

"A thorough and accessible guide to how to make the most of your film festival experi-
ence, especially if you are a first-timer trying to crack the code."
— Pamela Koffler, Killer Films,
Executive Producer – *Mildred Pierce* & *Boys Don't Cry*

"...an essential guide for any filmmaker attempting to navigate the complexities of
international film festivals..."
— Elliot Grove, founder Raindance Film Festival, British Independent Film Awards

"Rona and Monika have done an excellent job encapsulating their careers as both
festival organizers and filmmakers to present a pathway for new artists to participate
in the film festival world. Their book should be an important resource for any festival
goer looking to better understand the history and opportunity of festivals around the
world."
— David Straus, Co-Founder of Withoutabox

"*The Complete Filmmaker's Guide to Film Festivals* is a remarkable resource for
emerging filmmakers just starting their festival submission process. With so many
film festivals and markets worldwide, this is an essential guide to help navigate the
various steps of the festival circuit"
— Rena Ronson, Co-Head, UTA Independent Film Group

"This book is an amazing resource — a comprehensive, user-friendly guide to the
before, *during*, and *after* of film festivals. It's like an all-access pass for filmmakers
looking to jump-start their careers."
— Howard Cohen & Eric d'Arbeloff, Co-Presidents of Roadside Attractions

"A must-read book for anyone wanting to understand the film festival circuit."
— Kirk D'Amico, President & CEO, Myriad Pictures;
Executive Producer – *Margin Call* & *The Good Girl*

"Pack your bags and grab your essential guide to maneuvering film festivals! *The Complete Filmmaker's Guide to Film Festivals* is a must-read toolkit for both new and veteran filmmakers embarking on the often bumpy film festival journey. The only complete roadmap you'll ever need to guide you through the complicated twists and turns of festival entry rules, marketing and promotion, distribution and what you to do when you show up! It will be your constant companion."
— Nana Greenwald, Executive Producer – *North Country*

"*The Complete Filmmaker's Guide to Film Festivals* is a detailed, easy to digest reference that opens up the whole universe of film festivals to the reader. It is essential for the film student who is about to embark on their first film. Edwards and Skerbelis elegantly guide the neophyte through the minefield of which film festival to enter, how to enter and finally how to sell your film."
— Gillian Gordon, Chair, MFA International Media Producing,
   Tisch Asia, New York University

"Learn the dos and don'ts of launching your film on the festival circuit with Edwards and Skerbelis as your personal guide."
— Zanne Devine, Producer – *Easy A;* Executive Producer – *Cinema Verite*

"You want to get your film in front of an audience, sure, but more importantly you want the right audience — be it fans, buyers or producers. Rona Edwards & Monika Skerbelis have turned the business of film into an art form, outlining the proper strategies that will get your film not just seen, but noticed, on the festival circuit and beyond."
— Robert Grant, SCI-FI-LONDON Film Festival

"*The Complete Filmmaker's Guide to Film Festivals* pulls off quite a trick: it's both an invaluable primer for newcomers and a great refresher for veterans. Required reading for all levels of festival expertise!"
— Julian Higgins, Writer/Director – *Thief,*
   winner of the Student Academy Award and College Television Awards

"Rona Edwards & Monika Skerbelis have pooled their extensive insider knowledge to create an invaluable resource for filmmakers who too often launch themselves into the festival world without a reliable map. Short filmmakers in particular will find this guide invaluable as the authors have gone out of their way to include extremely helpful information specifically tailored for them."
— Kim Adelman, author of *Making It Big in Shorts*

"A must read for any serious filmmaker embarking on the festival path. It's like getting a front row seat and a degree in film festivals from industry pros who guide your every step."
— Julie Sisk, Director, The American Pavilion

"Traversing the thousands of film festivals held annually all over the world is a challenge faced by most filmmakers. With *The Complete Filmmaker's Guide to Film Festivals* in hand you are superbly equipped for this journey. Edwards & Skerbelis, who led us previously through the thickets of development in their book, *I Liked It, Didn't Love It (Screenplay Development from the Inside Out)*, offer here a soup to nuts and back again primer on all you need to know to promote yourself and your film. Enjoyably readable as well as instructive, they provide many useful tips, contacts, charts and checklists to enable you to do the best for your film — at the point when you are most in need of help — when the film is made and you start looking into how to promote it. Thank you Rona and Monika for making my life easier — as I travel the world judging, entering and visiting film festivals I will carry your book as my passport to success."
   — Gabrielle Kelly, Film Festival Judge/Programmer, Associate Arts;
      Professor, NYU Film School Tisch Asia

"Edwards and Skerbelis have done it again. Their first book, *I Liked It, Didn't Love It*, took the lid off the development process in Hollywood. Now they bring us their unique expertise and a crash course on navigating the byzantine film festival world. This comprehensive guide is a must have if you're serious about launching your film or your career on the festival circuit."
   — Cari-Esta Albert, Producer, *The Truth About Cats & Dogs*

"When I was a student filmmaker, no one shared with us how to submit our films to film festivals or what to do with our short films. This book is a brilliant masterpiece that contains information for filmmakers and producers who want to know where or how to submit their films to festivals. Highly recommended for all budding and aspiring filmmakers."
   — Sharon Loh, cinematographer – *Sandcastle*
      (official selection International Critics' Week Cannes Film Festival)

"The film festival world can be a confusing mess for new and experienced filmmakers alike. There is a large gap between the myth and reality of the film festival experience. Although it can be rewarding, the process can also be overwhelming. *The Complete Filmmakers Guide to Film Festivals* is a fantastic tool for navigating the labyrinth."
   — Doron Kipper, Writer/Director – Award-winning film, *Misdirection* (3rd Place, Drama – College Television Awards from the Academy of Television Arts & Sciences Foundation and Official Selection @ over 20 Film Festivals)

"Whether you're a seasoned veteran or just starting out, *The Complete Filmmaker's Guide to Film Festivals* will help you every step of the way — from pre-production to that potential big sale at Sundance."
   — John Halecky, Director – *Fish & Chip*; Film Festival Panelist/Juror

"Want to get the most out of a film festival? Edwards and Skerbelis offer insight on how best to maneuver the festival circuit."

— Rosanne Korenberg, Entertainment Attorney, Producer – *Half Nelson*;
Executive Producer – *Hard Candy*

"Rona Edwards and Monika Skerbelis are amongst a rare breed of industry veterans who care to take the time to educate and assist emerging filmmakers in what is an often times daunting, frustrating, and complex business. In *The Complete Filmmakers Guide to Film Festivals*, they once again come to the rescue of the first-time filmmaker, thoughtfully guiding them through the myriad of decisions and requirements with which they will be faced as they navigate the ever-growing, ever-expanding film festival circuit. It is not only a complete guide to film festivals, it is the go-to guide to film festivals, and how to use film festivals to launch a career. It should be on every film school's reading list, no question."

— Harrison Reiner, Producer/Co-writer – *Amar a morir*, winner of the Best Spanish Language Film Award at the Santa Barbara International Film Festival,
co-founder – the Writers Institute for Diversity in L.A.

"Not only do they give you the ins-and-outs of film festivals, Edwards' and Skerbelis' inclusion of multiple resources makes this book invaluable for anyone looking to do the festival circuit."

— Matthew Terry, filmmaker/screenwriter/teacher/columnist

"This is a useful analysis of film festivals, told simply and straight to the point. I especially liked the history of the festivals, something I had not read before!"

— Sydney J. Levine, SydneysBuzz Indiewire Blog Network

"Having taught at many film festivals, I'm aware of the hurdles filmmakers face once their project is 'in the can.' If you are one of those filmmakers, I've found the perfect book to help you face those challenges — *The Complete Filmmaker's Guide To Film Festivals*. Seasoned pros, Rona Edwards and Monika Skerbelis take you by the hand and guide you through the festival process, giving you valuable tips and advice on such subjects as selecting the right festival for your project, the submission process, navigating the various film markets, making the most of your festival, and keeping your dream alive! To make things even better, they've done some of the homework for you by including interviews with festival insiders and providing resource listings!"

— Kathie Fong Yoneda, script consultant, workshop leader,
author of *The Script-Selling Game: A Hollywood Insider's Look At Getting Your Script Sold and Produced*

The Complete Filmmaker's Guide To

film

FESTIVALS

YOUR ALL ACCESS

PASS

To Launching Your Film On The Festival Circuit

Rona Edwards & Monika Skerbelis

MICHAEL WIESE PRODUCTIONS

Published by Michael Wiese Productions
12400 Ventura Blvd. #1111
Studio City, CA 91604
(818) 379-8799, (818) 986-3408 (FAX)
mw@mwp.com
www.mwp.com

Cover design by MWP
Cartoon illustrations by Steve Tatham.
Photos courtesy of Pula Film Festival, Walter Harris, Mary Jo Godges, Renee Sotile, Kim Noonan. Unless otherwise indicated, photos are by Monika Skerbelis and Rona Edwards.

Printed by McNaughton & Gunn

Manufactured in the United States of America
Copyright © 2012 by Rona Edwards and Monika Skerbelis

Library of Congress Cataloging-in-Publication Data

Edwards, Rona
 The complete filmmaker's guide to film festivals : your all access pass to launching your film on the festival circuit / Rona Edwards, Monika Skerbelis.
     p. cm.
 Includes bibliographical references.
 ISBN 978-1-61593-088-3
1. Film festivals. 2. Motion pictures--Marketing. 3. Motion pictures--Distribution. 4. Made-for-TV movies--Marketing. 5. Made-for-TV movies. 6. Film festivals--Directories. I. Skerbelis, Monika- II. Title. III. Title: Guide to film festivals.
 PN1993.4.E39 2012
 384'.806--dc23
                          2012003000

TABLE OF CONTENTS

"Work begins after the film is made!"

A BRIEF HISTORY OF FILM FESTIVALS

"Before there was Sundance, there was Venice..."

- What is a Film Festival?
- How Film Festivals started and their function today
- Who runs a Film Festival?

DOING THE RESEARCH

"Someone's got to be analytical even if you are the creative type!"

- Researching and Targeting Film Festivals
- Top Tier Film Festivals
- Short Films and student filmmakers
- Niche festivals & sidebars
- The Oscar: Academy qualifying film festivals & Student Academy Awards
- Financial Considerations
- Screenwriting competitions at festivals

SUBMITTING TO FILM FESTIVALS

"Target Shooting"

- Importance of a logline, genre and hook
- Determining the audience for your film
- Clearances & Releases
- Submission Process: Entry forms
- The Programming Director & Film Screeners
- Duplication formats

ACKNOWLEDGMENTS

We wish to thank all the industry pros who sat down to answer our questions about their film festival experiences and insights into what filmmakers should be aware of as they embark on the festival circuit: Howard Cohen, Eric d'Arbeloff, Kirk D'Amico, Pamela Rosenberg, Tony Safford, Harris Tulchin, and Laurie Woodrow. Thanks also to the filmmakers who shared their experiences with their very candid answers: Jay Duplass, Mark Duplass, Rosanne Korenberg, Mary Jo Godges, Renee Sotile, Lorette Bayle, Jen McGowan, and Beth McElhenny.

Our deepest gratitude goes out to Michael Wiese and Ken Lee for their support and vision taking on this book to publish. Thanks to our copyeditor Matt Barber, for keeping us grammatically correct. We want to thank Steve Tatham for creating those wonderfully humorous illustrations for each chapter's heading in lickety-split time. A big thank you goes out to Jeff Black, our knight in shining armor who found us Steve and has been an amazing sounding board of support and a great friend over the years.

Monika would like to personally thank Rosanne Korenberg and Zanne Devine for exposing her to the film festival world while they were at Universal Pictures as studio executives attending the Sundance Film Festival back in 1991, and in subsequent years. She thanks the Big Bear Lake International Film Festival in Big Bear Lake, California, for bringing her on board, programming films since its inception, and Sandy Steers who she now shares the co-presidency with for keeping her sane.

She thanks her American Pavilion colleagues, Walter Harris, the director of the student programs, Lynne Howard, managing director, and Julie Sisk, who founded The American Pavilion and the student internship program, for hiring her as the director of the Emerging Filmmaker Showcase at the Cannes Film Festival.

Heartfelt gratitude goes out to Tina Miller for her support and for tolerating hundreds of DVDs laying around the house waiting to be watched, and thanks to her family for understanding why she even watches so many films. Thanks to pals, Cari-Esta Albert, Elizabeth Hunter, and Jacqueline Carlson for all their festival support. And to Rona Edwards for her continued friendship, support, business partnership, and sharing many festival moments together in the past and in the coming years.

Rona would like to thank all the filmmakers she's met at the many film festivals over the years who have given her a bird's eye view of the festival experience. A big thank you to film directors Meredith Ralston and Eric Williams, who made her a part of their award-winning films that rode the festival circuit to victory with those coveted prizes, and to the many students she's taught over the years; she wants them to know she's learned just as much from them as they have from her. To all the panelists she's had the pleasure to moderate at the many festivals she's been invited to over the years, she can't thank them enough for being so open and sharing their wealth of knowledge with all the emerging and seasoned filmmakers attending these panels, workshops, and sessions. She'd like to dedicate the book to her late mother and father, Edward and Ruth Goldstein, who always encouraged her life in the entertainment industry. To her "sister and brother," Susan and Alvin Bornstein, she can't thank them enough for all their support, good food, and company; and just being there when she needs them most. To Anne Beatts for being a great roommate at the Big Bear Lake

International Film Festival every year and Nana Greenwald for her continuing encouragement. To Jude Garrison, for always being my angel of support. And last but certainly not least, to Monika Skerbelis, a big thank you for being a true friend, colleague, and business partner, without whom this book would not have come to fruition.

Rona and Monika have been invited to many film festivals as guest speakers and panelists after their first book, the critically acclaimed *I Liked It, Didn't Love It: Screenplay Development From The Inside Out* was published. They want to thank those festivals that have invited them to share their knowledge and network with rising as well as experienced filmmakers. And to all the future film festivals, film markets, and emerging filmmakers showcases still to come, we've got our lanyards and we're ready to network, watch movies, and share our ever-evolving wisdom.

INTRODUCTION

"Work begins after the film is made!"

HOW MANY TIMES HAVE YOU gone to a film festival and it's been a whirlwind of overwhelming choices? Should you go to the filmmaking panels and seminars, or just watch films? And if so, which films? Feature films, documentaries, short films, animated films?

If you're a filmmaker who is screening a film, it is even more overwhelming. Not only do you need to prepare your film for its presentation, you need to publicize it. So, where do you start? How do you begin? You can't just show your film and be done with it. You need to network, promote, and try to create *heat* so that the industry insiders attending the festival will take notice. And, just possibly, your film and your work will lead you to the next step in your career — a job in Hollywood writing, directing, producing or starring in a studio-financed film. Or your aim might be getting the financing for your next indie film about your dysfunctional family's idiosyncrasies. Isn't that your ultimate goal?

No more raising the money yourself or using your credit cards to make a film. No more mom and dad lending you their house to shoot in for five days, turning their lives upside down. No more mom preparing lunches for the crew. A film festival can be your ticket to financial independence or, at the very least, to get others to believe and invest in your talents — but you have to know how to infiltrate the circuit so that you and your film get noticed.

The Complete Filmmaker's Guide to Film Festivals will help you prepare for the multitude of film festivals to which you've already submitted your film or target the ones you're about to submit to, so you don't make the mistakes countless filmmakers make, especially at their first film festival. Not having a strategy! On numerous occasions, filmmakers who discover our online film festival course, Maneuvering Film Festivals, stated they wished they had taken it before they embarked on the film festival circuit. Some take the course anyway and find they are accepted into more festivals, and some even win awards, because of the invaluable information in that course. And now, we've included this useful information, and more, into one cohesive volume, based upon our experiences attending, creating, programming, and judging film festivals over the past 12+ years.

In order to know what you should and shouldn't do, and what you should do first, you need to understand the basics. *The Complete Filmmaker's Guide to Film Festivals* is chock full of resources, providing filmmakers with exercises, illustrations, sample forms and formats to use in order to help ease the way and prepare seasoned veterans as well as up-and-coming filmmakers for the ultimate film festival experience.

Most films at film festivals are what we call independent films, in that they are financed by individuals, smaller production companies, credit cards, family and friends, all with the hope of getting a distribution deal and notoriety at some of the major film festivals. But with such intense competition, filmmakers shouldn't be discouraged if they don't get accepted into the highly publicized festivals. Don't count out some of the smaller, more niche-oriented ones because, as you will discover throughout this book, some of those festivals have given more than one filmmaker a kick-start to their career. We will give you the tools to discern which festivals may be right for your film and how to make the most out of the fast-paced, adrenaline rush of the occasion.

Most filmmakers think the hard part is making the film. However, after the film is made, there's much more work to be done. The real work begins after the film is in the can. And while you may be exhausted, take a short vacation and then start laying out the groundwork for the festival circuit. A film is no good if no one sees it. And you can't rely on someone seeking *you* out. You have to create the buzz, and film festivals offer a great opportunity to do just that.

While your initial goal is to get your film distributed, there are other opportunities for a filmmaker such as yourself to gain some traction for other facets of your career. So what are some of those goals needed to have a successful festival experience?

- Acceptance into the festival.
- Promoting your film.
- Win festival awards.
- Getting distribution for your film.
- Making industry contacts.
- Promoting your next film.
- Promoting your career.

- Promoting your film company.
- Follow up with relationships.

You, as part of the creative team behind the film (the director, writer, actor and/or producer) need to strategize on the best festivals suited to the film and prepare the appropriate promotional materials as soon as the film is completed, if not sooner. You will either be faced with hiring a press agent or doing your own press. In addition, you'll want to make sure there's an audience to see your film. Lastly, you'll need to make the most out of the networking opportunities that most film festivals offer and learn to not only promote your film, but yourself as well.

But to do this takes planning — and a bit of money. Filmmakers usually don't think about this aspect until their film is done, and that is a huge mistake. But *you* should be thinking about the next step while you're making the film. *You* should be including a film festival line item in your budget that will help defray the costs and not surprise you later on with how expensive film festivals can get.

Today, with a film festival in just about every city, a filmmaker can go broke with the submission entry fees, not to mention the costs involved in attending the festivals. Doing research on the various festivals to understand the type of films they screen and recognizing your own film's niche possibilities will help you determine which festivals are right for you up front so that you'll be able to include the costs in your film festival budget.

Top film festivals like Sundance, Cannes, Toronto, Berlin, and Venice can help a lower-budget film gain exposure and even win awards. Take the small Irish musical *Once*. It was shot in three weeks and made for less than $150,000, yet it earned a spot on the Sundance Film Festival schedule and won the World Cinema Audience Award. The filmmakers struck a deal with Fox Searchlight for North American rights. The stars, Glen Hansard and Marketa Irglova, went on to win the "Best Original Song" Oscar at the 2008 Academy Awards for their song, "Falling Slowly." The film was also named "Best Foreign Film" at the Independent Spirit Awards. This is a prime example of "the little engine that could." Who would have thought a small film like *Once*, shot on a very low budget, would make the splash it did — and it's not the only example we can give you. So we say, why not *your* film? If the end product is good, it will garner attention, but it's up to you to do the legwork, and make sure it gets noticed. Studios and production companies are always hungry to discover a fresh new voice. And they have been known to discover talent at film festivals.

Each year thousands of independent films earn coveted spots in top festival schedules with the hope of securing a distribution deal, but approximately 200–250 are acquired and make it to the local movie theatre. Some are sold Direct-to-DVD while short films might make their way to cable stations, mobile content, the Internet, and compilation DVDs. There are many ways to skin a cat, so think creatively and target the right companies for your film and know your marketplace. We'll give you some information in later chapters on the many possibilities that are out there for indie film distribution.

A LITTLE ABOUT US

Monika has worked the festival circuit for many years. While she was an executive at Universal Pictures, she attended the Sundance Film Festival to watch short films and scout new talent to bring to the motion picture creative group's attention. In addition, she attended many of the film schools' short film programs, met new filmmakers, and helped to discover emerging talent, some of whom have successful careers today.

Since 2000, Monika has been programming films for the Big Bear Lake International Film Festival in addition to helping turn a mom and pop festival into an important event. As the Artistic & Programming Director, she has met many filmmakers from around the world and introduced them to the appropriate industry insiders. As Programming Director for the American Pavilion Student Programs' Emerging Filmmaker Showcase at the Cannes Film Festival, she oversees a program of short films that screen during the festival at the American Pavilion. In addition, she had her own short film screened at the Cannes Film Festival's Short Film Corner.

Rona has been on panels and on juries of numerous film festivals around the world. She's had two of her own films exhibited at various festivals where they won awards. She has produced numerous films in her own right and has worked as a development executive in both television and feature film.

Witnessing firsthand, she has seen the films that receive buzz and the filmmakers who make their own buzz.

It's fascinating to see how filmmakers market themselves. It's a skill that has to be learned — but if you have the product to back up your promotion, and you have the where-withal to persist and take advantage of all the opportunities afforded you at these events, you most assuredly will succeed at landing the right company for your film, and elevate your career in the process.

The Complete Filmmaker's Guide to Film Festivals is intended to help support your dream and your vision in a pragmatic yet creative way. It offers concrete suggestions on how to promote your project and get it noticed amidst all the other films vying for the same attention. Sometimes there's no explanation as to why one film gets noticed over another, but one thing is for sure, aside from whether the film succeeds as a film, it is the promotional strategy behind the film that could determine the filmmaker's success at a festival and each festival thereafter.

We hope that, in reading *The Complete Filmmaker's Guide to Film Festivals*, filmmakers will be inspired and confident to start their festival trek, armed with the knowledge, tools, and support necessary to elevate and screen their work in front of appreciative audiences. There's nothing like view-ing a film with an enthusiastic crowd of people who are there for the love of cinema. If you follow these steps, you will most assuredly have a rewarding and fulfilling experience, knowing you have done the hard work and now can reap the benefits.

Rona Edwards
Monika Skerbelis
Los Angeles, CA

A BRIEF HISTORY OF FILM FESTIVALS

"Before there was Sundance, there was Venice..."

HOW FILM FESTIVALS STARTED AND THEIR FUNCTION TODAY

TODAY, THERE ARE THOUSANDS OF film festivals worldwide that allow filmmakers a chance to exhibit their films to audiences of diverse cultures and countries. There is not much written about the history of film festivals and how they evolved into yearly *must see* events. While there have been books and publications that specifically list festivals around the world, no one has explained why they came to be. In the early days of film, it was all about how to exhibit this new art form to the public. Movie theatres were born and audiences flocked to the darkened halls, sitting with a bunch of strangers, all having a shared experience of watching a film. Whether it was a prize fight, the funeral of an assassinated president, or a ballerina dancing, the world became fascinated with this celluloid medium right from the beginning. It took 30+ years before film festivals would take hold. It was the early 1930s when the first film festival was established. But film clubs and societies had been cropping up in the 1920s in major metropolitan cities in Europe, South America, and North America. The clubs offered a way for filmmakers and cinephiles to showcase films while sharing and discussing ideas. The London Film Society was one of the first film clubs formed in 1925 to screen films that were banned from many European theatres due to political content. With such founding members as author H.G. Wells and playwright George Bernard Shaw, the group would discuss filmmaking and current trends and issues. The next logical step after film societies was to showcase films as part of a "curated" program over a number of consecutive days.

Film festivals, as we know them today, initiated in Europe and have spun out to nearly every corner of the world. And though we'll be discussing some of these festivals at length in other chapters, it is important to note their history and how they began.

EUROPE PAVES THE WAY

The first recognized film festival was the Venice Film Festival in Italy. On the evening of August 6, 1932, Rouben Mamoulian's *Dr. Jekyll and Mr. Hyde* opened the festival on the Venice Lido as part of the 18th Venice Biennale, "Esposizione Internazionale d'Arte Cinematografica." The Venice

Venice.

Biennale was formed in 1895 as an organization dedicated to the arts. The Venice Film Festival began with the support of businessman and politician Count Giuseppe Volpi of Misurata, who also presided as the chairman, as a way to promote Italian cinema and tourism under the umbrella of La Biennale. For the first time, a festival presented films from all over the world in one city, where people could gather and view them together. Other films screened at the first legendary festival were *It Happened One Night* by Frank Capra, *Frankenstein* by James Whale, *Zemlja* by Aleksandr Dovzenko, *A Nous La Libertè* by Renè Clair, and *The Champ* by King Vidor. Today, La Biennale continues to support art, cinema, music, theatre, dance, and architecture, and is one of the top-tier film festivals in the world.

By the late '30s and early '40s more festivals began to emerge in Europe. The Moscow International Film Festival, supported by the head of the USSR at the time, Joseph

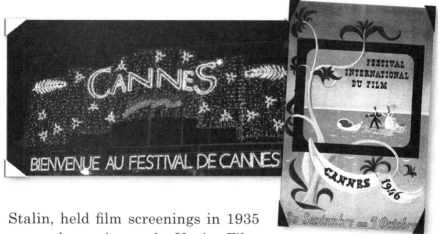

Stalin, held film screenings in 1935 as an alternative to the Venice Film Festival, but it was halted by World War II and then did not become an annual event again until 1959.

France's Festival International du Film, or as it's commonly called the Cannes Film Festival, was first presented in September 1939, and was originally to be presided over by Louis Lumière, one of the early pioneers of cinema and public exhibition, but the festival had to be postponed after the opening night film, *The Hunchback of Notre Dame,* directed by William Dieterle, thanks to the outbreak of World War II the next day. The festival didn't re-emerge until after the war in 1946 but was interrupted again in both 1948 and 1950 due to lack of funds, though it has been continuous ever since. In 1952, it moved to the spring months of May after gossip columnist Elsa Maxwell suggested that, rather than holding it in September after the long summer tourism, they hold the festival in the spring and have the opportunity to screen more films at that time of year before they premiered at other festivals. It quickly became an important postwar cultural event and still attracts to this day major film industry executives, producers, celebrities, and journalists from countries near and far. These days it is considered the biggest film festival in the world.

Other notable post-war film festivals that continue today include the Locarno Film Festival located in the Swiss-Italian mountain town and the Festival Internazionale del Cinema Di Salerno in Italy. In addition, the Karlovy Vary International Film Festival located in the Czech Republic was launched in 1946 but then skipped two years, 1953 and 1955, respectively. Regardless, it is still considered to be one of the oldest and most respected film festivals in the world.

Scotland's Edinburgh International Film Festival, established in 1947, is considered the longest *continuous* running film festival in the world, beating out Venice because the Venice Film Festival ceased during the war from 1943 to 1945.

Regarded as one of the premiere top-tier film festivals, Germany's Berlin International Film Festival (also known as the Berlinale) was formed in 1951 at the suggestion of an American officer, Oscar Martay, who was stationed in Berlin in 1948 to oversee German film producers and their activities post war. In 1950, with money loaned by the American military administration to kick-start the festival, Martay organized a committee consisting of a British counterpart, members of the Berlin senate, and several German producers. The initial festival opened with the film *Rebecca* directed by Alfred Hitchcock and starring Joan Fontaine and Laurence Olivier. Ms. Fontaine was also one of the first actresses to attend as a special festival guest and Martay received a Golden Bear for his efforts.

As festivals started popping up in other regions, so too was the need to distinguish them from each other. The 1950s brought a surge of new film festivals worldwide as organizers took note that these festivals were good for their cities and good for the film business. For example, the Pula Film Festival in Croatia (the former Yugoslavia), inaugurated in 1953, presented the films on an outdoor screen in the Vespasian

Courtesy of Pula Film Festival

Pula Film Festival.

Arena (much like the Coliseum in Rome), and now is considered one of the top open-air festivals, holding 8,000 people.

Festivals started popping up in India, Australia, Spain, Argentina, England, Ireland, Canada and eventually in the U.S. circa 1957.

NORTH AMERICA JUMPS INTO THE FOLD

The Yorkton Film Festival, Canada's first dedicated short film festival, was first held in 1950, way before the renowned top-tier Toronto International Film Festival originated in 1976. Toronto started as the "Festival of Festivals," screening films which won awards from other festivals around the world.

One of the oldest U.S. film festivals is the San Francisco International Film Festival, which has held a continuously competitive film festival since 1957. The first films to screen at San Francisco's festival were Akira Kurosawa's *Throne of Blood* and Satyajit Ray's *Pather Panchali*. There is some argument that states the Columbus International Film Festival, originally called the Columbus Film Festival and Chris Awards located in Columbus, Ohio, is the oldest, but it focused more on education through media, not on foreign or independent narratives. Regardless, they are both considered some of the longest running festivals in the United States. In 1959, Movies on a Shoestring, otherwise known as The Rochester Film Festival, was created and is considered the oldest continuously run short film festival in the United States.

The '60s brought us the Houston International Film & Video Festival (1961), the Ann Arbor Film Festival in Michigan (1963), the Chicago International Film Festival, and the Nashville Film Festival (1967). The New York Film Festival, originally the Film Society of Lincoln Center, took root in 1969.

PAVING THE WAY FOR SUNDANCE

However, the biggest independent film festival and the most popular U.S. festival is, of course, the Sundance Film Festival, presented by actor/ director Robert Redford. Redford created an environment for filmmakers to make independent films true to their heart no matter how difficult the subject matter and without corporate or studio interference. He founded the Sundance Institute as a place for these artists to have their work supported, mentored, and showcased.

Established first as the Utah/U.S. Film Festival in 1978 by the Utah Film Commission as a means to bring more film-makers to Utah, it was founded by Sterling Van Wagenen and Charles Gary Allison with Robert Redford as chair-person. Their goal was to showcase retrospective films and independently made films that coincided with Redford's vision and pet project, the Sundance Institute. The first jury included film editor, Verna Fields; cinematographer and special FX wizard, Linwood Gale Dunn; actress Katherine Ross; indie writer/producer/director Charles E. Sellier, Jr.; director Mark Rydell; and costume designer-turned-producer Anthea Sylbert.

In 1985, the festival was experiencing financial difficul-ties and, so, Redford's Sundance Institute took control of it, renaming the festival a few years later — the Sundance Film Festival. Tony Safford, the former programming director for five festivals at Sundance in its infancy, stated that those beginning days in the late '80s were fraught with struggle as the festival tried to gain sponsors, films, audiences, and recognition. However, there was a certain amount of freedom and excitement in that struggle because it allowed them to try certain things that were fun and innovative. There was a sense of support and community from those who did attend. He added, "The tipping point for us was showing *Sex, Lies, and Videotape.* That was the film that put the festival on the map, domestically and internationally." The festival's influ-ence and reputation grew and grew, and grew since then. One favorite program during his tenure there was a retrospective of Samuel Fuller's films with Fuller attending, followed by a retrospective of John Cassavetes' films just before he died. "The filmmaker that emerged from this in 1991 was Quentin Tarantino with *Reservoir Dogs,* a film which combines the violence of Fuller with an improvised style of Cassavetes. One could almost chart that course toward Tarantino," Tony enthusiastically told us. "That those programs introduced

Fuller and Cassavetes to a new generation of filmmakers is something I'm proud of."

But in those beginning years, though hard to believe, Sundance had trouble finding enough films. Just getting the submissions in of some quality and convincing the distributors that they could also show their films, because at that time it was not yet an acquisition driven festival, was a struggle in itself.

Sundance became an important festival for identifying the latest filmmaking talent, sometimes catapulting writers and directors to fame overnight. It became the go-to U.S. film festival because it fostered unlikely studio fare, focusing on the content and talent such as Tarantino, Steven Soderbergh, Robert Rodriguez, and Kevin Smith. Sometimes new stars were born, and thus it became, and still is, a winter playground for industry executives, agents, talent, and distributors to rub elbows, screen films, and party in the Wasatch Mountains while discovering new faces to sign, produce or distribute.

With Sundance's success, film festivals in many large and small metropolitan cities, in addition to mountain towns, deserts, and beach resorts have popped up over the past twenty years. In fact, it has now become odd if a town doesn't have some sort of a yearly film festival.

WHAT IS A FILM FESTIVAL?

A film festival is an annual event showcasing new independent films or recently produced films, high profile and undiscovered talent, established and upcoming filmmakers, student filmmakers, and films from around the world. Festivals normally have two or more screens or venues to showcase films. Accepted filmmakers hustle to get their film noticed in the hope of obtaining distribution, favorable media film reviews, representation, or to showcase the actors' and filmmakers' talent. Festivals are a great place to launch an independent film and discover new talent.

They also provide an opportunity for filmmakers to network with each other and get feedback from general movie-going audiences. Some festivals offer educational outreach programs which serve students and local communities with panels, hands-on workshops on filmmaking, and seminars on screenwriting, distribution, music rights, acting, etc. Having an educational component attached to a festival provides sponsors with the needed grounds to justify their contribution to donate their services or money for a cause they desire to support.

Studios see the value in high-profile and foreign festivals to help promote their upcoming film releases. Other countries see the value in film festivals to promote films made in their region and to help generate a buzz for an Academy Award nomination.

Another recent addition to festivals is the integration of new media and showcasing the latest in digital technology and mobile content. More film festivals are adding "pitchfests" and "roundtables" where screenwriters and filmmakers have an opportunity to pitch their projects or listen to and chat with industry professionals within smaller groups.

We'll be examining all this and more in the coming chapters, but one thing has become increasingly clear — film festivals are a great launching pad for filmmakers and, for the layman, they're just fun to attend.

WHO RUNS A FILM FESTIVAL?

Festivals are usually created by either one person who has a dream to have a film festival in their community, a film society, a group of locals with a love for independent film, a city's film commission to promote their city's tourism and bring in more local filming, or a non-profit arts organization. Most film festivals are non-profit and they stay afloat by obtaining sponsors. Festivals like Sundance, AFI Film Festival, Tribeca Film Festival rely on corporate sponsorships from the likes of Audi, Southwest Airlines, Hewlett-Packard, American Express, American Airlines, Microsoft, Apple, etc. Foreign film festivals may get some financial support from their government.

Most festivals are a nonprofit 501(c)(3) organization in the U.S. and most countries have an equivalent of charity status. They are organized and run by a group of tireless dedicated volunteers and managed by a board of directors who may assemble a staff to help run the daily operation. For more information on creating a film festival in your hometown, stay tuned for Chapter 12 in this book.

CONCLUSION

The mission of most festivals is to highlight films with superior artistic achievement from filmmakers worldwide. They offer audiences and filmmakers alike an opportunity to enjoy an eclectic array of films they might not have the occasion to view anywhere else. In addition, they have an opportunity for those few days to network with others who have a love of film.

Organized film festivals have been around since the early 1930s. They began because people wanted to enjoy a communal filmgoing experience in which they would be exposed to new and established filmmakers, international cinema, and expand their world in a party-like atmosphere, all within a short span of time (3–12 days mostly). There's nothing like the intense environment of these festivals, where the days are filled with films, panels, and gatherings at the watering holes — offering new networking opportunities, intelligent debate and conversation, and new relationships. As long as there are movies, film festivals are here to stay. What their next evolution will be is anyone's guess, but we have a feeling that the world is getting smaller thanks to the Internet. With the studios making less movies, independent film will be in demand and what better way to showcase those films than at a film festival, wherever they may be.

DOING THE RESEARCH

"Someone's got to be analytical even
if you are the creative type!"

WITH THE 4,000+ FILM FESTIVALS that already exist worldwide, how do you narrow down your list and not bankrupt your bank account? By doing the research ahead of time and designing a strategy, both financially and creatively, you will generate a plan and budget for exactly what is needed so there won't be any real surprises. But you have to do the research, know what festivals to submit your film to and what those festivals cost, as well as what extras are needed to promote you and your film.

It takes time. Targeting the right festivals and understanding what you must do in order to make that festival work for you is one of the most important aspects of the post production process and one you won't regret if you start planning early.

RESEARCHING AND TARGETING FILM FESTIVALS

Where to begin? First off, you need to start your list of potential festivals. You have to organize them according to what time of year, when the festival is open for submissions, and what their requirements are. At the conclusion of this book you will find an appendix that is a comprehensive list of worldwide film festivals to get you started, but you should also check our website ManeuveringFilmFestivals.com for the very latest listings. Subscribing to magazines such as *MovieMaker*, *Filmmaker*, and *Indie Slate* will keep you abreast as to the latest goings on in the film festival world. They include film festival sections, provide insight into the festival circuit, and devote whole issues to the film festival experience. So if you can't afford to subscribe to these magazines, then you should at least keep your eyes open for those specialized issues.

The Internet is one of the best ways to keep filmmakers connected to what's happening around the world. It is safe to say that with the advent of the Internet, film festivals have grown by leaps and bounds. By exploring the many websites available, you can start collecting information. The more information you find out about these film festivals, the better equipped you'll be in deciding which ones work the best for you and your film. The following are a few websites to help you get started. Figure out if what they offer fits the criteria for your goals and your film. Make a list and from that list, strategize the six to ten film festivals you wish to submit your work to first.

Let's start with Withoutabox.com, the number one website used by 300,000+ filmmakers for festivals worldwide. Founded in 2000 by entrepreneurs David Straus and Joe Neulight, who had the foresight and wherewithal to recognize that having a site where both filmmakers and film festival programmers could interact, submit movies, and seek out potential festival films, they created Withoutabox.com, which has become an essential prerequisite for anyone who wants to go the festival route.

What makes Withoutabox unique is that it is a user-friendly site which not only helps filmmakers identify all the film festivals, it makes it much easier for them to submit paperless "call for entry" forms — also known as "submission" forms — to those film festivals registered via their site. A call for entry form is what the filmmaker completes in order to submit their work to the various festivals. With Withoutabox, the filmmaker need only fill this submission form out once and it's saved in the system. It's one-stop shopping, so to speak, and is free for filmmakers to sign-up.

Withoutabox.com offers filmmakers and film festivals a way to easily access information in half the time it would take otherwise. In addition, your press kit is uploaded and accessible to the festival programmers. The site also provides a message board for filmmakers to ask questions and get advice. Once a filmmaker signs up for their free account, they'll receive continuous info announcing festival call for entries and the approaching deadlines. Equally, film festivals also save time because they can view all the new films registered for their festival within Withoutabox's extensive database system. Filmmakers can also upload their films for the festival programming committee to review. Just think of the cost you'll save from not having to submit physical DVDs!

Also, film festival programmers have access to the synopses, photos, cast and crew information all in one nifty website.

Project details, Withoutabox.

Print

Touch
Directed by: Jen McGowan
submitted by **Jen McGowan**
in category: **Short**

Entry
Tracking ID: **10-0059**
Submitted: **January 20, 2010**
Terms and Conditions Signature? **Y**
Publicity Release e-Signature? **Y**

Foreign Titles

ENGLISH   Touch

3-Line Synopsis
Sometimes, the most personal connection in
your life occurs with a complete stranger.

3-Line Synopsis
Qu'arrive-t-il quand la connexion la plus
personnelle dans votre vie arrive avec un
inconnu complet ? Touche.

Programming Descriptors
FORMS:Narrative Fiction, Short
GENRES:Drama, Independent, Supernatural,
Spiritual
NICHES:Women
Exact Runtime
00 hr : 10 min : 58 sec
Date of Completion
January 2010
Country of Production / Filming
U S A / U S A

SHOOTING FORMATS
HDV *NTSC*

PREVIEW FORMATS
DVD Region0 *NTSC*

EXHIBITION FORMATS
DVD Region0 *NTSC, PAL, SECAM*
DVD Region0 *NTSC, PAL, SECAM*
DVD Region0 *NTSC, PAL, SECAM*
MiniDV *NTSC, PAL, SECAM*
HDCAM *NTSC, PAL, SECAM*
DigiBeta *NTSC, PAL, SECAM*
DVCAM *NTSC, PAL, SECAM*
.MOV (Quicktime)
.WMV (Windows Media)
.AVI (Audio-Video Interleaved)

Exhibition Info
Print Frame Speed: Color, Stereo
Film Sound: Dolby Digital
Aspect Ratios: 1.85 (USA)

Submission Contact
Jen
McGowan
Submission
Contact
Citizenship:
Gender:
Date of
Birth:

Production
Emile
Hanton
Producer
Citizenship:
Gender:

Jamie Robinson
Producer

Jen
McGowan
Director
Citizenship:
Gender:
Date of Birth:

Philip Lott
Producer
Gender:

Writing
Colin Pink
Writer
Citizenship:
Gender:

Jen McGowan
Adaptation
Citizenship:
Gender:
Date of Birth:

Cast
Lily Knight
Lead Actor
Rachel
Kanouse
Lead
Actor

Withoutabox: sample control panel view displaying film information.

Filmmakers get a discount using the site while film festivals are charged a percentage of the cost of the submission. Even though it costs the film festival a percentage of the entry fee, the time saving factor more than makes it worthwhile. It's a win-win for all who sign up.

To top it off, Withoutabox was acquired by Internet Movie Database (imdb.com), a subsidiary of Amazon.com, and now provides filmmakers with a way to get even more exposure for their films via Amazon's various media sites.

Filmmakers can now create their own profile on IMDb, listing their film and credits, thereby giving them more legitimacy in the entertainment world. They can upload trailers and photos for a fee. In addition, CreateSpace, another subsidiary of Amazon.com, brings a whole digital distribution outlet for filmmakers to earn royalties by selling their DVDs on Amazon or having their films downloaded by the consumer through their Video-On-Demand (VOD) system. However, you don't want to have distribution on the Internet until you've nearly completed your festival run as it might negate premieres or other such requirements deemed in each festival's guidelines.

For European short film submissions, Shortfilmdepot.com provides a service similar to Withoutabox and is a good source for targeting international short film festivals. Currently, Clermont-Ferrand Short Film Festival & Market as well as São Paulo International Short Film Festival are just two of the festivals utilizing Shortfilmdepot, amongst many others.

Other websites that help filmmakers pinpoint festivals as well as offer general festival information are:

- Filmfestivals.com — lists worldwide festivals by month, date, etc.;
- Filmfestivaltoday.com — online site to locate film festivals;

- IndieWIRE.com — leading source for independent films and festivals;

- Filmthreat.com — website created by Chris Gore, author of *The Ultimate Film Festival Survival Guide;*

- Shortfilmcentral.com — international database to locate short film festivals;

- Filmfestivalworld.com — helps filmmakers launch their films on the festival circuit;

- Festivalfocus.org — a directory of film festivals and independent films;

- Britfilms.com — a directory of international film and video festivals.

While these websites are a great resource, you should not discount reading the two Hollywood trade papers: *Daily Variety* and *The Hollywood Reporter*. They cover film festivals extensively throughout the year, not only in print but on their websites. In addition, don't discount *Screen International* as a major source for the international marketplace.

There are many more websites and information to be found through newsletters, e-zines, and magazines. This is not a complete list, but these are the *crème de la crème* of resources, which we believe are just the tip of the iceberg. You need to do research, utilizing these resources, and then you'll discover which ones work best for you. You'll probably discover more websites as you dig through the myriad of information each site imparts because every day new websites pop up with more in depth content.

Targeting the right film festivals is only the beginning, but by doing so will save you time and money. You'll set up a budget for each festival so that you're prepared for the expense and you'll strategize the festivals that will do the most good for your film and for your career.

TOP TIER FILM FESTIVALS

THE A-LIST FILM FESTIVALS are top tier because they attract the buyers of films, including studios, foreign and domestic distributors, and other production companies. They are the destinations where films make the biggest splash and attract star talent to walk red carpets. Studios and distribution/production companies throw parties to show off their slate of films and the talent involved. It's an opportunity to garner publicity and buzz. Industry reps from all over the world converge at these few select festivals and markets throughout the year. They include Sundance, Berlin, Cannes, Venice, and Toronto.

The major festivals offer both non-competitive as well as competitive categories. In the competitive categories, some festivals award films with both jury and audience honors. By winning these awards, a film can garner interest and most likely distribution. Review their websites to understand each of their submission guidelines so you can determine if the festival is right for your film.

SUNDANCE FILM FESTIVAL — PARK CITY, UTAH, USA (JANUARY)

The Sundance Institute, founded by Robert Redford, has a strong commitment to independent films and emerging filmmakers.

They also offer excellent screenwriting and producing programs year-round. For eleven days in snowy Park City,

Monika and Rona.

about 40,000 attendees made up of film industry insiders, powerful producers, studio execs, and major celebrities, watch approximately 200 films. The whole Hollywood film industry just about stops when the Sundance Film Festival takes place. Agents, managers, producers, and executives from each studio attend the festival not only looking for films to acquire, but to discover new talent. A good percentage of the films screened gain some form of distribution. With a strong documentary competition, a section for indigenous films, and a celebration of music composers and performers, the festival bridges the gap between elite Hollywood and independent filmmakers.

BERLIN FILM FESTIVAL — BERLIN, GERMANY (FEBRUARY)

Over the years, more and more people are going to Berlin. The Berlinale Film Festival showcases films in competition and out of competition. More American product is appearing at the festival, plus they have a lot of venues. The Panorama screenings are great for documentaries and independent films. It's also one of the first festivals to have a strong platform for gay/lesbian-themed pictures. Lastly, they have the largest kids-to-teen film festival called Generations. All of this is going on at one time!

The screenings are open to all except for the market screenings which attract a strong European showing. Berlinale encourages young filmmakers just out of film school by offering what they call the Berlin Campus — 700 students apply from all over the world; they get housed in dorms and take master classes. Filmmakers, whose films are in the festival, are invited to speak at those classes. Berlin is good at organizing parties and it's a very welcoming, friendly festival. Not limited to European and American films, Berlinale also has a wide spectrum of Asian, African, and South American cinema as well. "Dietrich Kosslich [head of the Berlin Film Festival] has taken a festival that had lost its charm and shine and made it into the festival it is today," one producer told us. They emphatically state that Berlin is where the deals get made.

FESTIVAL DE CANNES — CANNES, FRANCE (MAY)

By far the largest film festival and film market worldwide, the Cannes Film Festival presents almost every form of film-making including documentaries, short films, and features. Over 10,000 buyers and sellers attend the *market* (Marché du Film). Over 5,000 journalists cover the festival and 30,000 people from all over the world attend the twelve-day event in one of the most picturesque places in the world — the French Riviera. It's not just about the countless parties catered at restaurants, hotels, apartment suites, and yachts along the Mediterranean, it's also about the showcases and sidebar events offered throughout the festival.

The Short Film Corner (SFC) is one of the premiere markets for filmmakers showcasing short films to buyers, who watch the films in cubicles on computer screens or at film screenings set up by the filmmakers in one of the many screening

Cannes Palais.

Cannes Film Festival Short Film Corner.

rooms. The SFC offers ample networking opportunities for filmmakers that's not just limited to the bigwig affairs of sophisticated Cannes.

The official award selection includes the Palme d'Or, Un Certain Regard, and the Directors' Fortnight. The Cinéfondation's competition supports student films from schools around the world offering cash prize awards to help finance the student's next film. The festival also includes tributes and the Cinéma de la Plage with outdoor film screenings on the pristine sandy beaches along the croisette.

Cannes Cinema de la Plage.

The Marché du Film is the premiere marketplace for buying and selling films to territories around the world. Booths are provided for buyers to meet with filmmakers in order to sell their films.

The International Village is peppered with tents along the beach where representatives from various countries and film commissions promote filmmaking incentives from their

Cannes Marché du Film.

Cannes International Village.

regions and offer respite for the weary feet of their fellow countrymen where one drinks cappuccinos while taking meetings in the comfort of the pavilions.

The American Pavilion, founded by Julie Sisk in 1989 and supported by corporate sponsorships, is one of the few with a restaurant. It also offers a film student internship program in which students work within the Pavilion as well as at some of the film market production and distribution companies, gaining valuable experience working with top-notch pros. Panels and roundtables offer great insight for festival attendees and students have the opportunity to learn from the great masters.

Other important events are the Producers' Network where producers from all over the world discuss current industry trends. Keynote speakers address breakfast meetings and there's an opportunity for speed pitching ideas.

The Cannes Film Festival website is translated into eight different languages. That's more than the United Nations' official languages. Cannes is so large it can be overwhelming. So you really need to do your homework before you arrive in order to make the most out of all that the festival has to offer.

VENICE FILM FESTIVAL — VENICE, ITALY (SEPTEMBER)

The Venice International Film Festival is the oldest festival run by La Biennale di Venezia, a cultural institution formed in 1895 to encourage artistic visions in cinema, art, architecture, dance, music, and theatre. The film festival is one of its proudest offshoots. Because the timing of the festival is in September, it showcases motion pictures that could potentially go on to become Academy Award nominated films. Filmmakers compete to win the Golden Lion award. Each year, the festival welcomes major stars and directors as they converge on the Lido and canals of the historic city. By the

photo courtesy of Walter Harris

Venice Film Festival.

way, Venice bestows the Corto Cortissimo Silver Lion for the Best Short Film.

TORONTO INTERNATIONAL FILM FESTIVAL (TIFF) — TORONTO, CANADA (SEPTEMBER)

TIFF is an eleven-day non-competitive festival, screening over 300 films. An unusual aspect about this festival is that each film gets at least two screenings. TIFF gets a lot of attention and is a highly regarded festival and that's why studio acquisition executives and industry professionals come here to scout new films and talent. It is also used as a platform to premiere studio films. Toronto is considered one of the largest showcases for Canadian films and the short film section only programs short films produced in Canada. Toronto is highly regarded as the gateway to the Academy Awards as it premieres films late enough in the year to garner Oscar buzz.

OTHER FILM FESTIVALS

Another thing to consider when determining which festival to submit your film to is who is behind the film festival. Who attends the festival? There are the obvious choices of Sundance, Toronto, Cannes, Berlin, and Venice, but there are smaller festivals that also attract industry execs. See who has attended past festivals. Has there been any success for the winning filmmakers? Did they get noticed? Did they get an agent? Did they sell their film? Were people there who could offer good, solid advice? Was there a chance to network with well-known filmmakers and industry professionals? Check out the credentials of the jury. The festival websites are the first place to investigate as they'll have pictures and press releases illustrating the past festivals and who of note has participated.

American festivals, both large and small, like Tribeca, Telluride, South By Southwest (SXSW), AFI, Santa Barbara, Palm Springs, Seattle International Film Festival, Newport Beach, Chicago, Cinequest, Mill Valley, Miami, and the Los Angeles Film Festival, have the advantage of attracting Hollywood industry professionals who attend in order to scout films and new talent. European film festivals like Rome, San Sebastian, Locarno, Rotterdam, and London film festivals also draw the major European entertainment industry.

Many regional festivals present tribute awards to top talent and filmmakers which in turn brings in Hollywood executives. This gives filmmakers an opportunity to network and mingle with pros they may not have an opportunity to meet elsewhere. We attended the Mendocino Film Festival as invited guest speakers and had the opportunity to mingle with Sydney Pollack and Laszlo Kovacs. It was a well-organized smaller festival located in a beautiful historic California coastal town. When we were invited to the

Monika and Rona with Roger and Julie Corman at the Bangkok Film Festival.

Bangkok Film Festival, we sat and conversed with Roger and Julie Corman over lunch.

Smaller festivals will take advantage of celebrities and top entertainment honchos who live in their communities and will help promote the festival. So taking a look at the kind of industry draw a festival has might also determine your choices of festivals.

SHORT FILMS AND STUDENT FILMMAKERS

FOR SHORT FILMS AND STUDENT FILMMAKERS, the following festivals are important because industry professionals such as agents, managers, producers, executives, short film distributors, buyers, and festival programmers attend these festivals to sign, option, or distribute, or select films and discover filmmakers.

- Sundance Film Festival — Park City, Utah (January)
- Flickerfest International Short Film Festival — Sydney, Australia (January)
- Clermont-Ferrand Short Film Festival — Clermont-Ferrand, France (January/February)
- Aspen Shorts Film Festival — Aspen, Colorado (April)
- International Short Film Festival — Oberhausen, Germany (April)

- Festival de Cannes — Cannes, France (Short Film Corner) (May)

- Munich International Short Film Festival, Munich, Germany (June)

- Palm Springs Festival of Short Films — Palm Springs, California, USA (June)

- Toronto Worldwide Short Film Festival — Toronto, Canada (June)

- Short Shorts Film Festival — Tokyo, Japan (June)

- The DC Shorts Film Festival — Washington D.C. (September)

If you get accepted to one of these — there's no doubt you will get some notoriety and have a stronger opportunity to find a prospective buyer for your film and/or use the screening to help create a "buzz" to get into other festivals. All of the festivals above, with the exception of Toronto Worldwide Short Film Festival and the DC Shorts Film Festival, are Academy Award qualifying film festivals which we'll talk about later.

Student films sometimes have their own category at film festivals with a separate award presented for Best Student Film or Best High School Film. If you do your research, you will find many film festivals specifically geared toward the student filmmaker and some of those are associated with a college or university. So check the festival's guidelines to make sure they accept films that might be outside of their domain. The website, *studentfilms.com*, is a good resource for information about student festivals and there's a section where you can ask advice. We have targeted a few of the student film festivals below:

- Ivy Film Festival; largest student run film festival — Brown University, Providence, Rhode Island (April)

- Fresh Film Festival; student films and first feature films — Prague, Czech Republic (August)

- Rhode Island International Film Festival/New England Student Film Festival; geared toward students in the New England area — Newport, Rhode Island (August)

- BestFest America Student Film Festival — San Diego, California (September)

- Angelus Student Film Festival — Los Angeles, California (September)

- European Student Film Festival; for high school students from across Europe — Prague, Czech Republic (November)

- International Student Film Festival — Hollywood, California (November)

- NextFrame Student Film Festival; organized by the UFVA (University Film & Video Association) — presented at a different University each year (August)

We have mentioned a few festivals geared toward students to get you started, but there are many more out there. Most festivals program student films within the short film screening blocks so the work will not be singled out as a student work but rather as one of many short films within the festival.

Student filmmakers sometimes get a minimal discount at festivals. The Los Angeles Film Festival doesn't charge entry fees for high school submissions. Most film schools at universities have what is called a "festival coordinator" who handles film submissions. Student filmmakers should know who that person is and make every effort to discuss their film goals with the coordinator at their school. School coordinators must develop relationships with the festivals and their programmers. Their goal is to make the school look good and to do that they must promote the students' work.

NICHE FESTIVALS AND SIDEBARS

DETERMINE THE TYPE OF FILM YOU HAVE and take advantage of festivals that have specific programming needs. For example, if it's a horror film then consider submitting to festivals like Shriekfest, H.P. Lovecraft Film Festival or festivals that specialize in that particular genre. So many festivals have specific themes (horror, comedy, family, etc.) or specific subject matter (gay/lesbian, African American, Latino culture, dance, politics, food, pets, etc.). For instance, if your film has a Jewish or Greek character, you may want to submit to one of the many Jewish and Greek film festivals out there. There are 160 Jewish Film Festivals around the world! If your film revolves around a mountain location then you may want to consider submitting to film festivals that are located in mountain towns. A film dealing with surfing would have potential at any of the festivals located along the coast. A festival like Slamdance may be more open to screening edgier films than other festivals. It doesn't hurt to email the programming director and ask them if they accept a specific genre.

Also some festivals offer what are called "sidebars," meaning that they spotlight something different each year. One sidebar could be films directed by women, Asian films, films about animals, or Native Americans. Sidebars offer more opportunities for showcasing your material.

Also, check out each festival's website to see what type of films have screened and won awards in previous years. This will help in distinguishing which festival might be right for your particular genre.

It is important to understand which film festivals can be beneficial to the filmmaker but keep in mind that smaller "destination" festivals can be more fun. Destination film festivals are set in beautiful surroundings or places of interest that offer people simultaneous events in sporting, touring, wine tasting, and other activities outside of the film festival.

We suggest you do an Internet search for festivals in your area. Meanwhile, here are some niche or theme-oriented festivals (keep in mind most cities have at least one of these below):

GAY/LESBIAN-THEMED FILM FESTIVALS:

- London Lesbian and Gay Film Festival — London, England (March)
- Provincetown International Film Festival — Cape Cod, Massachusetts (June)
- San Francisco Int'l Lesbian & Gay Film Festival — San Francisco, California (June)
- Outfest, Los Angeles Gay & Lesbian Film Festival — Los Angeles, California (July)

FAMILY & CHILDREN'S FILM FESTIVALS:

- Generations, Berlin Film Festival — Berlin, Germany (February)
- International Family Film Festival — Los Angeles, California (March)
- Seoul International Youth Film Festival — Seoul, Korea (July)
- Los Angeles Children's Film Festival — Los Angeles, California (October)
- Chicago International Children's Film Festival — Chicago, Illinois (October)
- Heartland Film Festival — Indianapolis, Indiana (October)
- Kids First Film Festival (Traveling Film Festival) (all year round)

DOCUMENTARY FILM FESTIVALS:

- Big Sky Documentary Film Festival — Missoula, Montana (February)

- DOCNZ International Documentary Film Festival — Auckland, New Zealand (March)

- Full Frame Documentary Film Festival — Durham, North Carolina (April)

- Hot Docs Canadian International Film Festival — Toronto, Canada (April/May)

- Sheffield Doc/Fest — Sheffield, England (June)

- Silverdocs — Silver Springs, Maryland (June)

- Hot Springs Documentary Film Festival — Hot Springs National Park, Arkansas (October)

Once you've gathered this information, you can then make intelligent decisions of what festival to enter that will help your film and help you kick start your career by getting noticed where it counts. Not every film will get into Sundance but many go on to other festivals that also can be beneficial to the filmmaker.

One last piece of advice for targeting film festivals is to submit your film to the town where you or your cast members grew up and/or went to college, should that town have a film festival. Festivals love showcasing local talent. If the city where your film was shot has a film festival, make sure you submit it to that festival.

Always make sure you check the rules and regulations since qualifications vary for each festival. For instance, most festivals want some sort of premiere status and don't want any films screened at other film festivals prior to screening at theirs. Some won't allow films that have already shown on the Internet. And still others require that the film be produced within the twelve months preceding the festival. So check those guidelines for the criteria before charging up your credit cards.

THE OSCAR: ACADEMY QUALIFYING FILM FESTIVALS AND STUDENT ACADEMY AWARDS

THE ANNUAL STUDENT ACADEMY AWARDS is a national competition for college and university students organized by The Academy of Motion Picture Arts and Science and the Academy Foundation. The competition supports student filmmakers who have not used industry professionals during the making of their films. Medals and grants are presented to winners for animation, documentary, narrative, and alternative filmmaking. Full-time students in a degree-accredited U.S. college or university can apply. In addition, three foreign student films are selected from CILECT (Center International de Liaison des Ecoles de Cinema et de Television) in which each affiliated college or university can submit one entry for consideration. Films should not have a running time of more than forty minutes.

A student film can be eligible to enter the Academy Awards' short film competition the following year. Films are evaluated by the short film committee based on the quality of the production and originality. A few of the past winners have been Robert Zemeckis, John Lassiter, and Spike Lee.

To be considered for an Academy Award for animated or live action short film (no more than forty minutes running time), your film needs to play in a theatre in Los Angeles County on three consecutive days with two screenings a day. These need to be paid admissions. However, if your film wins an award at one of the Academy qualifying film festivals, you are automatically eligible for consideration. You can obtain an updated list of Academy qualifying film festivals and requirements for feature films, documentaries, live action short films, animated short films, and student films from the Academy at oscars.org.

Having your film win at an Academy qualifying film festival will offer your film the opportunity to be considered for an Academy Award nomination! So targeting those qualifying film festivals should probably top your list of film festival submissions.

You should know that the Academy frequently revises their rules and regulations, so always check on their site for the most recent listings.

FEATURES AND DOCUMENTARIES

To become Academy qualified for a feature length film or documentary, you need to have your film screened in a theatre and publicly exhibited for paid admission on seven consecutive days in both Los Angeles and Manhattan. If you have a short subject documentary (under 40 minutes including credits), you only need to screen it in either L.A. or New York City. Check the Academy's website for complete requirements.

LIST FOR ACADEMY AWARD QUALIFYING FILM FESTIVALS

Short Film Awards Festival List

CHANGES ANNUALLY — CHECK www.oscars.org FOR CURRENT INFORMATION

AFI FEST (California, USA)
Grand Jury Prize for International
Short Film
www.afi.com/onscreen/AFIFest

**ACADEMIA DE LAS ARTES Y
CIENCIAS CINEMATOGRAFICAS
DE ESPAÑA (SPAIN)**
Goya Award for Best Short Fiction
Goya Award for Best Short Animation
www.academiadecine.com

**ACADÉMIE DES ARTS ET
TECHNIQUES DU CINÉMA
[CÉSAR] (FRANCE)**
Best Short Film
www.lescesarducinema.com

**ACADEMY OF CANADIAN
CINEMA & TELEVISION [GENIE]
(CANADA)**
Best Live Action Short Drama
Best Animated Short
www.academy.ca

**ACADEMY OF MOTION PICTURE
ARTS AND SCIENCES [Student
Academy Awards] (California,
USA)**
Gold Medal - Alternative
Gold Medal - Animation
Gold Medal - Narrative
Gold Medal - Foreign Film
www.oscars.org

**ANN ARBOR FILM FESTIVAL
(Michigan, USA)**
Best of the Festival
www.aafilmfest.org
Lawrence Kasdan Award for Best
Narrative Film
Gus Van Sant Award for Best
Experimental Film
Chris Frayne Award for Best Animated
Film

**ANNECY FESTIVAL INT'L DU
CINEMA D'ANIMATION (FRANCE)**
Le Cristal d'Annecy
Special Jury Award
www.annecy.org

**ASPEN SHORTSFEST (Colorado,
USA)**
Animated Eye Award
Best Comedy
Best Drama
Best Short Short
www.aspenfilm.org

**ATHENS INT'L FILM FESTIVAL
(Ohio, USA)**
Best Narrative
Best Animation
Best Experimental
www.athensfest.org

**ATLANTA FILM FESTIVAL
(Georgia, USA)**
Best Animated Short
Best Narrative Short
www.atlantafilmfestival.com

**AUSTIN FILM FESTIVAL (Texas,
USA)**
Narrative Short Jury Award
Animated Short Jury Award
www.austinfilmfestival.com

**BERLIN INT'L FILM FESTIVAL
(GERMANY)**
Golden Bear - International Shorts
Competition
www.berlinale.de

**BERMUDA INTERNATIONAL
FILM FESTIVAL (BERMUDA)**
Bermuda Shorts Award Winner
www.biff.bm

**BILBAO INT'L FESTIVAL OF
DOCUMENTARY & SHORT FILMS
(SPAIN)**
Grand Prize of the Bilbao Festival
www.zinebi.com

**BRITISH ACADEMY OF FILM
AND TELEVISION ARTS [BAFTA]
AWARDS (ENGLAND)**
Best Short Film
Best Short Animation Film
www.bafta.org

**CANADIAN FILM CENTRE'S
WORLDWIDE SHORT FILM
FESTIVAL (CANADA)**
Best Live Action Short Film
Best Animated Short Film
www.worldwideshortfilmfest.com

**CANNES FESTIVAL INT'L DU
FILM (FRANCE)**
Palme d'Or (Short Films)
www.festival-cannes.fr

**CARTAGENA INT'L FILM
FESTIVAL (COLOMBIA)**
Best Short Animation - Golden
Catalina Indian
Best Short Fiction - Golden Catalina
Indian
www.festicinecartagena.org

**CHICAGO INT'L CHILDREN'S
FILM FESTIVAL (Illinois, USA)**
Adult Jury First Place Animated Short
Adult Jury First Place Live Action
Short
www.cicff.org

**CHICAGO INT'L FILM FESTIVAL
(Illinois, USA)**
Golden Hugo for Best Short Film
www.chicagofilmfestival.org

**CINANIMA INT'L ANIMATION
FILM FESTIVAL (PORTUGAL)**
Grand Prize
www.cinanima.pt

**CINEQUEST FILM FESTIVAL
(California, CA)**
Best Short Narrative
Best Short Animation
www.cinequest.org

**CLERMONT-FERRAND
INTERNATIONAL SHORT FILM
FESTIVAL (FRANCE)**
International Grand Prix
National Grand Prix
www.clermont-filmfest.com

**CLEVELAND INTERNATIONAL
FILM FESTIVAL (Ohio, USA)**
Best Short Narrative
Best Animated Short Film
www.clevelandfilm.org

**DAVID DI DONATELLO AWARD
[ACCADEMIA DEL CINEMA
ITALIANO] (ITALY)**
Best Short Film
www.daviddidonatello.it

**ENCOUNTERS INTERNATIONAL
FILM FESTIVAL (U.K.)**
Brief Encounters Grand Prix
Animated Encounters Grand Prix
www.encounters-festival.org.uk

**FESTIVAL DE CINE DE HUESCA
(SPAIN)**
International Short Films Contest -
Danzante Award
Iberoamerican Short Films Contest -
Danzante Award
www.huesca-filmfestival.com

**FLICKERFEST INTERNATIONAL
SHORT FILMS FESTIVAL**
The Coopers Award for Best Film
The Yoram Gross Award for Best
Animation
www.flickerfest.com.au

**FLORIDA FILM FESTIVAL
(Florida, USA)**
Best Narrative Short
Best Animated Short
www.floridafilmfestival.com

**FOYLE FILM FESTIVAL
(IRELAND)**
Best Irish Short
Best International Short
Best Animated Short
www.foylefilmfestival.org

**GIJON INT'L FILM FESTIVAL
FOR YOUNG PEOPLE (SPAIN)**
Premio Principado De Asturios Al
Mejor Cortometraje (Best Short Film)
www.gijonfilmfestival.com

THE HAMPTONS INTERNATIONAL FILM FESTIVAL (New York, USA)
Golden Starfish Best Short Film Award
www.hamptonsfilmfest.org

HIROSHIMA INT'L ANIMATION FESTIVAL (JAPAN)
Grand Prix
www.urban.ne.jp/home/hiroanim

KRAKOW FILM FESTIVAL(POLAND)
The Golden Dragon
www.kff.com.pl

LOCARNO INT'L FILM FESTIVAL (SWITZERLAND)
Golden Leopard - Best Short Film, International Competition
Golden Leopard - Best Short Film, National Competition
www.pardo.ch

LOS ANGELES FILM FESTIVAL (California, USA)
Best Animated/Experimental Short Film
Best Narrative Short Film
www.lafilmfest.com

LOS ANGELES INT'L. SHORT FILM FESTIVAL (California, USA)
Best of the Fest
Best Foreign Film
Best Drama Film
Best Comedy Film
Best Animation Film
Best Experimental Film
www.lashortsfest.com

LOS ANGELES LATINO INTERNATIONAL FILM FESTIVAL (California, USA)
Best Short
www.latinofilm.org

MELBOURNE INT'L FILM FESTIVAL (AUSTRALIA)
The City of Melbourne Grand Prix, Best Short Film
Best Fiction Short Film
Best Animated Short Film
www.melbournefilmfestival.com.au

MONTREAL FESTIVAL DU NOUVEAU CINEMA (CANADA)
Best Short Film – International
www.nouveaucinema.ca

MONTREAL WORLD FILM FESTIVAL (CANADA)
First Prize - Short Film
www.ffm-montreal.org

MORELIA INTERNATIONAL FILM FESTIVAL (MEXICO)
Best Animated Short Film
Best Fiction Short Film
www.moreliafilmfest.com

NASHVILLE FILM FESTIVAL (Tennessee, USA)
Best Animated Short
Best Live Action Short
www.nashvillefilmfestival.org

NEW YORK INTERNATIONAL CHILDREN'S FILM FESTIVAL
Best Short Film
www.gkids.com

NORDISK PANORAMA – 5 CITIES FILM FESTIVAL (Five Nordic Countries)
Best Nordic Short Film
www.nordiskpanorama.com

OBERHAUSEN INT'L SHORT FILM FESTIVAL (GERMANY)
Grand Prize of the City of Oberhausen
www.kurzfilmtage.de

OTTAWA INT'L ANIMATION FESTIVAL (CANADA)
Best Independent Short
www.animationfestival.ca

PALM SPRINGS INT'L FESTIVAL OF SHORT FILMS (California, USA)
Best of the Festival Award
Best Animation
Best Live Action (15 minutes and under)
Best Live Action (over 15 minutes)
www.psfilmfest.org

RHODE ISLAND INTERNATIONAL FILM FESTIVAL (Rhode Island, USA)
Grand Prize, Best Short
www.film-festival.org

RIO DE JANEIRO INTERNATIONAL SHORT FILM FESTIVAL (BRAZIL)
Grand Prix - International Competition
Grand Prix - National Competition
www.curtacinema.com.br

ST. LOUIS INT'L FILM FESTIVAL (Missouri, USA)
Best of the Festival
Best Live Action Short Film
Best Animation Short Film
www.cinemastlouis.org

SAN FRANCISCO INT'L FILM FESTIVAL (California, USA)
Golden Gate Award Narrative Short
Golden Gate Award Animated Short
www.sffs.org

SANTA BARBARA INT'L FILM FESTIVAL (California, USA)
Bruce C. Corwin Award - Best Live Action Short Film
Bruce C. Corwin Award - Best Animation Short Film
www.sbfilmfestival.org

SEATTLE INTERNATIONAL FILM FESTIVAL (Washington, USA)
Best Narrative Short Film
Best Animation Short Film
www.seattlefilm.com

SHORTSHORTS FILM FESTIVAL (California, USA)
Best of Festival Award - Grand Prix
www.shortshorts.org

SIGGRAPH (USA)
Best of Show
www.siggraph.org

SLAMDANCE FILM FESTIVAL (Utah, USA)
Grand Jury Prize for Best Narrative Short
Grand Jury Prize for Best Animated Short
www.slamdance.com

SOUTH BY SOUTHWEST (Texas, USA)
Best Animated Short
Best Narrative Short
www.sxsw.com

STUTTGART INT'L ANIMATION FESTIVAL (GERMANY)
Grand Prix International Competition
www.itfs.de

SUNDANCE FILM FESTIVAL (Utah, USA)
Jury Prize in Short Filmmaking
Jury Prize in International Short Filmmaking
festival.sundance.org

SYDNEY FILM FESTIVAL (AUSTRALIA)
Dendy Award – Best Australian Short Film – Live Action
Yoram Gross Animation Award
www.sff.org.au

TAMPERE INT'L SHORT FILM FESTIVAL (FINLAND)
Grand Prix - International Competition
National Main Prize (under 30 minutes)
www.tamperefilmfestival.fi

TRIBECA FILM FESTIVAL (New York, USA)
Best Narrative Short
www.tribecafilm.com

UPPSALA INT'L SHORT FILM FESTIVAL (SWEDEN)
Grand Prix
Best Children's Film
www.shortfilmfestival.com

USA FILM FESTIVAL - NATIONAL SHORT FILM & VIDEO COMPETITION (Texas, USA)
Fiction First Place
Animation First Place
www.usafilmfestival.com

VENICE INT'L FILM FESTIVAL (ITALY)
Corto Cortissimo Silver Lion - Best Short Film
www.labiennale.org/en/cinema

ZAGREB WORLD FESTIVAL OF ANIMATED FILMS (CROATIA)
Grand Prix - Best Short Film at Festival
www.animafest.hr

FINANCIAL CONSIDERATIONS

FILMMAKERS WHO HAVE RECENTLY GRADUATED film school have their minds spinning and pocketbooks trembling trying to decide which film festival they should submit their film to, knowing that certain festivals hold the potential for their talent to be discovered. Aside from the entry fee, most film festivals require filmmakers to pay for their own travel and accommodations. Submitting a film to a festival doesn't necessarily mean acceptance and a screening. It goes through a process which we will discuss at length later. But, make no mistake — it can get costly and it can be very over-whelming. Festivals charge an entry fee of anywhere from an early deadline fee of $25 to a late deadline fee of $100. There are many foreign film festivals like the New Zealand International Film Festival, Italy's Taormina Film Festival, Poland's Tofifest International Film Festival, and Ireland's Corona Cork Film Festival that do not require any entry fee for submissions.

These film festivals want to encourage international partic-ipation and feel that the excessive shipping costs and international money orders required by foreign filmmakers to pay for entry fees is prohibitive. So, they decided that they would do away with entry fees in favor of attracting more worldwide submissions from outside of their countries. With sites like Vimeo, YouSendIt, and others, filmmakers can upload their films for programmers to view and save time and shipping costs.

Some festivals like the Daytona Beach Film Festival, DC Independent Film Festival, and Tiburon Film Festival have no entry fees for students. A lot of the no-fee festivals are targeted toward a specific genre or a theme like the Bicycle Film Festival, showcasing films about bicycles using music, art, and film.

(This is for an average 3-day trip, however, if you stay longer you should include those additional costs in these estimates)

These are approximate estimates only. You will need to do your own research for these and other festivals to have a more accurate accounting for your budget.

EXPENSE ESTIMATE FOR FESTIVALS
(Travel from Los Angeles)

NAME OF FILM FESTIVAL	ENTRY FEE	TRANSPORTATION			FOOD	LODGING (per night)	ADVERTISING	FESTIVAL PASSES & EVENTS	TOTAL (approx)	FESTIVAL DATES
		AIR	CAR/TAXI	GAS						
Sundance Film Festival	$50.00	$215.00	$135.00	$70.00	$150.00	$150 -$300	$ 500.00	$300.00	$1,870.00	1/20/11 – 1/30/11
Clermont-Ferrand Short Film Festival	FREE	$900.00	$30.00 Taxi	–	$100.00	$78.00	$500.00	–	$1,608.00	2/4 - 2/12/2011
Mill Valley Film Festival	$35.00	$275.00	$100.00	$75.00	$100.00	$250.00	$200.00	–	$1,035.00	10/6 – 10/16/11
Breckinridge Film Festival	$40.00	$230.00	$100.00	$75.00	$100.00	FREE	$200.00	$175.00	$ 920.00	6/9 – 6/12/11
Hamptons Film Festival	$55.00	$300.00	$100.00	$75.00	$100.00	$300.00	$200.00	–	$1,130.00	10/13 – 10/17/11
Big Bear Lake Film Festival	$35.00	–	–	$35.00	$75.00	$75 -$150	$50.00	$75.00	$ 300.00	9/15 – 9/18/11
Big Bear Lake Film Festival (Day trip)	$35.00	–	–	$35.00	$25.00	N/A	$50.00	–	$ 145.00	915 – 9/18/11

Transportation = Air Fare, Car Rental, Bus, Train, Gas
Food = Meals, Drinks, Snacks
Lodging = Hotel per night
Advertising = Postcards, Posters, Scotch Tape, Staple Gun, Promotional items

Because submission fees can add up, some filmmakers will contact the festival directly to try to get a "fee waiver." A "fee waiver" allows a filmmaker to submit the film without paying the entry fee. However, most festivals are non-profit organizations and rely on the submission entry fees to help financially support the festival so they cannot afford to waive them. Some festivals feel that by waiving entry fees would destroy the integrity of fair competition for all filmmakers. After all, if you waive one fee, why not another? Conversely, it poses the question, why should one film rate a fee waiver over another?

Sometimes the programming director will allow the film-maker to submit their film with the understanding that if the film is accepted into the festival they will still have to pay the entry fee. In addition, they might get a reduced rate equivalent to the early deadline fee.

A programming director might see a film at another festi-val and, if they like the film, they might invite it to be in the festival. Most likely the filmmaker will still have to pay the entry fee. However, if this happens to you, make sure that the programming director puts your film through the official channels in spite of the fact that it wasn't submitted in the usual fashion. It's best to pay the entry fee and pay attention to the official guidelines.

So now you have an understanding of the different types of film festivals and the cost involved to submit to them. You don't want to have your film finished and then discover you have no money left to submit to festivals.

To attend a festival like the Sundance Film Festival, it could cost the filmmaker at least $1,500 for three days and that does not include promotional materials for your film. You can find ways to cut costs and get your accommodations down to around $60 a night if you share a condo with ten other filmmakers or friends, where you might have one large room with five beds and two bedrooms for couples. You might be able to cut back on your transportation expenses by taking a shuttle from the airport in Salt Lake City to Park City instead of renting a car, especially since parking is prohibited in most areas during the festival and there's shuttles that take you to the different venues anyway. You can shop at the local grocery store for food instead of eating out all the time. These are things you must take into consideration when planning your expenses for each festival. Granted, some festivals will be less expensive.

Here's how a festival like Sundance might breakdown:

Entry Fees might run anywhere from early deadline $35 to late deadline of $75 for short films and anywhere from $45–$100 for feature films and documentaries.

Advertising costs for postcards, posters, scotch tape, staple gun, etc. — $500;

Travel/Transportation Expenses can run $600 (airfare and car rental). If you drive, include fuel, if you rent a car also include fuel, if you take a shuttle it might cost $35–$40 per person/shared ride;

Hotel Accommodations are at least $150 per night;

Meals can be at least $45 per day unless you eat peanut butter and jelly sandwiches;

Drinks run upwards of at least $30–$50 because you do want to network at the local bar parties;

Festival Passes, including access to all film screenings, hospitality suite, seminars, and event parties can run from $300 to $3,000 for express passes. Individual movie tickets cost $15. Usually one Filmmaker Pass per film entry is given free and that pass may not include all the events and parties.

Keep in mind prices go up and down all the time (mostly up) so the above is an approximate estimation for this festival. You will have to do your own cost estimate prior to going but, for now, this will give you an idea.

If you do your research on the film festivals you wish to enter, you can calculate an estimated cost and include it in your overall production budget. You'll save yourself a head-ache later on when you realize how expensive it can get. Be prepared — spend your money wisely!

SCREENWRITING COMPETITIONS AT FESTIVALS

IF YOU ARE A SCREENWRITER, there are a number of film festi-vals that also have screenwriting competitions. Check with each individual festival for the requirements and provisions for such a competition as some are only for feature-length screenplays, some include short film scripts, and some are genre-specific. It's not a bad idea if you're already submit-ting your completed film to the festival to enter one of your screenplays into the screenwriting competition. Make sure that the judges for the competition are industry insiders so someone reading your material might actually be able to help you with your career goals. For instance, Iris Yamashita was discovered at the Big Bear Lake International Film Festi-val's Screenwriting Competition. Her screenplay, which won first place, was read by one of the competition jurors, Cathy Tarr, who works at CAA. She gave the winning script to Paul Haggis (*Crash*) who then gave it to Clint Eastwood. Eastwood was impressed and proceeded to hire Yamashita to write *Letters from Iwo Jima*. The rest is history and Yamashita is now an Oscar-nominated screenwriter. All thanks to connections made at the Big Bear Lake Screen-writing Competition.

Similar to the film call for entry section, Withoutabox.com has a dedicated section for entering screenwriting competitions. The call for screenplays section lists 100+ screenwriting competitions along with their deadlines.

Here is a partial list of film festivals with screenwriting competitions:

- Slamdance Film Festival Screenplay Competition
- Austin Film Festival Screenplay Competition
- Big Bear Lake Screenwriting Competition
- Moondance Screenwriting Competition
- Jacksonville Film Festival Screenplay Competition
- Eerie Horror Film Festival & Screenplay Competition
- DC Shorts Screenplay Competition

CONCLUSION

WHILE YOUR FILM IS BEING SHOT or in post production, that's the time to start your research on what film festivals to target. Plan accordingly so that you budget the right amount of money for each festival. It can really mount up. By doing this, it will diminish some of the financial burden by knowing the submission costs in advance and help you meet submission deadlines.

It takes a lot of time to prepare for and attend a festival but it will be a memorable experience. You'll meet people that will become your friends for life and others whom you will work with in the future (maybe even on your next project). You'll benefit by meeting entertainment professionals who can help further your career. But planning is everything. Coming up with a strategy that works for the promotion of your film and getting the most out of the festival circuit will be repaid to you a thousand times over.

If you're lucky enough to already have a film shot, it's time to start putting together a list of film festivals where you would like to screen your film. Don't forget the regional and niche festivals that have industry professionals attending in addition to festivals that are less than a 150 miles from where you live so that you can attend even for a day trip, if need be, and save some money. And don't forget to target the Academy qualifying festivals.

EXERCISES

1) Create an estimated expense report for targeted film festivals. Include:

- **a.** entry fees
- **b.** transportation (airline, shuttle/taxi, gas)
- **c.** food
- **d.** lodging
- **e.** advertising and promotional materials
- **f.** festival passes
- **g.** time away from family/home/work

SUBMITTING YOUR FILM

"Target Shooting"

SO YOU'VE COMPLETED YOUR FILM. You're now thinking to yourself, how do I get it out there? How do I get it seen? The logical answer is to hit the film festival circuit road. It is there that you and your film could get noticed. Your goals of making a career out of moviemaking might become a reality. But how do you go about this? What festivals should you submit to? What do you need to move forward?

Before you totally move forward, let's take a step back and look at the film you want to present.

IMPORTANCE OF A LOGLINE, GENRE AND HOOK

Most film festivals, or for that matter anyone in the business, let alone your audience, will want to know what your film is about. The clearest and most concise way to present your film in that way is with a "logline." A logline is one or two sentences that describe the story of your film.

Usually, you begin with a protagonist doing some sort of action with an outcome or a protagonist with a desire who will do anything to achieve that desire but there's a greater obstacle in their way. It may also convey the tone of the piece. But above all, it tells the story in a succinct way. Generally we don't use the character's names in loglines unless the film is based upon a true story. However, a DVD jacket and festival program guide may have the character's name listed with the actor's name in parenthesis. This is important for attracting viewers if you have recognizable actors.

You might begin creating your logline by working with the following exercise:

This is a film about...

A (_____) who wants (_____) and (_____) happens.

You can also start your logline this way:

When a (*character*) does (*activity*) to (*other character*), they/he/she discover (*outcome*).

There are many ways to write a logline. The idea is to give the gist of your story at its most basic but still retain the essence of the characters, who they are, what they want, and what's in their way of getting it. Sometimes you can add the outcome. For example: *A psychiatrist helps a kid who sees dead people only to discover that it isn't the kid who needs help.* Or, you could be a spoiler and write the logline this way: *A psychiatrist helps a kid who sees dead people only to discover that he, himself, is dead and that he has issues he must resolve with his life.* Either way would work to describe the movie, *The Sixth Sense.* Usually, however, you don't want to spoil the surprise ending.

They used to be called "*TV Guide* loglines" because if you look in a *TV Guide* magazine, you'll see a one-sentence synopsis of a movie or episode and it is from that which will determine what you want to view that night on the telly. Or your Sunday paper probably lists all the feature films playing in the theatres along with their one- or two-sentence loglines. It's important to create a logline that entices or whets the appetite of the audience you're targeting to watch the film, much as it is important to pitch a logline in order to get a meeting or send your material to a prospective buyer. Something about it must be accessible, interesting, and compelling to make the spectator choose it over all others.

You will need this for every submission entry form, festival program guide, and to pitch your film to industry professionals at the festivals. It is not the *theme,* which is the message of the movie, nor is it the *hook,* which is ultimately that "something" that will bring an audience in to see your film and "hook" them. Sometimes the hook is the *high concept* of the idea. It is also not the *tagline*, which is used for marketing purposes to entice an audience. For example, the tagline for *The Sixth Sense* is "I see dead people." That's very intriguing, though the story is really not about that. The story is about the psychiatrist.

Some festivals call the logline a synopsis and require a three-line description. Most likely they will want a few types to choose from so you not only have to prepare the short synopsis (i.e., logline) but you should also write a 125-word synopsis and a 250-word synopsis. If you use Withoutabox, they use the word *synopsis* instead of *logline*.

No matter what, you will need to hone your film down to a few sentences and create a few choices of synopses that will be employed throughout your festival run and beyond. So it's imperative to get it right.

A logline can also be used when you make phone calls to convince executives at studios and production companies to attend the screening of your film. The person taking your call will most likely ask what the film is about. Therefore, it is important to give them something that will grab their attention quickly. That's where a logline comes in handy. If they like the logline, they might ask additional questions and most likely will be open to watching the film. It also doesn't hurt to have a logline ready if you happen to be standing next to an executive or producer in an elevator, attending an industry party, or if Sam Mendes happens to be sitting next to you on an airplane. They're a captive audience but that doesn't mean you should engage them in endless conversation — having a logline will avoid cornering them. With a logline, you won't take up a lot of time and they can respond quickly. It piques their interest and they know immediately if it is a genre or an arena of film they might be attracted to.

A logline can also be used to invite distributors, agents, managers, executives, and programming directors to attend your film festival screening. If you send invitations out to your contact list, make sure the logline is placed right after your opening paragraph, inviting them to attend. If they can't make the screening, offer to send them a copy of the film for their own personal viewing, but also set up a time to follow up or meet with them. The logline will either get their attention and make them want to see your film, or it will tell them it's not a subject or story they're interested in at this time. Either way, it's a fast and easy way to garner interest in your film.

Writing a logline takes practice, but if you can get this practice down pat, it will only help you learn how to pitch your ideas for future film projects.

When you're writing your logline, you might consider adding the genre to it. For example: "This is a romantic comedy about…" Additionally, your DVD/Blu-ray jacket should also include the genre and a paragraph synopsis of your film.

GENRE

A genre is the category in which your story fits. It represents the tone of your piece. For example: drama, comedy, thriller, horror, sci-fi, biography, etc. Don't describe your film in multiple genres — all that tells us is that you're unsure of what genre your film truly is. A romantic thriller or a fantasy comedy is fine, but stating more than two genres generally is hard for an audience to grasp. Again, it's about being concise and clear so that people will get the type of film you've made right away.

All call for entry submission forms require a genre to be listed. Festivals need to know how to program your film for audiences so it helps if the film's genre is unambiguous. Some festivals may highlight the genre or have a block of films dedicated to a specific genre as part of their programming or sometimes as a special sidebar.

Also, if a film falls into a niche category (Asian, women, youth, children, student, gay & lesbian, Jewish, etc.), know what that niche is and state it in your promotional materials, flag it in a letter to the programmer, and in the letter section on Withoutabox.

HOOK

A hook is that certain something that grabs an audience, makes the film accessible, and also points out a special quality of the story that might be refreshing to a viewer. It's what reels an audience into the theatre to see the film.

It might be a high-concept idea in which the idea is easily reducible to one line and has immense public appeal. Like the hook of a song that grabs the listener, so, too, must the hook of a story grab the viewer. For example, the hook in *Memento* is that it's a story told backward and the audience has to put all the pieces together along with the protagonist. Some more examples include:

- *Cool Runnings* — There is no snow in Jamaica yet a Jamaican bobsled team enters the Olympics;
- *Calendar Girls* — Women over 50 pose for a nude calendar;
- *(500) Days of Summer* — A hopeless romantic recounts his 500-day relationship;
- *Juno* — A teen interviews prospective parents for her unborn baby;
- *Little Miss Sunshine* — A 7-year-old girl gets her dysfunctional family to drive cross country so she can compete in a beauty pageant;
- *Hard Candy* — A young girl's revenge on a pedophile;
- *The Cove* — The secretive and illegal practices of capturing dolphins by a Japanese company;
- *Logorama* — Living in a society filled with logo consumerism;
- *Twins* — Danny DeVito and Arnold Schwarzenegger as "twins."

Sometimes a hook seems very similar to a logline but it's not. The logline recounts story and character, the hook recounts the high concept. Note that a hook should not be confused with a theme. A theme is what the main character learns along the way or what the moral or message of your film is and what you want the audience to take away with them.

The hook is sometimes confused with a tagline. Remember, a tagline is a marketing line that you might see on a poster. It's a catchy, memorable phrase that sometimes becomes part of our vernacular culture.

Some popular taglines include:

- "The search for true love begins outside the box" (*Lars and the Real Girl*)
- "A family on the verge of a breakdown" (*Little Miss Sunshine*)
- "They dropped everything for a good cause" (*Calendar Girls*)
- "Here comes the bribe" (*The Proposal*)
- "Trust Me" (*Liar Liar*)
- "Only their mother can tell them apart" (*Twins*)

Now it's time to answer the following questions about *your* film:

1. What is the logline?

   - A one- or two-sentence synopsis of your film.

2. What is the genre?

   - The type of film into which it best fits. Is it a comedy, drama, action, romantic comedy, etc.?

3. What is the theme?

   - The moral of your story. The message you want your audience to get from your film.

4. What is the hook?

- That "something" that grabs an audience, possibly something different from other films of its nature. Something that is accessible to your audience. The higher concept.

5. What is the tagline?

- The line on a movie poster that entices one to see your film. A memorable, catchy phrase.

Those five questions will help you determine what festivals to submit to and will break your film down to the bare bones.

DETERMINING THE AUDIENCE FOR YOUR FILM

As you peruse the 4000+ film festivals open to you, it's a good time to determine who exactly your audience is, and what festivals would be the best fit in order to usher in the right crowd.

Some festivals might be open to edgier work or films with a more personal vision while other festivals might focus on movies shot in their cities or towns. Others might be inclined to screen films that have locals attached as stars, producers, writers, and/or directors. Some festivals may only want wholesome family entertainment. If you have a horror film, you might want to make sure you submit to festivals that are open to screening bloody, gory, and possibly more graphic films. Some festivals stipulate no nudity or profanity. It's important to find out the requirements of each festival you target in order to determine what festivals are right for your film.

In addition, you want to make sure you fill every seat in the venue and create "heat" or a "buzz" for your film. But how do you do that when you're a stranger in a new town? We will discuss how to get the most out of local publicity and you will also learn a number of ways to generate interest in your film as well as you, the filmmaker, in Chapter 4 and 5.

Once you determine your target audience, you can then strategize what groups to promote to, what festivals might accept your film, and ultimately how to create the "sizzle" needed to get noticed by that audience.

If the film deals with elderly issues, then you may want to publicize at local senior citizen centers, retirement resorts, as well as Rotary Clubs, Elks Lodges, and senior clubs, etc., with flyers and posters in the town where your film is screening.

If children are positive role models in your film, then try targeting schools, parks, and recreation centers, libraries, and Boy and Girl Scout organizations.

If art and music play a significant role, then target coffee houses, music stores, art galleries, local artistic groups, and music teachers. If your film has a spiritual bent, then you should market it toward those groups best able to appreciate its perspective. The list for any of these will keep growing as you contact one group and ask them who else you should contact. These are merely suggestions to give you the impetus to think outside the box. Reach out to those people who you know will enjoy and get the most out of your film. Sometimes, you can arrange a screening of a film in the same city as the festival at another venue (after it's premiered at the festival) and start to generate more followers and supporters. This creates a viral support system that extends itself to Facebook and Twitter. The idea is to make sure that you target an audience for your film, and that people are talking about it.

When we say targeting an audience, we mean once you get your promotional items and press kit ready to go, you have more potential opportunities to publicize your movie to specific audiences.

Once you decide who your audience is, don't just rely on the film festival to supply your audience. Don't rely solely on the film festival moviegoers — expand your audience to include those that might not necessarily attend a festival. You can go outside the festival itself and into the town touting your film to get people into the theatre that will "get" your movie.

CLEARANCES AND RELEASES

Clearances are very important. This should be taken care of while producing your films. Filmmakers enter festivals and end up not having the complete rights to sell their films to distributors because they have not gotten the proper clearances. These include music clearances, photos, clips from movies or shows, etc. In the case of a documentary, some might be considered "fair use" — a limited use of copyrighted material that doesn't require permission for the use of criticism, comment, news reporting, scholarship, teaching, and research. However, most need clearances. It is up to the filmmaker to get these clearances, not the festival. Even to the point of shooting a documentary scene where someone, somewhere, has a song playing in the background and you can hear it in the soundtrack of the film, needs to be cleared or taken out.

Music in particular is the bane of a producer's existence. If you use music, the music has to be "cleared," meaning a written agreement allowing you to use the music from the record company, artist, and composer, whoever has the right to give you the rights to use the song or composition in the movie. It's always expensive. Where once you could get free festival rights, it is becoming increasingly harder these days, though you might be able to get festival usage fee for a mere $250 a side; meaning for the performance rights as one side and the publishing rights as another side, so the total would be $500. If you have someone else aside from the original artist perform the song, then you only have to pay one side — the publishing. You should also negotiate all the rights for that music in steps should you get a distribution deal, theatrical release or a television broadcast, and that could end up in the tens of thousands of dollars for that one song.

Too many productions have gone down the tube because the proper legal advice was not taken or not even received. Oftentimes, the filmmaker cannot warrantee or guarantee ownership because they did not get release forms signed or did not clear music. If you have a piece of artwork behind an actor, it too needs to be cleared by the artist for use as well. If you are using original music, then you need to have an agreement with your composer.

If you are making a documentary, you need to get release forms signed by all the participants allowing you to use their voice and likeness on screen and for publicity purposes. If you have actors, you need to make sure you have signed contracts with them stating you have the right to use their likeness in publicity in addition to a buyout of their services (a buyout means you pay them for their services and owe them no more unless designated under union rules if the production is union. If it's non-union, you want to make sure you use non-union actors and buy them out or have them grant you the right to use their services if they're unpaid). The same thing applies to all the other participants including crew members so no one can come back later and say you owe them anything more than what was agreed to in the original contract or agreement.

There are specialists in this field who do nothing but clear music, clips, stills, character names, etc. It is important to seek advice or have a good producer on your project who has already collected clearances and releases during the production phase of the film. There are attorneys who specialize in clearance and copyright whose advice might be worth seeking so that you have all your i's dotted and t's crossed. Otherwise, it can be a nightmare for a filmmaker to find out that he or she can't sell their film because nothing was cleared in the movie and it can't be shown for public exhibition.

SUBMISSION PROCESS — ENTRY FORMS

Once you target the festivals, you will need to fill-out a "call for entry" form. Even if you use an online service like Withoutabox (which you should), you will still need to fill in the following information:

- Logline
- Genre
- Sound Ratio (Dolby Stereo, Dolby Digital, DTS, etc.)
- Aspect Ratio (4:3, 16:9, etc.)
- Year of completion
- Running Time
- Country of Production
- Shooting Format — the format in which the film was actually shot — e.g., 16mm, 35mm, Video, MiniDV, DVCam, BetaSP, HiDef
- Exhibition Format — formats available to screen at the festival — e.g., 16mm, 35mm, DVD, BetaSP, DigiBeta, HDCam, DVcam, HiDef, Blu-ray or digital media files: MPEG, MPEG2, .MP4, .wmv (Windows Media Video), .mov (Quicktime). Make sure you pay attention to NTSC versus PAL formats for the region.

All film festivals have different requirements so pay attention to the technical requirements in the festival guidelines. Projectionists need the *sound* and *aspect ratio* so they can project your film with the best quality. There is no room or time at festivals to correct or make sudden adjustments in film projection because it will send a ripple of scheduling headaches within the program. If you need your volume played higher or your color bars are one minute long instead of five seconds, add a note in bold letters with instructions to the projectionist. There is nothing worse than having to sit in the theatre and watch a minute of color bars. The programmer programmed the film for a certain block of time and, now due to those lengthy color bars, it may have added to the running time, making the film block longer and throwing off everyone else's scheduled time so they miss other movies or events at the festival. You do not want an unhappy audience.

Because of the various exhibition formats these days, most festivals have moved toward digital projection via a computer or hard drive. Therefore the films on DigiBeta, BetaSP, DVD or a digital media file are copied onto a fast hard-drive. This expedites the process of screening dozens of films back-to-back, switching between DVD, Beta, and other formats. It will cut the time in between films and play a whole short film block automatically, one after the other, with one click of the remote. Also, if the short films and documentaries are copied onto this hard-drive, it makes it easier to pull a film from one theatre over to another screen if a problem arises. That's why it's important to label your DVD, media file or film with the aspect ratio and sound requirements so it's transferred correctly.

We've already stated that the country or city of origin can be important for certain film festivals if the film was shot local to that film festival. For instance, if you shot some of your movie in a mountain or beach town, you should flag it in a cover letter to the programmer of that city's film festival as a local production and it will give you better odds at being accepted into the film festival. If you live in Santa Barbara you could be considered for the Santa Barbara Film Festival local filmmaker showcase. And if you add an addendum to your letter stating you are a local and will be bringing dozens of family members and friends to the screening, what programmer could resist a full house?

Also, if you, your cast, or even your crew graduated from high school or college that has a film festival in its town, submit your film to those festivals and flag it for the programming staff so that they realize you graduated from that area. The same also applies for where you were born. You can add this information either in a cover letter sent with the screener DVD or you can write it in the cover letter section on Withoutabox when you submit to the festival.

The country is also important because some festivals may have a sidebar showcasing films from a specific country or they may be highlighted in a short block of international films.

For the completion year, use the date you start submitting your film to festivals. Most festivals accept films within a one-year period, but some will accept a three year copyright date. If your film is balancing on the expiration dates for eligibility, it couldn't hurt to contact the programming director and ask if your film would be considered for that year's film festival anyway.

If you've screened another film in previous years at a particular festival, make sure you let the programming staff know this by mentioning it in your cover letter or on your entry form. Be sure and state the name of the film that screened in order to tickle the programmer's memory.

As you embark on submitting your film to various festivals, it will help to keep a simple submission checklist — so you can do the appropriate follow up for each submission. It's a great way to keep tabs on your budget and how much you are spending on entry fees.

FESTIVAL SUBMISSION CHECKLIST EXAMPLE

TITLE: TITLE OF MY FILM

CATEGORY: FEATURE FILM/SHORT FILM/DOCUMENTARY

DATE SENT	FILM FESTIVAL	EARLY ENTRY FEE	EARLY DEADLINE	REGULAR ENTRY FEE	REGULAR DEADLINE	LATE ENTRY FEE	LATE DEADLINE	SCREENING REQUIREMENTS	FOLLOW-UP	RESULTS
6/15/11	Sundance Film Festival 1/19/12 – 1/29/12	$45.00	8/15/11	$75.00	9/2/11	100.00	9/23/11	35mm, 16mm, HDCam	12/6/11	Accepted
1/5/11	Los Angeles Film Festival 6/16/11 – 6/26/11	$50.00	12/3/10	$60.00	1/14/11	$70.00	2/24/11	35mm,16mm, HDCam, DigiBeta	5/15/11	Accepted
3/15/11	Hamptons Film Festival 10/13/11 – 10/17/11	$60.00	4/1/11	$75.00	5/13/11	$95.00	6/10/11	35mm, HDCam	9/15/11	
6/15/11	Venice Film Festival 8/31/11 – 9/10/11	–	–	60 Euros	6/24/11	–	–	35mm, DVD	7/15/11	

FESTIVAL SUBMISSION CHECKLIST

TITLE:

CATEGORY:

DATE SENT	FILM FESTIVAL	EARLY ENTRY FEE	EARLY DEADLINE	REGULAR ENTRY FEE	REGULAR DEADLINE	LATE ENTRY FEE	LATE DEADLINE	SCREENING REQUIREMENTS	FOLLOW-UP	RESULTS

ROLE OF THE PROGRAMMING DIRECTOR, PROGRAMMERS AND FILM SCREENERS

Do you ever wonder who determines which films are accepted into a film festival? How are the films selected? Why are they selected? It's not just about selecting the best films but also the films that fit together well. Sometimes it has to do with getting the most short films into a film block so the length can be a determining factor as to why some films are accepted and others not. It's part of the job of the programming director to make it all fit together and create a successful slate of films that represents the festival in a positive light.

Festivals have a programming team that consists of a programming director, programmers, and screeners. Some programmers are assigned specific types of films to track and program: feature film programmer, documentary programmer, shorts programmer, student film programmer, international programmer, and sidebar event programmer.

Sundance Film Festival receives 10,000+ submissions each year, while Slamdance and Tribeca Film Festival each receive 5,000+. The size of the festival will depend on the number of screening venues and screening time slots, coupled with the length of the festival.

Sundance Film Festival's director of the festival, John Cooper, provides the artistic vision of the festival while Trevor Groth, the director of programming, oversees the programming of the films, the programmers, and the 50+ screeners who watch thousands of films in order to determine what makes the final cut. Their job is to help Cooper finalize the film program by recommending the best films that fit within the Sundance milieu. Tribeca Film Festival has a smaller staff with at least 14–16 programmers and, in 2011, they screened 88 features and 61 short films from 5,600+ submissions. Slamdance states they had 40 programmers last year, with half of them screening features and the other half viewing shorts, and showcased 83 films at the 2011 festival.

Monika has functioned with five to eight screeners. Unlike Sundance, Big Bear receives approximately 400–500 film submissions per year. Regardless, each film gets its fair shake with at least three to five of those screeners reviewing every film submission.

Programmers and screeners at festivals are looking for well-made films that will appeal to general moviegoing audiences as well as generate industry interest and distributors acquiring films; films that have some sort of message or films that transport the viewer into another culture and/or a different way of life.

Such qualities include:

- New Voice and Originality — is this a new *take* on a familiar subject or is the filmmaker a risk-taker with a vision of his or her own?

- Storytelling Skills — does the story take us to places we haven't been, does it draw us in, in a unique and refreshing way?

- Diversity — does it showcase diverse groups of people; will it appeal to those people as well as cross-platform to others?

- Inspirational — is it touching and does it provoke an emotional feeling?

- Well Acted — does it have believable and interesting characters that are also accessible to an audience in some way?

- Production Values — Professional sound and camera work that evoke the essence of the film in a way that rises above the norm;

■ Strong Editing — Creating a tight story with just the right pacing to keep an audience engaged;

■ Appeal to local community or demographic — The programmer understands the local atmosphere and will thus program specific films to appeal to their towns and cities. For example, if the festival is located in an area with a religious and/or wholesome community, a programmer may not want to screen a film with a lot of cursing.

Story, direction, sound, and performances are some of the strongest elements a film should have. Bad sound and acting can flat-out kill a potential spot on the schedule.

A well-made film with some of the above criteria may find a spot on festival schedules. Sometimes it isn't about the film, but the running time or theme might help tip a film into acceptance.

When a film is logged into the festival's database system and a tracking number is assigned, it is given to the film screeners to watch. Though not all festivals are alike, suffice it to say that each screener rates each film with whatever rating system the festival utilizes. In some festivals, film screeners rate each film with a rating system from 1 = poor to 5 = excellent, and write a brief evaluation of the film backing up their rating. This enables the programming director to make the final selection of films screening at the festival. Films that receive a 4 or 5 rating from three or more screeners are the first considered for selection. The 4 or 5 rating shows the programming director that the film has merit and should connect with the audience. The films that get a 3 rating are the ones that have to battle it out for a place on the schedule. If the selection committee is on the fence, the film running time will be considered, or if they think the filmmaker will attend the festival, it might push a film into the competition. Films that receive a 1 or 2 rating from three screeners become a quick pass.

Some festivals have Jury Awards. The highest rated films evaluated by the initial film screeners for each category are kicked up to the Jury (usually made up of industry professionals) and they may make the final selection. In addition, most festivals have Audience Awards for each category. A ballot for voting is given to audience members as they enter the theatre and are collected at the end of the film as they leave. Most ballots have the film titles listed along with a rating score of one to five for attendees to rate each film. A volunteer ballot counter tallies each of the film ratings for all the categories to come up with the average score. The highest score wins the audience favorite.

Winners may receive money, a statue, a certificate, and/or a prize from a prize award sponsor.

Just because you met or know the programming director, screeners or jurors, does not mean that you will secure a place on the accepted film schedule. Knowing them will help make sure your film doesn't get lost amid the hundreds of film entries and, in turn, may help increase its chances of acceptance into the festival if the programming committee is on the fence about it. However, it isn't always about the filmmakers. It's about creating a cohesive and entertaining program that is very much like piecing together a great big puzzle or editing a film so that it makes sense. The programming director wants variety, versatility, quality, and entertaining films that can cover a whole multitude of subject matters. They have to manipulate the time slots so that the programming, seminars, and panels opposite each film will attract audiences. Then they have to lock those time slots four weeks before the festival and send the schedule off to the printer for the program.

DUPLICATION FORMATS & DVD SCREENERS

Films are screened in one or more movie theatres or venues utilizing 35mm, 16mm, BetaSP, DigiBeta, MiniDV, DVcam, DVD, HDcam, and Blu-ray. Once your film is accepted into the festival, the programming director will request an exhibition preference. As mentioned earlier, some festivals are moving toward digital projection via a computer by copying the films onto a fast hard-drive so be sure and check with the programming director or the festival guidelines on their website for the right exhibition format.

When you submit to a festival, they will require one to five DVDs for their screeners on staff who will evaluate the film. Having a few DVDs available for screeners will get the film

Example of a DVD with necessary information.

through the screening process faster so be prepared for this additional expense and time.

Some festivals are beginning to accept films emailed for the screening process by utilizing sites like Vimeo or Yousendit to name two. Withoutabox recently added the function for filmmakers to have programmers view submitted films on their server.

Make sure you have professional DVDs burned and have the correct region and format for the country you're submitting to unless it's an all region disc. Most American festivals will not accept PAL. Above all, check out the DVD before you send it. Many festival programmers encounter problems with DVDs that will not play on newer decks. Sometimes a DVD has a menu but no film included or the film stops and starts or it becomes pixelated. Another issue is the "play link" is not enabled. Avoid putting self-made stickers on the DVDs because they will damage the DVD decks. Also, some programming screeners will not watch a film if it has a self-made sticker glued to the disk. Have your title and contact information professionally printed if at all possible or, at the very least, write on the disc with a permanent marker. We've seen some DVDs with a small white box next to their contact information where you can write the Withoutabox tracking number.

Dubbing costs have come down in price so it is not unusual to get professional copies made for as low as $2.50 a DVD for a quantity of 100 including the title, contact info, and length printed on the DVD.

You usually have one shot with programmers and their screeners. Therefore, you need to make sure you put your best foot forward. It is important to make it an easy experience for the programmers to view your work.

ENVELOPES, DVD, CD CASES AND SLEEVES

You don't need to spend a lot of money for mailers. You can submit your DVD for as low as 84¢. Some of the recommended mailing envelopes and DVD cases are:

- Bubble Wrap cushioned mailers;
- Stay Flats self-seal mailers are good for CDs and DVDs;
- Slim DVD jewel cases or paper DVD sleeves;
- DVD cases with second hub for double DVD or CD; a good deal if you want to put your DVD on one side and a CD Electronic Press Kit on the other side, with an outer sleeve for artwork on the inside. Make sure the screener DVD has its own sleeve because it will be separated from the rest of the information when it goes to the screeners.

Avoid using those brown Jiffy padded envelopes with recycled paper fiber. They're hard to tear open without losing the fibers, making a mess for the person opening the mail. And you don't want the programming staff starting on the wrong foot in viewing your film! Go with the bubble wrap envelopes instead.

CONCLUSION

Your film is ready to go. You know what festivals you're going to target. Now utilize the tools to get your film out there. Sign up for Withoutabox and set aside two hours to explore the site. Fill in the information necessary to get noticed and begin your festival exploration.

Do your research with the festivals so you have an understanding of the type of films they screen and how you can promote your film to a target audience.

Using Withoutabox will certainly save you an enormous amount of time filling out entry forms, but make sure you understand each of the categories requested. Provide all the information they request and make sure you take advantage of the cover letter if you have something special to share — e.g., you're from that city or the film was shot there, or maybe your lead actor will attend the festival (if it's someone notable). However, don't write a lengthy letter about where your film screened or how much the programming director is going to enjoy the film. Keep it simple and short.

This is a lot to get you started but there's still so much more you'll need to do to prepare yourself. Next up: creating your promotional materials and getting ready to go to your first festival.

EXERCISES

1) Ask yourself the five questions about your film:

- What is your logline?
- What is your theme?
- What is your hook?
- What is your genre?
- What is your tagline?

2) Determine three target demographic audiences for your film.

3) Using the Submission Checklist illustrated in this chapter, list the festivals you want to submit to and include the cost for the early, regular, and late deadlines. Note the dates for those deadlines and the festival date itself, whether they require a premiere, screening format, date sent, and a date to follow up. In addition, include a final resolution section that lists *Accepted* or *Rejected* next to the festival and any other comments that might be important to note.

4) Sign up for a Withoutabox account and start filling in the information about your film.

SAMPLE COVER LETTER ADDRESSED TO PROGRAMMING DIRECTOR OR PROGRAMMING TEAM

Feel free to change it around, but keep it simple, short, and clear

Date

re: "Title of Film"/WAB Tracking #_____

Dear Programming Director (WRITE THEIR NAME),

I am submitting my romantic comedy feature film, MY FILM, for inclusion in your festival. Your festival would provide an ideal environment for the World Premiere (or U.S. Premiere, West Coast Premiere, East Coast Premiere, etc.)

It has just been selected to screen at the NAME THE FILM FESTIVAL in June and it recently won an audience award at NAME THE FILM FESTIVAL.

Thank you for your consideration. I look forward to your response.

Sincerely,

Filmmaker Name
Title of Film
WAB#12-0315
Phone
Email

YOU'VE BEEN ACCEPTED... NOW WHAT?

"Yikes! What do I do now?"

STEVE PARHAM '11

YOU'RE JUMPING FOR JOY, CALLING all your friends and family, and then it hits you...You have only a few weeks before the festival date to prepare your promotional materials and strategize what you hope to gain from the experience. If you've been prepping all along — from production through post production until now, you are ahead of the game but there's probably a few things you didn't think of to do that will help boost your profile at the festival. If you haven't done anything to pave the way, you better get cracking!

PROMOTION

What is promotion? It's utilizing any press, posters, flyers, and merchandising to help brand your film and yourself. You want people to be talking about you and your film. You want to cultivate an audience for your film so that you can win audience awards and create the necessary buzz to elevate the film's profile. You do this by promoting it and yourself.

The first thing to do on the list is to put together an Electronic Press Kit (EPK). An EPK should have the trailer or trailer/website link, poster and/or postcard, bios of people involved in the film, and production stills. It can be sent via the Internet as a compressed PDF file along with an additional video media file, or as a hard copy sent via snail mail (though this is less used these days) as well as integrating the text and media files on a DVD for easy handling. An EPK is a valuable asset for prepping the local press and the potential audience prior, during, and even after your film has screened.

You should be thinking of the kinds of material you want included in your EPK while you're shooting the film and, most assuredly, during post production. It's important to take candid photographs of your cast and crew while on the set. More festivals are using thumbnail photos on their website to help give moviegoers a quick visual idea of what the film is about. In addition, having someone, whether it's an assistant or a producer, collect information on the cast and crew, in order to incorporate it into their bios for the EPK, could help to spin a story if the film is accepted into a festival that is in the hometown of a cast or crew member.

Once you've put the EPK together, paper the town with it!

BUILDING YOUR PRESS KIT (EPK)

Right now, it might seem like a daunting task to put all of this together. In the long run, it will be enormously beneficial as it will help you focus on how to market your film and how to describe it concisely. Once your EPK is completed, it only need be tweaked for specific outlets, but, for the most part, you will have your selling tool and be well on your way to promoting the project you've spent years bringing to fruition. Don't stop and short change yourself now.

Your press kit should include the following:

- **Cover letter** with all your contact information, phone, website, email address, running time of the film, year it was produced, country or origin where it was shot, and list any film awards it may have won. In addition, here's a good place to flag if your film fits into a niche or genre for festivals that specialize in those kinds of films or have sidebars highlighting them. Here's also where you can point out whether any cast or crew are local hometown heroes or residents.

- **Postcard** — The postcard should have a version of your poster on it with a dynamite tagline on the front and notable cast and crew members in the credit block. On the backside, include your contact information, website, running time and format, country of origin, and upcoming screenings if you have them — make sure you include the date(s), time(s), and place(s) of those screenings. There should be an area to put a stamp, mailing address and/or an Avery label to promote any last minute additions or screenings. And if there's room, include a short logline. If you've won some awards at festivals, promote it by adding the festival laurels that correspond with your award. If you've already been accepted at other festivals, feel free to use the "Official Selection" laurels from those festivals. All you have to do once you're accepted is ask the festival for the "Official Selection" laurels or make them up your-self if the festival doesn't provide it. More on this later.

Festival "Laurels" example.

- **Logline** — One to three lines describing your film; in addition, write a 125-word synopsis as well as a 250-word synopsis of your film (just like you did for Withoutabox).

- **Cast and Crew list** — On a separate sheet, list each actor's name followed by the name of their character as well as the crew along with their titles.

- **Production stills** — One or two photographs at 72 dpi for the website and at least one at 300 dpi resolution for potential printing in newspapers, magazines or festival programs (if you have a star in your film, make sure the photos include that star so you get some press out of it).

- **Production notes** (sometimes called a "Back-grounder") — Production notes can be like a diary of some of the events that happened on the way to making your film. Sometimes they can be additional bios on the creative people behind the scenes as well as biographies of any notable actors, though you can have a separate section for that. Sometimes if the project is based upon underlying rights, it can be discussed here how the film-maker secured the rights and what the steps were in bringing it to the screen.

- **Bios** — Biographies of your director, producer(s), writer(s), and any pertinent actors should also be included, possibly with an approved publicity still of each.

SAMPLE CAST & CREW CREDITS
Title of Film

Format varies, but the character roles are listed on one side while the actor portraying that role is listed on the other side. The same applies for the crew list with the crew position on one side and the person credited with that function is on the other side.

Cast:

Sue Miller	Sandy Hunter
Laurie Brown	Beth Hunter
Tina Edwards	Cindy Hunter
Robert Garrison	Jacob Hunter
Miles Black	Boyd Nogood
Morris Randall	Sheriff Peters
Albert Jones	Guard #1
Jesse King	Guard #2
Bree Knowlton	Bank Teller
Dana Bark	Citizen
Bobby Glue	Man on Buggy
Shelby Bizou	Director/Writer
Anne Woods	Producer
Elizabeth Pierre	Producer
Maddie Mae	Co-Producer
Kelly Parrott	Executive Producer
Dilbert Green	Cinematographer
Mark Downey	Editor
Tina Foote	Production Designer
Cindy Williams	Set Decorator
Mary McHenny	Casting
Blue Reynolds	Make-up
Phillip Griffin	Sound Editing

HOPE IN HEAVEN

Directed by Meredith Ralston
Narrated by Kiefer Sutherland

"They call me dumb-dumb."
– *Mila, a 20 year old bar girl trapped in the Philippines' sex tourism industry.*

Mila works at Heaven, a little bar on "blowjob alley" in Angeles City, the Philippines. Once the site of the United States Clark Air Force Base, the city is now one of the busiest and sleaziest sex tourist destinations in Southeast Asia. Mila lives in tremendous hope that someday, a customer will rescue her from Heaven and take her to America.

In the Philippines, prostitution is not just lucrative business – it's an industry. Hope in Heaven, by filmmaker Meredith Ralston, examines the country's sex trade and young women it traps. Seen through the eyes of two idealistic female students and a male university professor, the film captures two years of Mila's life and the people who befriend her. The poverty and squalor she lives in, and her hope that one day a foreigner will rescue her, are both poignant and heartbreaking.

Hope in Heaven is part of a five-year development project funded by the Canadian International Development Agency (CIDA) in cooperation with Mount Saint Vincent University (MSVU) and Saint Mary's University, of Halifax, Nova Scotia, Canada. Ralston, a member of MSVU's Women's Studies and Political Studies Departments, was the co-project director in the Philippines' project. It was here she met Mila and felt compelled to depict her story on film for the world to see. Hope in Heaven is her fifth documentary.

The film depicts the social hygiene clinic where hundreds of young women line up daily for health checks in primitive conditions. Following these visits, the women are issued passes certifying their good health. They wear these badges around their necks or on their bikinis while dancing for the Western men. Interviews with prostitutes, mama-sans, community workers, academics and clients expose the complexity of prostitution in two very different cultures. More sobering, seventeen girls (some as young as ten years old) are rescued from a casa, a local brothel and caught disturbingly on film.

Once the film was completed, Ralston knew she needed a powerful voice to convey the magnitude of the devastating conditions in Angeles City. Her first and only choice for the narration was actor Kiefer Sutherland. With strong Canadian roots and a stronger social conscience, Sutherland was readily on board.

Production notes ("Backgrounder") example. For the documentary *Hope in Heaven* aka *Selling Sex in Heaven.*

- **Director's statement** — Include a paragraph or two of what attracted the director to the project or why he or she wrote it (if they did), how it all came together, and what the film means to the director.

- **Film reviews** — If the film has been reviewed and it's favorable, a good copy of the review(s) should be included and remember to add the newspaper's company logo above the review and date.

- **Trailers and film clips** — Make this short and sweet and, above all, entertaining and intriguing. Don't give away the whole film in the trailer, just enough to whet the appetite. If you choose a film clip, choose one that will draw an audience in, either by a good performance, an hysterical piece of comedy or a shocking dramatic moment. Again, if you have any stars in your films, showcase them in your clips or trailer.

It sounds like a lot of work, doesn't it? Well, there's no doubt about it that it is a lot of work. You thought making a movie was hard, but it doesn't stop there, it just begins! Rather than being overwhelmed by all that needs to be done, start at the top and check each item off. Sometimes when you are putting together one thing, it coincides with other important promotional efforts, so you kill two birds with one stone. If you're lucky enough to have someone work with you, like a PR person or marketing maven, or if it's a joint effort between producer and director, it will get done even faster.

These days festivals want you to submit a press kit *only* if you have been accepted into the festival. This is because they can get some of that information already off Withoutabox. If a festival needs an image of your film to send to the press, they can grab it quickly from Withoutabox. If they need a logline, that, too, they can get from Withoutabox. So while you thought putting a press kit together might be a lot of work, if you've filled out all the information on Withoutabox, you already have a head start with your EPK.

COVER LETTERS

The cover letter that accompanies your press kit should be concise and to the point. There's no need to go into any great detail as the press kit takes care of that. Start by saying, "Per our conversation, enclosed (or attached) please find a press kit for my film, *One Festival Down, Dozens to Go*, which will be screened at the BLANK BLANK Festival on January 19, 2013. Please contact me if you have any questions." Make sure you use your letterhead so your contact information is right there, or if you send an email with an EPK attached, make sure your contact info is somewhere in the email and the name of your press kit file is the same title as your film. This will help the festival locate the EPK by its title on their computer. Make it short and sweet and let your press kit do the talking.

LOGOS, STATIONERY, BUSINESS CARDS

It's a good idea to create a logo that will help brand your company as well as your movie. Your logo will appear on your business cards in addition to your company letterhead. Your logo will also appear on your website. It can be clever but should be easy to read. It can also simply be the name of your movie (if it's not too long of a title). Whatever you do, create a logo that you won't tire of because you will have to live with it on your DVD cases, stationery, business cards, postcards, etc., for a long time. You can create a logo yourself in Photoshop, Illustrator, or other graphic design programs, or you can hire someone who is an experienced graphic designer. If you hire a graphic designer, try and negotiate for them to create the whole package — DVD cover, DVD label, stationery — including business cards and envelopes as well as letterhead, backgrounder/production notes design, postcards, posters, bookmarks or other promotional items, which are called "giveaways," in order to promote your film directly at the festival. One suggestion is to go to an art or design school and hire a student. You'll probably pay a lot less and get someone who is equally as talented. Just make sure you see samples of their work and interview the designer to discuss your ideas to make sure you are both on the same wave-length as to how you perceive the final product(s).

POSTCARDS

Marketing is key to getting people to attend your screenings. Postcards (3×5 or 4×6) are a great way to alert industry professionals so they can attend screenings of your film. It's also good to have them on hand when you attend film festivals to place in filmmaker lounge areas (sometimes called Hospitality Suites), the venues or to just hand out to people in passing, almost like a business or calling card.

Your postcard should include artwork and the title on one side and possibly even have a credit block like movie posters have. It could look like a mini movie poster in fact, and should have a tag/marketing line that symbolizes your film.

You've already seen examples of taglines in a previous chapter, but here are some additional festival films and their corresponding postcard taglines:

- "For girls like Mila, there is no Hope in Heaven" (the award-winning documentary *Hope in Heaven* aka *Selling Sex in Heaven*)
- "Is it possible to love someone for who they are, not for who you want them to be?" (the award-winning short *Still Me*)
- "What if you could REMEMBER every day of your life?" (the award-winning documentary *Unforgettable*)

Postcard examples.

- "For sale: Craftsman style house. Three bedroom, two baths. Fireplace, hardwood floors. Haunted."
  (the short *Repossessed*)

- "Talking Causes Witnesses"
  (the award-winning feature *Winter's Bone*)

So many times we see postcards without contact information. Imagine an executive, a buyer, or even a programming director from another festival wanting to get in touch with you. They pick up a postcard only to find out later at the office that there is no contact information! This is why it's so important to have your contact information on all your materials. That's the whole idea of promotion: to get people to see your film and to promote yourself and your movie. If they can't contact you easily, they may give up and go on to the next talented filmmaker from the festival. Above all, you want to be creative enough so your postcard sticks out from all the other postcards, reflecting the tone of your film, and, like a commercial, has that phrase or jingle that will stick inside people's heads.

POSTERS

Posters are what will initially attract an audience and get them interested in seeing your film. It's advisable to have one or two mounted on poster board because some venues will not allow you to tape or pin posters to the walls. Some festivals will provide tacky putty which will not damage walls or columns. Others offer bulletin boards where filmmakers can staple their information — make sure you bring your own staple gun and have some tape on hand. However, an easel bought at the local art supply or stationery store is your best bet. Bring it to the film festival (these easels usually fold up and can fit in your luggage, but make sure you have your name and phone number written on it). Placing the poster on the easel in an area where there is strong foot traffic, such as near the entrance to the theatre, inside the hospitality room or near the ticket sales area is guaranteed to attract attention.

The poster should have a striking still photograph or graphic from the movie with the title easily readable. If you have notable stars in the film, include their names boldly. Have a credit block like a professional movie poster and a marketing tagline that will hook your audience into coming to the screening just like you have on your postcards. It's about branding your film — you want people to see the poster and know the name of the movie with just a glance because they saw the picture or the tagline somewhere else (postcards, flyers, etc.).

Posters displayed at Sundance.

Be sure the print is legible and that the credit block is bold and large enough to read (a common mistake made by filmmakers). You don't want your potential audience squinting to read your poster. Also, make sure you have the screening time and venue prominently displayed on it. Some filmmakers fasten a sheet of paper, or a removable sticker, advertising the screening time and venue across the poster thereby making the poster reusable for other film festivals. If your film has won awards or has been an official selection at other festivals, you might consider adding the festival's laurels to the poster like you have on your postcard.

In addition, it's good to have some standard 8.5" × 11" flyers duplicating the poster just in case the posters are too large to display in certain areas.

PRODUCTION PHOTOS

Make sure you have photographs that were taken on set during production as well as photos taken from the film itself — high-resolution (300 dpi) for publications and low-resolution (72 dpi) for websites. Some festivals require a photograph that characterizes the film for their festival souvenir program. Again, if you have any notable actors, make sure you showcase the fact that they are in your film. Still photographs can be 4" × 6" since they will be reduced to about a 1" × 1" or 2" × 2" image for a festival program or website. However, newspapers may require larger stills as it's easier for them to reduce and keep the resolution crisp versus trying to enlarge one that has already been reduced. With digital cameras and photo programs such as Adobe Photoshop, photos can be adjusted just right and sent as jpgs, tiffs or gifs to newspapers and publications via email with no resolution lost. Always make sure you save your images as the title of the film and not something generic like "still" or "photo." In this way, it will be easier for the recipient to locate the image when they download it to their computer.

PROMOTIONAL ITEMS

If you've been to a festival, then you know one of the fun parts of promoting your film is to come up with interesting items and merchandise like hats, key rings, matchbooks, bookmarks, mugs, pins, and pens to promote your film. If you contact the festival in advance, some might be happy to include your promotional merchandise in the complimentary filmmaker gift bags that are normally given to participants at the festival for free, though some might charge you for the extra added promotion. This helps get the word out on your film and gives attendees something to remember your film by.

Wearing custom screen printed t-shirts with your film's image is another great way to promote your film during the festival. If your actors or crew attend the festival, make sure they're wearing the t-shirts as well. Also, by having some on hand to give away to volunteers to wear or even creating a contest in which a name is drawn prior to the screening so that some lucky attendees will win a t-shirt, might also help in attracting attention for your film and getting people into the theatre during your screening time. Create a promotional team out of the filmgoers by enlisting them to help advertise your film. Baseball caps, t-shirts, buttons, and water bottles with the graphic from your film or or just the title will attract interest if you have festival goers, your cast, and crew marching around town subliminally advertising the film by wearing or carrying these items. Two filmmakers, Renee Sotile and Mary Jo Godges, attended festivals dressed in real-life astronaut suits, handing

Courtesy of MJ Godges & R Sotile

Mary Jo Godges and Renee Sotile in their astronaut flight suits.

out postcards to promote their film, *Christa McAuliffe: Reach for the Stars*. This brought attention to them and their film. They caused quite a stir and everyone wanted to meet them, curious about why they were wearing those suits, which in turn created an even bigger audience for their film.

David Klein, who created Jelly Belly candies and the subject of a documentary about his life and the company he created, attended a festival with his producer son, wearing a cowboy hat and jacket covered in what looked like Jelly Bellys. Before the screening, they handed packets of Jelly Bellys to the attendees.

These are just two examples of how to create word-of-mouth buzz and gain attention and support for your film.

Having promotional merchandise is a terrific way to get people to remember your film. These items can be expensive to produce so it will take some homework on your part to comparison shop for the best deals. If you've hired a graphic designer to design your logo and posters, make sure they design a few promotional items as part of your overall deal with them. Art directors and production designers usually have a good "in" to inexpensive places to duplicate these items. Above all, include some money for these things in your post production budget. These items do make a difference in not only getting audiences to see your film but also as a way to get noticed by industry professionals. If you use pens, bookmarks or matchbooks, make sure there is contact info on them even if it's just your website. If it's a graphic that illustrates the point of your movie, make sure that graphic is splattered all over the place and utilized on your posters, flyers, postcards, letterhead, etc. You want to spark interest and yet be different. Regardless, there should be continuity of style and graphics throughout all your materials to keep the branding of your product consistent. The more a person sees the same clever art, the more he or she will remember it and your film!

Consider using the climate where the film festival is taking place as a way of creating unique items. For example, if it is a winter festival in the mountains or a cold location, chapstick or knit ski hats would be appropriate. For summer festivals, consider items like sunblock, hats, visors, or water bottles. Sometimes food like granola bars or candy displaying the graphic from your poster is another way to draw attention. M&Ms offer personalized candy. Imagine a bag of M&Ms with the title of your film on them? Just make sure you have your screening time, screening location, and website written on the package itself or somehow attached to the items.

You want to hype your film, capture audiences, and draw attention away from the hundreds of other films screening at the festival. Walk the streets or hire some students to walk around the town and hand out your promotional items to potential attendees. It's a great feeling when people ask for an item that you've run out of and is in demand. You're creating "heat" for your film.

Judd Saul holding FRAG promotional items at the American Pavilion/Cannes Film Festival.

Soundtrack CDs are another good use of promoting your film as long as you own all the rights to the music. Again, and we can't say this enough, make sure the cover has the name of the film, a credit block, pictures, and contact information on the sleeve, back, and/or front cover.

ESE Film Workshops online mug.

WEBSITES

It's a no-brainer that creating a website is a great way to promote yourself and your films. However, you want a domain name that search engines will pick up and drive traffic to your film's website. When you create a domain name, be careful not to make them long. Some filmmakers use the movie's name as the domain name and add "the movie" or "the film" after it. The trick is to make it short and easy. You can list your other work, your bio, contact info, photographs, upcoming festivals, and trailers. You should create a blog, Facebook, Twitter, and Foursquare account and have people contribute their thoughts and discuss your film, the subject matter, and/or the filmmaking. This can all be embedded on your website. If you've hired a graphic designer to help with your logo, stationery, and other design materials, you may want to see if they have website experience and negotiate an overall deal that would include designing your website as well. The idea is to have consistency of style and branding for you and your film in all forms of media. Don't make it too complicated. Make it easy to navigate with stylish colors and cool novelties such as downloading a screensaver or a bookmark. You can also have a link to your electronic press kit and a page for your rave reviews. In the end, having a great, easily accessible website will save you money in the long run.

Websites should have the following information:

- Contact Information
- Synopsis
- Bios
- Cast & Crew list
- Trailer
- Press Kit with Media Images (hi-res and lo-res for media to easily download)

- Press Releases & Reviews
- Screenings and Festivals
- Awards

Some filmmakers will create a separate email address such as a gmail or hotmail account to use specifically for film festivals or for any communication regarding the film itself, so their personal email accounts don't get corrupted by potential spam mail. Create folders in your account to archive and file away important emails. Student filmmakers also create these accounts to keep their information separate from their film school accounts. These email accounts should either be your name or the film's title.

The following filmmaker's websites are easy to navigate and serve as good examples with useful ideas:

www.teacher1986.com — *Christa McAuliffe: Reach for the Stars* is a documentary about the heroic teacher who brought the nation to tears when the Space Shuttle challenger exploded in 1986. Directed by Renee Sotile & Mary Jo Godges, the website is a good example on how to sell a documentary DVD to the general public and educational organizations.

www.unforgettabledoc.com — *Unforgettable*, directed by Eric Williams (*Mad City, Out of Sync*) is a documentary that follows his brother who has hyperthymesia, an autobiographical memory, through one eventful year. The website is loaded with trailers, news interviews, and humor. Plus he even sells "I'm No Brad Williams" t-shirts at the Unforgettaboutique.

www.touchthefilm.com — *Touch* is an award-winning short by Jen McGowan about two strangers who make an important connection while waiting for a train. This site is very clear, pristine, and provides exactly the right amount of information. It is very accessible.

www.themousethatsoared.com — An animated short, directed by Kyle Bell, *The Mouse That Soared*, is about a flying circus mouse who reflects on life thanks to two well intentioned songbirds. The website is set up to look like a circus poster nailed to a brick wall, with the trailer, drawings, and an unbelievable festival listing of laurels. The crew navigation button links directly to the IMDb page.

www.solitarymovie.com — *Solitary* is a feature film that won a few awards at festivals and received distribution. Directed by Greg Derochie, *Solitary* is a mystery thriller about an agoraphobic woman who's trapped inside her house and thinks that her husband is conspiring with her shrink to drive her insane. The trailer is front and center on the website and all the information you need is easily clickable.

Top mistakes filmmakers make and should avoid on their websites include:

- Contact information isn't easy to locate;
- A short description of the film is not included;
- Website is consistently not working properly or the links are broken;
- Trailers or footage buffers load slowly;
- If you're using your production company's domain name, still buy a domain name that's the title of your film and point it to your website;
- Website is not easy to navigate;
- Website doesn't give enough of a "feel" for the film and what it is about;
- Website doesn't promote any prominent talent, i.e., actors, directors, and crew of note;
- There's nothing unique or clever about the website.

The one thing we've learned about websites is that you have to constantly maintain them — you need to check them often because, for some strange reason, links get broken and text goes askew for no apparent justification — except the web gremlin that attacks them. You need to check up on your site every so often to make sure things are running smoothly. If you have a blog, keep blogging. Information on your site needs to be snackable, meaning in small bites. A website needs to be sticky. It needs to have people keep coming back and lingering on it. And to do that, it should be entertaining, informative, and updated continuously, otherwise it will become inactive and at the bottom of the Google search.

EMAIL DATABASE

There are many software programs that allow you to sort and create email and snail mail databases. We like to use Filemaker Pro, however you can also use Excel and other Rolodex-type programs to create your comprehensive database. There are also some great email marketing sites where you can archive your email blasts like iContact, Constant Contact, and Patron Mail. These email sites charge around $10, for under 250 emails, up to $150 a month depending on the size of your email list and how often you want to send out the email blasts. These sites can save a lot of precious time and make it easy to send 2,000 emails at a click of a button. The first thing you must do is to create an email database so you can notify everyone when you are accepted into film festivals, win awards, and to generally stay in touch with miscellaneous announcements. One idea is to have an email contact list available at your screenings and get your audience to sign up for periodic news.

Use your postcard design in the body of an email that will then be sent to your list, advertising acceptance into festivals, future screenings, and any awards your film might win along the way.

Another way to promote yourself and your film is to create an e-zine — that is your own flyer or magazine which is geared to your festival and career activities, and is sent via email. You could also offer tidbits of knowledge in these e-zines which might help other filmmakers. Along with advertising yourself and your film, it is important to give the person taking the time to read your e-zine something in return — information about a festival, insight into filmmaking, something of that ilk, will set your e-zine apart from others.

There is a lot of software out there that will help you in designing a format in which you can just plug in information as it's applicable for each mailing.

Use your database to send out your emails or e-zines and you've taken the first step in promoting yourself on the web. Always include your email address and website in your email blasts should people want to contact you or require additional information.

PRESS AND PUBLICITY

You've gotten most of your press kit done. It's time now to write a press release for your film. Most newspapers in small towns don't have a lot of reporters to cover these events. By sending them your press release, they can use it verbatim and not have to pay someone to cover it and Bingo! You get free publicity. OR, the press release may cultivate interest in you and someone may actually interview you for the local paper. Press releases are also a good stepping stone for promoting you and your film for all kinds of publicity possibilities. You can send press releases to the local television stations, local newspapers, local magazines, and radio stations as an introduction. Keep in mind that magazines in particular have a longer lag time (usually up to 4 months in advance of a story). Try and do some research via the web to find a contact name at each business. The press release should also be included in your press kit and can be adapted and changed depending on what you are publicizing at any given time.

A press release has a simple format. Across the top, it should state "FOR IMMEDIATE RELEASE" or FOR RELEASE BEGINNING (Type the dates a week prior to the film festival in that city)." Add your logo to the top center of the page.

Below that, come up with a headline or title for your potential "article" on your film. You want the release to have all the pertinent information yet include some human interest angle so that the press release could be printed "as is" in a newspaper or publication. (See sample press release on page 92.)

Now that you have your press release written, it's time to contact those prospects to promote yourself and your film. Start by contacting the programming director, or whoever is your festival contact, and get the contact information for the local press in the area. Once you receive that, start your plan of attack!

TELEVISION PUBLICITY

Upon acceptance into a film festival, make sure you contact the local TV and cable stations for an interview. You can start by sending your press release. You can also call them first and speak to their marketing or public relations person. Ask them the best way to send them information on you and your film. It could simply be an email to the contact person or general information address. If there is a particular television show you are targeting, contact the producers or host of that program. Ask them if you can send your press kit either via email, CD/DVD or in hard copy and point them to your website to review your trailer. Explain that your film has been accepted into the local film festival there. Please check the local station's website in case they have specific guidelines for press submissions.

[ADD FILM LOGO]

FOR IMMEDIATE RELEASE...

"HEAVEN" DESCENDS ON FILM FESTIVAL

Selling Sex in Heaven, a powerful film about sex tourism in the Philippines has been accepted into the ESE Film Festival for the 2012 event. Produced and directed by Meredith Ralston, the film follows the true story of a young girl, Mila, who works at a bar called Heaven in *blowjob alley*. The film, narrated by Kiefer Sutherland, illuminates the ever-pressing problem of sex tourism in this part of the world and the victims it creates.

[From here explain a little about the filmmakers and how they came to do the project or if there's a notable star, make note of that. If there is a website for additional info, include that here as well.]

[Be sure and put when and where it's going to be screened:]

The film will screen on Monday, January 19th at 4:30 pm at the ESE Theater, 264 S. La Cienega Blvd, Suite 1052, Beverly Hills, CA 90211. The filmmakers will be present for a Q&A afterwards.

[Be sure and put a fact sheet within your press release:]

WHO: Award-winning Filmmaker, Meredith Ralston

WHAT: 47-minute documentary, SELLING SEX IN HEAVEN

WHERE: ESE Theater (give address)

WHEN: 4:30 pm, January 19th

FOR MORE INFORMATION CONTACT: **[You or whomever you want to be the contact person should they require more info — PERSON, ADDRESS, PHONE, CELL PHONE, EMAIL ADDRESS, WEBSITE]**

After sending your information, follow up with that person to see if you can do an interview and/or send them the trailer to show on TV. Ask them how long the trailer should be — depending on the network it could be 30 seconds, but for truly local stations, they may allow up to two minutes. Most filmmakers don't realize that local stations love to put new content on their network and a trailer is a great way to promote your film. If you are able to, be sure and add extra frames to the trailer, advertising where and when the film will be presented. Make sure you know what format they need in order to broadcast the film at their station.

Above all, after sending your press release and/or your press kit, be sure to follow up, offer yourself as an interview, or if you have a star accompanying you to the festival, get them to be interviewed as well. If you are granted an interview, don't forget to bring a copy of your poster and have one of those fold-up easels handy so that you can display it in the camera shot behind or beside you so audiences can see it and identify the film easily when they attend the festival.

NEWSPAPERS AND PUBLICATIONS

Doing your research on the web will uncover a myriad of local newspapers and publications in which you can get free publicity. Armed with your press release, which could be printed verbatim, be sure and include a photo from the movie or of your star, if the star is notable.

Start by surfing the web to see what local newspapers are in the area as well as online local news sites. Find the name of the editor for the entertainment section. Try calling them directly and letting them know that a press release is being sent to their attention. See if you can email them your electronic press kit, too. And, as with the TV stations, always, always follow up with them after a few days or so either via email or on the phone. Try and get them to do an article on you or at the very least print your press release. Ask them what you can do to help them out in order to facilitate this. Make it easy for them to do the article on you by having that great press release! Remember, newspapers have deep websites and are always in need of filling them up with news. Print has less space. If you're lucky, your article will be in print and on the site. But, either way, you will get free publicity.

RADIO STATIONS

Last but not least, contact the local radio station(s). Find a contact person at the station to whom you can send your press kit and press release, much like you've done for the TV stations and newspapers. If there is someone who does entertainment, go directly to them. Otherwise, start with the station manager who will most likely connect you to the right person.

With the web, it's easy to find out what radio, publications, local online news sites, and television stations are in the area. You can use the press kit and press release you've put together for all your promotional needs, though you may need to change or amend some things to make it applicable to whatever medium from whom you're trying to get press. Sometimes a news producer or radio host will interview you on the phone and use clips of it throughout the day on the air.

Now that your press kit is out there in the world, and you've set up some potential press, it's time to get ready to go to the festival!

CONCLUSION

You may have a festival or two lined up, so now you need to draw attention to your film by utilizing all promotional and marketing opportunities out there to create a buzz and get the word out. If you haven't done so yet, start creating a website for your film even if it is only one page to begin with. To sum it up, this is an inexpensive way to promote your film. You need a site easy to navigate with information to access quickly by festival attendees, press, potential distributors, and programming directors. You want to list your upcoming festivals with screening dates, times, and venues. Also, keep past festivals up on your site so site visitors can see the various festivals your film has screened at. Your website can also be used as a way to sell your film, so make sure you have a section available to purchase a copy of the DVD. An audience member may get home and decide they would like to own a copy of your film or want someone they know to see it.

Make sure you have postcards at the festival to hand out and be creative and come up with inexpensive ways to have t-shirts, key rings or other promotional items available to distribute. Start collecting email addresses now so you can begin an email campaign to alert family, friends, and industry professionals about each of your screenings.

By thinking ahead and being proactive in your promotional campaign, it will help you have a successful festival run.

EXERCISES

1. Create a specific email account for your movie;

2. Create a website;

3. Create social networking accounts and a fan page. Make sure they're all linked;

4. Create a YouTube account for your trailer;

5. Create a Vimeo account so you can easily direct press, festival programmers or potential buyers to view your film in a private areas. Make sure you check the private settings; otherwise, your film will be public and become ineligible for some festivals.

MAKING THE FESTIVAL CIRCUIT WORK FOR YOU

"Confidence goes a long way (or is that experience?)"

BY NOW YOU SHOULD HAVE a good idea of what festivals you will submit your film to, including the cost, and expenses related to those festivals. You should also have a head start on putting your promotional and marketing items in motion. You might have been accepted into a few film festivals already and are gaining traction. However, you can't just sit there and do nothing but allow your film to play. It's time to make that festival circuit work for you.

What do you hope to get out of that experience? How can you make the most out of the contacts you meet?

Most filmmakers attend festivals with a few promotional materials such as posters, postcards, and a business card, but there's so much more that can be done to really elevate your profile. Part public relations, part promotion, a filmmaker's work takes place before, during, and after the festival. Remember, it's not just about your film that's screening, it's about you, the filmmaker; your next project, your company, and the strategy you've set up to accomplish your goals. Do you need to find representation? Distribution? Create relationships with film industry execs and filmmakers? How about garnering more exposure for your film than just relying on the festival program? Start a checklist of what your goals are and how you can achieve them. This is just the tip of the iceberg but it will put you on the right track to getting the most out of your festival experience. You can always add to your list. However, get started — because there's a lot to do! As long as you're clear on who to contact and how to get your film noticed (thereby getting yourself noticed), you should treat each day leading up to the festival and during the festival itself as one more rung on the ladder to a successful experience.

ROLE OF THE FILMMAKER

The filmmaker's role at the film festival is to promote his/ her film and network with peers and industry professionals. This is not only an opportunity to promote your current film exhibited in the festival, but also to tout your next project, and make important contacts for talent, financing, and representation for future films. Don't expect that the festival will promote your film. True, you will be listed in a program and be on the schedule — it's up to you to get your name and your movie out there in the eyes of the festival goers and industry machine.

- How do you get noticed?
- What kind of promotion is necessary?
- How can you be clever enough to stick out from the pack?

It is worthwhile to attend festivals whether you have a film in them or not. You can still meet industry pros and hand out postcards of your film regardless of whether you have a film in the festival. It's important to observe what happens at a festival. What films stick out, and why? What you can do to promote your own film?

It is also an opportunity to network with other filmmakers and compare festival notes. You might learn about festivals that weren't on your radar that would be perfect for your movie. It is also a great way to discover new talent and writers for future film projects.

If you can't attend a festival, always send someone from your crew or above-the-line talent to represent the film at the screening and the awards ceremony. There is nothing more depressing for festival organizers then presenting ten awards and having only two filmmakers in attendance. You went through the trouble of submitting to the festival, so get the most out of it by attending it, if you can. Make sure you send postcards ahead and send out your press release regardless of whether you are in attendance.

When a film wins a competition, it is the director who usually receives the award. Some festivals like the Method Film Festival showcase the work of actors in indie films and present over a dozen awards to performers. The San Sebastián International Film Festival has the Donostia Lifetime Achievement Award which they present to two or three actors. The Hollywood Film Festival honors emerging actors, casting directors, and presents additional awards for the Best Mobile Short, Video Game, Music Video, Commercial,

Advertising, and Website Content. With all these awards, it's important to show the festival your appreciation by showing up and/or having someone there to accept the award.

UTILIZING THE TALENT INVOLVED WITH THE FILM

If your film has noteworthy onscreen talent involved, will they be willing to accompany you to the festival to help promote the film? This can be difficult if the film is not in the same city where they live, and you might have to pay for their transportation and accommodations unless they are more than willing to do so. However, some festivals might be thrilled to have celebrities attend and may be willing to help sponsor that star by paying for a hotel and even for the trip there. Further, the festival organizers might ask that celebrity to present one of the filmmaker awards or sit on a panel. It doesn't hurt to ask the programming director just in case. If a notable producer, writer, cinematographer or editor is involved, they, too, may add to the appeal of your film, especially having them as guests during the Q&A session following your film.

If your film is based upon a true story or is a documentary, having the subjects of the film accompany you to the festival is also a treat, not only for the audience but for the local press. You can utilize their participation in order to promote more buzz and thereby create more publicity for yourself and your film.

Don't worry if it's just you at the festival. There are many ways to skin a cat; this is just one way to help generate the buzz needed to rise above the pack. There are other ways that we'll explore as well. Remember, in the end, you have to do what works for you and your film. These are merely suggestions. Pick wisely, do your homework, and go full steam ahead.

PROMOTING YOURSELF AND YOUR FILM

Some filmmakers have set aside some funds for a publicist. If you can afford a publicist, it might be worth your while. However, you need to be able to pick the right one. Publicists charge for their expenses and a monthly retainer whether they get you interviews or not. Take a look at some of the more successful indie films that had little to no backing from any conglomerate and see how their press was handled and who handled it. Pick the one you think would be on a similar track as your film. Let them contact the publications, radio, and television stations; get you interviews and additional publicity for your film. It may be expensive to hire one, but, if you have a good publicist, it will help generate more exposure. That being said, the key word here is "good" publicist. Unless you know them personally, you need to talk to others who have used them and find out their flaws as well as their strengths. The main thing is to not just rely on them to get you what you need. A writer can't totally rely on their agent to get them work and neither should a filmmaker rely solely on a publicist to generate all the publicity. Yes, it's their job, but you'd be making a terrible mistake to sit back at this juncture in your embryonic career hoping they do a good job for you and allowing prime opportunities pass you by. We've seen it all too many times that a publicist's monthly retainer for four to six months has generated far less than what you could have done for yourself. So why get a publicist and spend all that money? Because it couldn't hurt as long as you and the publicist sit down and discuss your strategy — what you expect of them and what you can do to help them achieve your goals. You must be on the same wave length. Keep in mind, it's an enormous amount of work to do it on your own so having that extra person on your team may be worth the expense.

If you can't hire a publicist, it's okay. There's still a lot you can do without one. Ask someone from the festival to help you find someone, pay them a small token, and get them to post your flyers and posters in the windows of the local businesses around the city or town weeks or days before the film festival. Do your research and ask in advance where the areas are in town that allow postings of festival events. Coffee houses and community bulletin boards are also a great place to display posters, flyers, and postcards. This is particularly helpful if you don't live in the town. Then, when you arrive, people will have become familiar with your film thanks to the flyers and posters. We know someone who went to the Palm Springs Festival of Shorts and her poster was the only one up in one of the local restaurants. When asked how she did it, she replied, "It was easy. I just called the festival office and asked." And *voila*, someone she hired did it for her ahead of the festival, laying the groundwork for promoting her film.

LOCAL NEWSPAPERS, RADIO, TELEVISION

Since your film may have been accepted into festivals housed in smaller towns, think of the wealth of opportunity for you to provide the local newspapers, radio stations, and even local TV stations with promotional material from your press kit as well as live interviews. If you have a website set up for your film, and you should by now, make sure your electronic press kit is accessible and that you're okay with giving "creative commons licenses" (*creativecommons.org*) on such materials, thereby allowing free usage of your trailer, articles, and press material to be utilized or embedded on other people's sites. We'll talk more about creative commons licenses in Chapter 8.

Contact the editors of the local presses and steer them to your site or email them your EPK. The same goes for the local radio and television stations. Follow up with them and let them know you're available prior to the festival as well as during the festival for any interviews and offer to help them out. After all, they need content and you're willing and able to give them free content. And, if you happen to have a star or known talent in, or associated with, your film and they are willing to help you with press, offer the local press an interview with not only yourself but together with your star. Though any publicity would be helpful, we strongly suggest you always be there with your star or subject of your film so that you, too, are part of the story. Why? Because it's not just about your film, it's about your next film and you as a filmmaker. It's about getting your name out there so that it's recognizable to the masses and, most importantly, to the industry itself. You can't think so narrowly — it's about more than this festival, this film, at this time. It's also about paving the way for your future.

Creating a blog, whether on your website or linking it to your site, as well as uploading your trailer to the video sharing website YouTube, Vimeo, and others, can help create a "buzz" for your film. You should have already created a Facebook group for your film and gotten everyone you know to join and become fans. Utilize Twitter and send out Tweets when you are accepted into festivals. Start contributing to film-related websites and blogs by offering new insight into the production of *your* film. This will help engage a new audience and involve them in following the status of your movie.

Create what is called "circuitry web-marketing." Circuitry means that if you have enough people travel through your website and click onto another website or page, and, from there, click onto another site, this creates a web of promotion. You can also allow other film-related sites to reprint some of your press materials or embed your trailer on their sites or blogs, thus you are creating circuitry or connections via the web. Having other filmmakers hook onto your website, blogs, or share comments on YouTube, Facebook, Twitter, and other social networking sites creates community awareness. Allowing them to embed videos such as your trailers, or link to your blog and website, creates the full circle. This makes your fans more invested and you'll gain more web traffic. It also will help your Search Engine Optimization (SEO) and bring your website to the top when consumers seek out indie films via Google and other search engine sites.

However, be aware that by posting your complete film on the Internet may disqualify you from entering festivals, may wane interest from distributors, and even disqualify you for an Academy Award. Do **not** upload your whole film unless you are at the end of your film festival circuit run and have exhausted all potential distribution opportunities. Then it becomes about having a place to go in order to show your work, like a virtual resume. That being said, as technology metamorphoses, rules and guidelines may change so it's always best to check each festival's individual requirements and guidelines prior to allowing your film to be broadcast over the Internet for online competitions and festivals. Posting your trailer as a teaser is perfectly acceptable. More on some alternative distributions and how the web fits into that later on.

EXTRA TIPS UPON ACCEPTANCE INTO A FILM FESTIVAL

If you are accepted into a film festival, contact imdb.com and make sure you have a listing on their site as a filmmaker. You may have to send them proof by having them go to the festival's website to view your listing and/or you may have to send them a copy of the festival program listing your film.

However, listing yourself on a site like IMDb will also help optimize search engines in finding you online as well as give your film more legitimacy. You can also link your IMDb account to Withoutabox.

Make sure you email all the other festivals you've submitted your film to and alert them to your acceptance into other festivals. This might nudge the festival programming director into deciding if your film should be included in their program. It just might tip the scale, so to speak.

NETWORKING

Most festivals offer a myriad of networking possibilities for the filmmaker. This is not the time to be shy about meeting new people. Boldness counts as long as you do it in a way that is not intrusive. Higher-profile festivals have all kinds of high-powered executives, distributors, other festival programming directors, actors, and agents attending. Some are there for their own films, while others are scouting out talent and looking for content for their respective outlets. The best way to make the film festival circuit work for you is to exploit your networking skills. When you are accepted into a film festival, find out who the jurors, panelists, and invited industry guests are who will be attending. Send them a postcard and/or an email introducing yourself to them and inviting them to see your film. Offer information about your film along with the time of your screening and, during the festival, make a point to meet them and possibly get them their own DVD copy of your film if they can't attend your screening.

One of the great things film festivals have to offer is the one-on-one networking opportunities available for everyone. It's easy to hobnob with other filmmakers, celebrities, film executives, agents, and managers in a social environment like a film festival. Some festivals have specific networking parties for the VIPs to mingle with the film-makers. It's just as important for filmmakers to get to know each other and support one another's films in the festival as it is for them to meet those high-powered indus-try types. These parties are the perfect place to do so in a social, more intimate way. A film festival is intense. People are thrown together for a few days or weeks. You begin to run into the same people over and over again at the screen-ings, in the eateries and bars, and walking the streets of the festival's village. You'll begin to recognize the same people and strike up conversations. Some will lead to last-ing friendships, others to representation and/or deals for future films or the acquisition of the film you have screen-ing in the festival. Seek out those people. Target the ones you think will be beneficial to your film and career. Don't be overpowering or aggressive. Many times we've met people, exchanged business cards, and had meetings with them back in Los Angeles weeks later. Of course, there might be those that never return a phone call and are just being polite because they're a captive audience at the festi-val; don't let that discourage you. It only takes one agent or manager to represent you, and only one buyer to release your film or license it for broadcast. So, how do you find out about the people who might be in attendance?

The film festival website is the first stop. There's usually a list of jurors and invited guest speakers. Check out what other films have been accepted so you can scout out those filmmak-ers. The festival program is your next stop because it is the finalized printout and will have the definitive list of films and biographies of people involved with the festival. Lastly, check out the film festival schedule of events. Make sure you attend as many as possible — filmmakers' breakfasts, opening night ceremonies and "after parties," panels and seminars, closing night events, and filmmakers' award cere-monies. Usually the opening night will have most everyone

Rona networking with filmmakers.

involved in the festival there. Jurors might be introduced then as well as other VIPs. Attending the educational panels and seminars will surely offer you opportunities to meet industry folks. There are usually question and answer periods following the panels, and, as you leave the event, possible encounters with those people you've already targeted on your strategy list.

Some festivals are so informal you could be standing in line with an agent or having a drink at the local watering hole, sitting next to that one important studio exec who might be interested in your film. And now that you've created a logo and a business card, you will have something to hand them. Better yet, you will encourage them to see a screening of your film by presenting them with a postcard and/or a promotional item. Many times, we've met people going down an escalator, waiting in line, or even at the airport going home (sometimes on the airplane itself), and were able to have informal conversations that led to full-fledged meetings in Los Angeles.

Your film was accepted into the festival, be proud of that and promote it as if it were the Oscars!

HARRIS TULCHIN'S
10 TIPS FOR A FUN AND PRODUCTIVE CANNES

The Cannes Film Festival is the most famous of all the film festivals. It is the single most important annual international conflux of major stars, directors, international sales agents, bank executives, and film business entrepreneurs. Consider using or modifying a number of the following techniques to navigate this and other film festivals.

1. THE PINBALL METHOD

The whole point of your Cannes trip is the sheer number of face-to-face business opportunities you can create. The market and festival offer such a range of companies, dealmakers, and personalities that a well-planned and executed Cannes stay can benefit your operations for years to come. For the budding dealmaker there are two basic philosophies to make the most out of your trip. The first is the pinball method, which means allowing yourself to roll with the action by putting yourself in places — be it the MTV party, marching the steps of the Palais at the hot premiere, taking drinks at the Bar at the Majestic, moving through the crowded halls of the Carlton Hotel and its many sales offices, dining on bouillabaisse at Tatou while people-watching, belting out a Karaoke tune at 4:00 am at La Chunga, or perhaps mixing with dignitaries at the beach party. At each venue you will bump into the people you need to get to know or catch up with. Remember though, Cannes is a marathon, so pace yourself.

2. THE MOHAMMED METHOD

A second approach has been perfected by Cannes veterans like Buckley Norris and Brian Kingman. It consists of taking a table out on the patio at the Majestic Hotel bar, across the street from the Palais, and simply sitting there all day long and well into the evening. Eventually, every person you want to meet, do business with, or catch up with, is going to pass through the Majestic Bar. If you have set the stage properly, they will sit at your table. The bottles of Perrier, the chilled champagne, playing cards, backgammon board, and a bevy of recognizable attractive performers, associates or executives will help reel in future business contacts.

3. HAVE A PLAN

As glamorously casual as Cannes may seem to an outsider, the successful insiders always go into each year's session with a set strategy in place. It helps to make a list of (and if possible, prior to Cannes, to set meetings with) the appropriate sales companies, producers, actors, directors, distributors, bankers, financiers, and the insurance guarantors that you need to meet to make your project a reality.

4. PUT IT IN WRITING, BUT BE THERE

Further to this goal, and regardless of what you're pushing, have something in writing. Make it short, make it smart. Whatever you do, do not bring a truckload of scripts to Cannes or a boxload of DVDs of your completed film to hand out at Cannes — nobody wants to take it, nobody wants to carry it, nobody has time to read it or view it, and nobody wants to have to pack it in their luggage when they leave. Be prepared to pitch your project or completed film on the spot and hand somebody one or two pages that have the critical information (synopsis, attachments, estimated budget or glossy one-sheet with artwork of your completed film and the like) clearly presented. Then follow up with a script or DVD stateside. Some sales agents or distributors will take the time to watch (but not carry back) a two- or three-minute trailer of your completed film.

5. REMEMBER: SELLERS ARE THERE TO SELL

The international sales agents at Cannes are there to sell movies to buyers, not look for new projects, and unless the company has a special acquisitions department, they do not have the time or the focus to hear pitches until very late in the market when the key foreign buyers have left. Do not pester sales agents for meetings to pitch a project or completed film. Be flexible, take a meeting when you can get one and make sure you follow up with them after Cannes.

6. THE PAVILIONS: WHERE TO MEET & GREET (AND REST YOUR FEET)

Of course, to pitch and to meet, a newcomer needs to know where the action is in the first place. We recommend that you spend time at the American Pavilion, the German Pavilion, and the various European Pavilions. Take the opportunity to meet other filmmakers, directors, writers, producers, and the key international dealmakers who are becoming more and more a force in the independent world. You'll also run into agents, managers, lawyers–they are all there. The Pavilion circuit runs numerous panels on everything from film financing to a roundtable of French directors, to digital filmmaking techniques and a one-on-one conversation between Roger Ebert and Harvey Weinstein. The luminaries who attend Pavilion programs run the gamut. The other advantage to the Pavilions is their status as the office away from home for many Cannes attendees. You should take full advantage (for a nominal fee at the American Pavilion) of the meeting tables, computers, mailboxes, internet access, telephone services, fax machines, and other business services that are essential when a deal pops up out of nowhere and requires immediate action. It also doesn't hurt that at the American Pavilion the Starbucks, Seattle's Best or Peet's Coffee (or whoever is the sponsor for that particular year) and accompanying insider chitchat is top drawer. The availability of the trade papers and the *Los Angeles Times* and *New York Times* and a constant stream of information also distinguishes the American Pavilion: keeping connected to what's going on both at the Festival and in the business in general is the key to Cannes.

7. CASUAL AND COMFORTABLE

While we are on the subject of Cannes essentials, here is a note on attire: make sure you have comfortable walking shoes or sneakers. Cannes may be the one place on earth where everybody still walks everywhere. Dress in casual clothes, except for the evening premieres, and official black-tie dinners, and make sure you bring a tuxedo or gown that actually fits comfortably. Do not wait until you get to Cannes to try it on. The shops on the Rivera are very expensive. Make sure you make friends with the concierge at the Majestic Hotel and tip him often. The Majestic is right across the street from the Palais and you will inevitably have your briefcase, handbag, dress shoes, marketing materials, or something that you will want to leave at the concierge's desk. You do not want to walk up the red carpet of the Palais with a bulky suitcase. The gendarmes will embarrassingly refuse to let you enter in front of all the paprazzi and TV cameras.

8. THE HOTEL DU CAP

A trip to Cannes is not complete without several stops at the **Hotel Du Cap**, but bring plenty of cash, as the food and drinks are pricey. Be sure to schedule and make reservations for lunches and late night rendezvous. This is where the major players play. The A-level industry movers, be they producers, directors, stars, executives, bankers or sales agents are all there. Make friends with (and tip generously) the Du Cap's Maitre d' so that you are given that strategically placed sunny table when you want to be in the sun next to this year's hot director.

Cannes in general and the Du Cap in particular follow "European Time." The serious action starts at Midnight and continues until 4:00 a.m. or 5:00 a.m. each morning. Even deep into the night, it has become increasingly difficult to gain access to the Du Cap bar. Arrive early for dinner and spend the entire evening once you have gained access. When you run into a connected colleague, it is a good idea to have him put you on the bar's invited guest list, or in the alternative, bring enough euros to tip the gendarme at the gate.

9. MAKE FRIENDS WITH A PUBLICIST

Cannes is a world most visibly driven by hype and heat. It is the Cannes publicists who rule the Festival, control the A-level events, the private black-tie dinners, the guest lists, and the other hot tickets. While there is usually a lot of pressure on these hardworking professionals to find tickets and place settings for unexpected additions to the entourages, sometimes they really do have extras. Be particularly nice to any publicists you meet and you might get lucky.

10. BRING YOUR ENTERTAINMENT LAWYER

Wherever you go, add one more important party to your entourage. **Make sure your entertainment lawyer is at your side at all times.** In addition to the key business contacts and introductions that your entertainment lawyer is likely to furnish, negotiations at Cannes can take place everywhere, and you never know when that napkin will become a deal memo. Enjoy Cannes and make it a successful and profitable trip for your career.

Used with permission from Harris Tulchin medialawyer.com and *The Independent Film Producer's Survival Guide: A Business and Legal Sourcebook* by Gunnar Erickson, Harris Tulchin, Mark Halloran.

UTILIZING THE POST-SCREENING Q&A SESSION

Most festivals allow filmmakers ten minutes for questions from the audience following the screening of their film. This is a great opportunity to get feedback and also to ask the audience questions about how they feel about the film. It creates debate and discussion, and generates even more "buzz" around your film. You can also steer the questions so you impart what you want to your audience. If your subject matter is important and you want to educate your audience, you can give them some hardcore facts on the issue. If you have a famous actor in the film, you can share stories about what it was like to work with them and offer funny anecdotes. Or better yet, as already stated, have that actor appear with you at the Q&A, and you can bet you're going to have a packed house. It's not a bad idea to have a friend in the audience who can start the ball rolling by asking a few planted questions, thereby creating a discussion, hopefully, amongst everyone in the audience.

Why have a Q&A after your film? Because it helps the audience get to know the behind-the-scenes stories and gives the filmmaker even more prominence. It also engages the audience to become involved with the journey you, the filmmaker, have gone through to bring this story to the screen. There are times when we may not have thought much about a particular film or documentary we've watched, but when we see the filmmaker's passion about the subject matter and learn what inspired them to make the film, we think of the film in a different light. In addition, this may increase your chance of getting a high rating and getting an audience award.

Most film festivals have someone introduce the filmmaker before the film screens. Encourage whoever is introducing your film to allow you one minute to welcome the audience and give a comment or two about the film before they watch it. Share a little anecdote or explain some little tidbit that will entice the audience. It's also a way of personalizing the experience for the moviegoer. They meet the filmmaker right up front and feel invested in what they are about to see.

This is a good way to pique the interest of audience members and encourage them to stay for your film (if your film is shown in a block with other films), or if some of your audience decides to make an exodus to another screening, they will have at least put your face to the film. Because films are programmed against each other, it is not possible for everyone to see every film. Sometimes acquisition executives, agents, managers, etc., who may really want to see your film, but choose to go to another film that's programmed against yours, end up seeing you at other screenings or at one of the festival parties. They may ask if you could send them a copy of your film. Don't take offense. Make it easier on those people and yourself by letting them off the hook and sending them the DVD instead. Discuss with them why you want them to see it and how you would love to hear their reaction to your film.

Putting a face to your film is important — it's also a calling card. Because that filmmaker had a welcome statement or Q&A, they're now memorable, and when seen on the street in passing, it's like running into an old friend. Be sure and greet those people. In Hollywood, it's all perception and it's not that much different at film festivals.

DEVELOPING PROFESSIONAL RELATIONSHIPS

Developing relationships with agents, managers, studio executives, and production companies is important because they can open doors for your future career opportunities. Meeting them in an informal setting like an after party at a film festival is a good way to strike up a casual conversation. Running into them at different screenings or panels, can help to solidify that relationship enough to reach the next level — which is to meet with them back in New York, Los Angeles, or wherever. That's your ultimate goal. Make sure you get their business card. Adding those all-important names to your database so that you can submit other projects and/or invite them to other screenings will help cement your name and brand you in a way that hopefully will keep the door ajar for future endeavors. Remember, you have something to offer. You've completed a film, no small feat in this economy and business. That's to be respected.

Always have something else in your back pocket. Meaning: what's your next project? Is it another independently financed film? Or is it a new script that you want to get representation for? This will give you something more to talk about. It lets those industry people know that you are thinking ahead, beyond this film. It also allows them to view you as someone who has more to offer and is thinking about the next few projects they'd like to make. Let's face it, an agent or a manager is interested in someone who is productive. They don't get paid unless you do and it would behoove them to sign clients who constantly are producing something, whether it's a new screenplay or another film. It gives them more ammunition, more to sell, and, therefore, more opportunities to make money off of you. An executive comes at it from a different perspective. If they like your work, they want to bring you into their production company, studio or network. They want to discover the next Duplass Brothers (*Cyrus*), Debra Granik (*Winter's Bone*), or Ryan Fleck (*Half Nelson*). It will make them look like heroes. By demonstrating you have more than one film up your sleeve will tell them you are someone they should be in business with. They might want your next film. There was one producer who said that he always liked to hire second-time directors because they already got their feet wet on a film and, now, were ready to get it right.

While it's important to promote the film you have in the festival, it's also equally important to promote you as a commodity. So you should always have other projects at various stages in the pipeline to market.

Don't forget to network with agents', managers', producers', and executives' assistants. Today's assistants are tomorrow's executives. They are the gatekeepers. Many times, it is the assistant who helps shepherd projects through. They help facilitate matters for their busy boss. Assistants are eager to discover the next Quentin Tarantino or upcoming talent to bring to their boss or company's attention. It will help them get promoted if they show that they have a great eye for talent. There's usually a swarm of lower-level execs or assistants at many mid-level and smaller festivals. They can be very helpful to an up-and-coming filmmaker. Try to cultivate those relationships.

The Los Angeles Film Festival has what is called "poolside chats" and "coffee talks" where filmmakers and industry pros have informal conversations. We've been to festivals who have devoted parties for assistants working in the film industry. Many film festivals offer ample opportunities to network at various get-togethers. It's where everyone lets their hair down in a casual atmosphere and the purpose is to meet other filmmakers. This is just the start of developing these relationships. It is up to you to follow up after the festival is over… when everyone puts on their business attire again and becomes more formal.

NETWORKING VIA FILM ORGANIZATIONS

While we're mostly talking about film festivals, there are a number of organizations where you not only promote your film and yourself but can also meet other filmmakers and industry professionals. Film Independent (FIND), Women in Film (WIF), Independent Film Project (IFP), monthly networking breakfasts offered by various organizations, local cinematheque groups, Writer's Guild lecture events, Academy of Motion Picture Arts and Sciences' screening events, pitchfests, classes at colleges, workshops, seminars, local filmmaking meet-up groups, and screenings offer ample opportunities for networking and making that all-important contact, which in turn will help promote your film and your career. People who attend these usually walk away with new contacts and friendships that last a lifetime. Seek out organizations in your own areas. Most cities have screenwriting or writers' groups; some have satellite organizations from some of the bigger organizations usually found in Los Angeles or New York. Certain film schools and states have alumni and filmmaking organizations reserved for those who have gone to those schools or come from those areas. All great opportunities to build your Rolodex and contact database, share information, and even make films together. It's also a way of publicizing your film when you do get accepted into festivals. You should be sending a press release, Tweeting, and Facebooking in order to cultivate an audience and awareness of not only the film, but your plans for the film. It's also a way of branding yourself — associating your name with your film and the many festivals you've attended because of it.

CONCLUSION

It doesn't have to cost a lot to promote your film. The most expensive portion is the trip expense to the festival or hiring a publicist. With the Internet, the sky's the limit in the potential marketing campaign a filmmaker can now create. Certain websites, local radio, and TV stations are in need of content, and if a filmmaker has created their EPK in a way that helps those outlets, via press releases and articles or even mock Q&A interviews with the filmmakers, you're already helping them out by giving them broadcast and print-ready content. Just be sure to contact them ahead of time, giving them enough leeway to include those promotional materials or to set up live interviews.

Creating a fan base via Twitter and Facebook (and other such sites) will engage your audience into support for your film. Possibly Tweeting from the festival will offer a bird's-eye view of the daily life of a festival participant. Or blogging before, during, and after a festival will involve your followers to support your film even more because you are giving them something back as well.

Above all, you want to brand yourself and your film so people begin to associate you with it, thereby promoting your name and getting it out there. Not only will your audience know you, but also those film industry VIPs who flock to the festivals will soon recognize your name and want to meet you. And isn't that the goal of networking anyway? Good honest hype goes a long way. If your film is good, people will want to meet you. More importantly, people will want to do business with you.

EXERCISES

1. Create three questions you want to ask your audience about your film.

2. Locate three film organizations in your area and attend a meeting.

FILM
MARKETS

"How do you say 'buy my film' in five different languages?"

A FILM MARKET IS NOT ALWAYS associated with a film festival. It is a meeting place for distributors and sales agents (discussed in Chapters 7 and 8) to mingle and to buy and sell product for international territories. A sales agent worth their weight in gold will attend at least six of the international film markets a year (AFM, Cannes' Marché du Film, Berlin's EFM, NAPTE, MIPTV, and MIPCOM). There are also several smaller film markets held in conjunction with film festivals. In addition, some focus on television sales in which films and TV shows are sold to the international television marketplace (some of which are noted above in the six essential film markets). Some short film festivals have their own film markets and film libraries where buyers and festival programmers go to scout films. We'll examine some of those marketplaces below.

FILM AND TELEVISION MARKETS

Sales agents and acquisition executives attend these markets to pick up films for their territories. Sometimes producers will have a few actors and a director attached to a screenplay, and then try to raise money at film markets by selling territories ahead of time which in turn helps to finance the production of the film.

While not film markets *per se*, we've included a few film festivals where the potential of selling a film is quite high in addition to the more prominent international film and television markets below:

- National Association of Television and Programming Executives (NATPE) held at various locations in the United States in January;
- The Sundance Film Festival held in Park City, Utah, in January;
- European Film Market (EFM) at the Berlin Film Festival held in Berlin, Germany, in February;
- MIPTV held in Cannes, France, in April;
- Marché du Film held at Festival de Cannes in Cannes, France, in May;
- The L.A. Television Screenings held in Los Angeles, California, in May;
- The Venice Film Festival held in Venice, Italy, in late August/September;

- The Toronto Film Festival held in Toronto, Canada, in early September;

- MIPCOM held in Cannes, France, in October;

- American Film Market (AFM) held in November in Santa Monica, California.

The Asian market has grown in recent years and it's not unusual to find Hollywood execs scouring the Hong Kong Film Market held in late March, the Shanghai film festival and mart in June, the Asian film market in Busan, Korea, in October; or the International Film Festival of India in Goa commencing the end of November; all seeking potential product for their studios and production companies.

Monika at Bangkok Film Market.

Bangkok Film Market.

Attending these markets is an eye-opening experience. Booths are set up, advertising the various films for sale. Hotels are taken over by sales reps who set up shop in lavish suites, meeting with the many distribution companies who bid on films for their countries. Sometimes the stars of the films may be flown in and the buyers are wined and dined in the hopes of making a good sale. Sales agents screen the films they represent all through the market as well as meet and greet prospective buyers from all over the world who are hungry for product.

The marketplaces also offer buyers a wide variety of product to choose from countries other than the United States. Some producers will attend these markets in the hopes of buying English language rights to foreign films. Producers like Roy Lee (*The Ring*) have made a career of buying up Asian films and selling them to American studios for English remakes.

So how does this help you, the filmmaker, who has your film screening at a market or film festival associated with a market? It's another opportunity to sell your film globally and widen your audience base. If you've made a deal with a sales agent, it's another chance to profit financially from your undertaking. Sales agents have long-term relationships with the many distribution houses in each country. They know what each country's tastes are and if your film is right for those territories. They represent your film amongst many films but they also have the power to introduce your film to an audience you might not have had without their expertise. We'll discuss sales agents and producer's reps at length in the next chapter.

If you have an agent or lawyer representing your film without the benefit of a sales agent, you have to make sure they are familiar with global distribution companies. They have to understand how to make such deals as there are a lot of intricacies involved. Don't be penny wise, pound foolish. Get someone who knows their stuff to represent you.

An important element at some film festivals for buyers and sellers is Cinando.com. It's a European film database serving the independent film industry. Registered market participants at Cannes, Berlin, AFM, Toronto, and the Hong Kong Film Market, to name a few, utilize this system because it offers screening times for films at the major festivals and provides film titles that are currently available for distribution, along with the contact information for the producers, buyers, and sellers attached to the projects.

If you choose to seek out buyers for your projects at these markets, it's best to contact them ahead of time in order to schedule a meeting. This way you'll be welcomed when you arrive and guaranteed a spot on their busy schedule. Companies with booths at the markets are easier for walk-in conversations. However, to get beyond the security at the hotels, it is best to have an appointment scheduled. Security is always tight at markets like AFM — you need a badge to get in. Make sure you register for the market in advance of arriving. Utilize the *market directory* they provide to pinpoint individuals you want to contact. In addition, research prospective buyer's websites to confirm that they might be likely candidates for your type of material. It's a good idea to have your trailer on your iPhone, iPad, iPod, or whatever mobile or tablet device you use, to show potential buyers.

Strategize each day at the market so you can be the most productive and get the most out of it. Take advantage of any panels where buyers and distributors share their thoughts about the trends and state of the industry. Have your business card available for everyone you meet and exchange cards.

When you get home, make sure you enter all the business cards you received into a database and list which film market you met the person at for future use. Follow up with a letter or email thanking everyone who granted you a meeting, or, for those that you met casually, remind them how you met and that you look forward to seeing them again. If they requested more information on your project or film or they want to see your screenplay, make sure you send it off to them in a timely manner while the market is still fresh in their minds.

A FILM MARKET PRIMER FOR PRODUCERS

We interviewed several producers in the hopes of finding out the lowdown on what to expect from and out of these film markets, as well as what a typical day would be like for them. Here's what we found out.

Before attending a film festival or film market, start by asking yourself several questions.

- Why am I going and what's the purpose? Usually it's for many different reasons. It takes a lot of work so you have to prep beforehand. If it's a festival or market you're not familiar with, then call people who are. Look at the events and the screenings;

- Identify what your needs are;

- Are you putting together packages? Meaning, are you looking for elements to package together: a director, actors, etc.;

- Are you looking for money? Do you already have a package and are you looking for money to produce the project?

- Are you looking for partners?

Marché du Film, Cannes Film Festival.

You should collect the trade articles (from *The Hollywood Reporter* and *Daily Variety*, etc.), so that you can target who you want to meet. These articles usually list who is planning to be there. Check out the film market's website to confirm who will be there. Download the list of attendees and blast them with invitations to your screenings. People love being fed at these festivals, so offer wine and cheese at a reception. It doesn't cost much and you'll get more people to attend your screenings.

Each festival and film market has its own agenda. You might be showing your film or you might be trying to sell your next film, or both! Whatever you do, you'll want to meet as many people as you can while you're there.

The good news is that there are many more options today; the bad news is, today, producers have to do it all. Therefore,

you must try to be open to whatever it is that crosses your path. The markets are changing worldwide. The amounts of money available from traditional financing is not as prevalent. You have to look for new ways to produce your projects.

So you need to ask and answer these questions:

- Have you any cast?
- Have you any financing?
- Where do you want to shoot the picture?

If you have answers to those questions, you can then target whom you want to meet at the various festivals and marketplaces, knowing you have something to sell that will entice those buyers for their specific countries.

One producer told us that the one festival and market she never misses is Berlin. "It's the most manageable festival and I get the most done at Berlin," she told us. There's more American product appearing there via numerous venues. They have the Panorama Screenings for documentaries and independent films along with the competition for the bigger pictures. You'll find many an acquisition executive at this festival and market.

So while the main festivals and markets that producers go to are Berlin, Cannes, AFM, Toronto, and Venice, there are some other festivals that are on their radar as well, depending on what projects they are trying to sell. San Sebastian is very easy to navigate and the people are very open. Other notables on our radar are Rotterdam, Melbourne, and London film festivals. It doesn't have that frenzy of Cannes or AFM.

Additionally, the Produced By Conference, sponsored by the Producers Guild of America, has transformed itself to not only being a place for prominent, well-seasoned producers to meet up with mid range and up-and-coming producers via roundtables and seminars, but also because of the International Production Showcase, it is metamorphosing itself into a true film mart as well. Rona took several meetings with film commissions and other international producers in attendance, in an effort to put together a number of movies from her slate of films. It was a great way to make contact in a short period of time over a great weekend spent on a major studio lot. Also, the conference sponsors ten winners who are producers with screenplays, as well as some funding attached, to come to the conference and meet with well-known Hollywood producers.

DIGITAL FILM LIBRARIES
AND FILM MARKETS

Some festivals have what is called a "film library" where film buyers and film festival programmers sit in stalls and watch films on computer monitors with headphones. This is a great opportunity to catch up on films they may have missed during their assigned screenings. The value in this is immense since it gives programmers and buyers additional means to acquire more product for their companies and more films to consider for other festivals. Most festivals have so many movies to display, that it's impossible to cover every film. This is just one more convenience festivals offer that inevitably supports the filmmakers.

Sometimes, a film may not be accepted to screen at the film festival, but is still eligible to be listed in the digital film library or film market. Palm Springs International Shortfest and Film Market has a great film library associated with their film festival that lists close to 3,000 short films available for viewing in their film market. Some are online to view via Withoutabox and others you can physically borrow on DVD after providing some form of I.D., like your driver's license. Newport Beach Film Festival has a library where you can view all the films screening at the festival, including

Short Film Corner,
computer booth, Cannes
Film Festival.

feature films and documentaries. The Short Film Corner at
the Cannes Film Festival screens close to 2,000 short films
in their digital library. Those films are no more than 35
minutes in length. The Cleremont-Ferrand Short Film Festival also has a video library listing over 5,000 titles.

Monika utilizes these film libraries to catch up on films
she may have missed at other festivals. If she is looking for
specific niche films, she will spend hours sifting through the
market catalogue finding specific films to view that might fit
the criteria of the festival she programs. One year, she was
looking for films about animals because the festival's sidebar showcase dealt with pets. She also keeps an eye out for
youth-oriented family films at short film markets.

Filmmakers are also allowed to view films in the library, but priority goes to industry buyers and distributors. Hanging out in the film library is a great way to meet other filmmakers and programmers from other festivals. Some filmmakers set postcards down in hopes that they will spark viewer's interest to watch their film.

Festivals with film libraries have a better chance of attracting serious industry pros who are searching for material to distribute or program as well as finding new talent. Short film festivals that have a library or film market connected to the festival should be on the radar for filmmakers who make short films. You could be passed on for a film screening at a festival but still be accepted into the film market.

PITCHFESTS AND ROUNDTABLES

A number of film festivals have pitchfests and/or roundtables associated with their festivals. A pitchfest gives filmmakers and screenwriters the opportunity to pitch their projects to agents, managers, production companies, studios, and networks. The organizers enlist as many companies as they can to participate in the pitchfest. Sometimes it's a few hours, or sometimes it's a one-day affair, and sometimes it's a weekend. Producers or writers have three to five minutes to pitch their projects to companies they target as being right for their material. The way this works is a bell rings, and the participants introduce themselves to the prospective buyer or representative, and then begin pitching their project. Sometimes the buyer will ask questions, request the material or pass on it right there. The executive, agent, manager or producer listening to the pitch might ask them to sign a release form and have them submit the project for consideration or contact them later after the pitchfest. When the bell rings again, the participant moves on to the next company's table while someone else sits in their place, or,

Typical Pitchfest room.

depending on how it's structured, they may have to queue up again and wait for the next bell.

A few more tips to have a successful pitchfest experience:

1. Network with other attendees to find out who they pitched to successfully;

2. Don't pitch to your top companies first; allow yourself time to practice your pitch before hitting your A-list;

3. Because those same A-list companies will have the longest lines, plan accordingly;

4. Make sure what you are pitching is right for the company you are pitching;

5. Have lots of patience.

A pitchfest affords newer filmmakers greater opportunities to open more doors and get to know more industry people. Where else can you meet reps from the major agencies, production companies, and studios in one fell swoop? For some filmmakers who have no relatives in the business or any real connections, this gives them the opportunity to network and introduce their work to people who normally would not even take their cold call.

Some writers have gotten representation from pitchfests while others have gotten their scripts optioned or hired to rewrite other projects already in development with those companies. A pitchfest also can be used to practice and hone a pitch for meetings you hope to set up later. People always ask us if they are worth attending, and after much consideration, we feel they do provide a good service to emerging writers and filmmakers. They are valuable to try at least once as long as you do your homework and make sure the pitchfest has real industry pros in attendance. Do your research on the companies via the pitchfest program/flyer and pre-event advertising. See what kind of projects they make or people they represent. The idea is to get your foot in the door and a pitchfest just might provide that entry.

Some festivals have roundtables that bring a limited amount of filmmakers together with industry pros, allowing more casual conversations which usually consist of Q&A in addition to advice for the filmmaker. Participants usually pay for the opportunity to meet these high-profile veterans and have a more intimate, one-on-one experience.

CONCLUSION

Films have a stronger chance of finding distribution and getting attention at film markets associated with film festivals, so it is important to target those festivals if you have a film or package to sell. In this global arena, hundreds of countries converge on film festival marketplaces to buy, sell, and network amidst their peers. There is no wrong or right. Maybe it would be good advice to just experience a film market without something to sell in order to scope out the layout of the land. Being prepared prior to going to the festival or film market is the number one priority in order to have a successful film market experience. Check out who is going to be there, do your research, and try to set up meetings so that your appointment book is filled.

If you are screening a film, email invitation blasts ahead of the market or festival and follow up to confirm that these distributors, acquisition executives, development executives, financiers, etc., are planning to attend. Buddy up with the assistant to make sure the meeting is on their boss' calendar and exchange local contact info with them in case there are changes or if you just want to confirm that they are attending the screening or meeting. Above all, do your research — know who you want to sell to, and have a good time!

PRODUCER'S REPS VS. SALES AGENTS

"Rep, Agent, Company — What's the Diff?"

SIDE FROM PROMOTING A FILM or a career, producers and filmmakers need to garner attention to their film via the many film markets associated with film festivals as previously stated. If there is no film market associated with a festival, then they should try to invite the appropriate people who can take their film to the next level — getting distribution.

Inexperienced filmmakers may need help selling their film. They may not have the contacts or wherewithal to work the marketplace. They may not have an agent or lawyer who can help facilitate those transactions. That's okay as there are a number of people whose function is to do just that. They're called a *producer's rep* or *sales agent, sales rep* or *sales company* (all names for similar functions). But how do you know if you need one or both or none? If you have a good agent or lawyer, that may be all you need to sell your film. So to help you out, let's define the difference between a producer's rep and a sales agent.

PRODUCER'S REP

A producer's rep (or producer's representative) is like a middleman who brokers your film by selling it to distributors for U.S. domestic buyers. However, sometimes they are involved in repping it for international distribution as well, though most likely you'll also need a sales agent. Much like a talent agent, they most often work for a commission, though sometimes a producer's rep might take a flat fee (especially for what they perceive as harder sales). These commissions can be anywhere from 5%–20% of the negotiated contracts. Some reps might charge a monthly fee in addition to or against their agreed upon percentage. Others might take an executive producer credit and fee from the budget if they help set it up or raise additional financing. There is no standard deal. Since there is no set norm, these deals are negotiable, though it will depend on how valuable your film might be in order for you to get a better than average deal. Whatever the case, make sure your deal is spelled out. You don't want any surprises when you receive a bill for expenses. Sometimes you can negotiate capped expenses and fees. It depends on how strongly the rep feels about your film and how much work it will take to sell it.

The producer's rep is a buffer between the buyer and the filmmaker. The buyer will want to flatter the filmmaker yet drive a hard bargain with the rep, so it's essential to have a producer's rep that has your best interest at hand. They make money off the sale. They also need to negotiate the term of the sale (length of agreement). In order to make the deal, sometimes a rep might short change the filmmaker by negotiating a longer term length thereby tying up the rights longer than what is normally acceptable as they are more interested in the money aspect of the contract rather than the finer points. Make sure you understand these two deal points — term of the deal and for how much money.

The size of the film and the amount of work involved will help determine the fee.

This cost along with reasonable expenses such as shipping, setting up screenings, travel, and food should all be considered and spelled out in your deal with a producer's rep. Some producer's reps are also attorneys, so you get twice the bang for your buck. Just having a producer's rep may not be enough. It is suggested you also have an attorney familiar with distribution deals. The producer's rep is responsible for submitting your film and negotiating the end result. A producer's rep's support of a project travels a long way with a distributor and sales agent. It can be the difference between putting your project on the front burner or not. So getting a producer's rep involved early on can help generate a buzz around your project. Where do you find them? They can usually be found attending the major film festivals where they peddle their client's films. Some sit on panels or conduct seminars at the festivals and markets, so make sure you check out what the festival is offering in the way of events.

Before signing with a producer's rep, filmmakers need to make sure they get an idea of the type of films the producer's rep has successfully represented. Filmmakers shouldn't have to compete for attention if the producer's rep is already representing a similar type film.

Some of the producer rep's responsibilities to a filmmaker are:

- Know the players in town at the studios, agencies, and programming directors at the top film festivals;

- Have a track record with experience selling films;

- Create a sales pitch and strategy to launch the film;

- Raise financing (if the film is not completed or is in script stages with talent attachments);

- Sell films and close deals in the best interest of the client;

- Sometimes arrange finishing funds for films in post production (this can be done with a sales company as well);

- Create a game plan, direction, and "buzz" for the film;

- Negotiate deals for U.S. distribution including theatrical, TV, cable, and home video/DVD distributors;

- Target major film festivals and obtain the best screening slot possible for the film.

A good producer's rep should have contacts and access to the end-user. Filmmakers should ask themselves if they are going to represent them and their film well, and explain all the options available to them. Producer's reps should not only have good contacts at one company but many in order to give your film the widest breadth of exposure. If you make your deal with a producer's rep for the U.S. market, then you need to make contact with a foreign sales agent also known as a sales rep or sales company. Sometimes a producer's rep can help you with this as well by recommending someone and then work in tandem with them.

SALES AGENT

A sales agent, on the other hand, sells your film to different territories worldwide outside of the U.S. (which usually includes Canada with the exception of Quebec). Territories can be sold by country or by incorporating a number of territories together, e.g., Spanish-speaking territories (which could cover Spain, Mexico, and parts of South America and Central America), or French-speaking territories (which would include not only France but Quebec as well). Since a sales agent is the same as a sales rep or sales company, for our purposes we will use sales agent to describe their function below.

Sales agents employ acquisition people (who go the festivals to scout films for worldwide distribution), sales, legal, marketing, distribution, and collection departments (meaning they make sure to collect the licensing fees from the different foreign distribution companies they make the deals with). A company acting as a sales agent for international distribution could include the U.S. market or *exclude* it. Most times they are hired strictly for foreign sales outside of North America (or English-speaking North America). Their job is to know all the foreign distributors and sell product to them. These distributors are then granted the rights to exploit films in their local territories for a licensing fee, usually for a limited term. There are many kinds of licensing including theatrical, non-theatrical (airlines, hotels, cruise ships, etc.), television (free, cable, pay TV, Pay-Per-View, Video-On-Demand, etc.) and home video (DVD and any future formats) as well as the Internet. The terms of these sub-licenses are subject to approval by the producer or via the sales agent. Sometimes a producer or sales agent may only license certain formats and not all to the same distributor.

They create marketing materials, attend film markets, and have a direct line to the buyers. They negotiate the contracts and give the producers reports while collecting the fees. For all

of this work, they usually receive an advance of money up front, or a percentage, or can also receive an advance with a larger or smaller percentage on the backend depending on the deal.

Sales agents are members of the Independent Film and Television Alliance (IFTA). This is an organization (formerly known as the American Film Marketing Association) that helps sales agents collect money due them from distributors, provides licensing agreements, lobbies the government on behalf of the independent filmmaking community, and conducts arbitrations when there is a dispute. They will also give you a list of IFTA members since the most prominent sales agents belong to the organization. In addition, you can obtain a list of all the companies that exhibit at the American Film Market.

When making a deal with a sales agent, make sure you cap marketing and entertainment costs so the company won't charge the filmmaker for every dinner they eat at the many markets and festivals they attend, and the parties they throw, against their expenses — especially if there are other films they are selling along with your film — you want to make sure you are not paying for them to sell the other films as well. While it is not easy to have an exact accounting of what was discussed with whom and how to charge that expense, capping prices for their expenses will help to prevent an exorbitant sum of money for "entertainment" and marketing. Make sure you know what films are on the company's slate and, because many sales companies represent a number of films, see what films your film is going to be packaged with. Make sure you are a strong link so that if they are selling your film in a package, you can make sure yours doesn't get lost amidst the other films and sold for less. A typical commission runs between 5% to 35% depending on whether the sales agent has been involved from the beginning of the film, helped obtain additional financing or contributed in some way to the development and/or production of the film. If the sales agent was appointed merely to sell the film, then the average rate is 15% commission on international sales.

Discuss up front what kind of sales estimates the sales agent thinks he or she can get for your film. What is the high as well as the low price it can get? You have the opportunity in negotiating your agreement with a sales agent to approve a high and a low price. If for some reason your film ends up getting an offer for a price lower than the approved prices, the sales agent should discuss this with you in order to get authorization, otherwise these prices are agreed to ahead of time and the sales agent will just make the deals in the different territories as per your already approved prices.

So, to recap, the sales agent is paid by recouping all allowable expenses (to be negotiated ahead of time between you and them), the advance, and the percentage, leaving the rest of the monies paid by the various foreign distributors they make deals with to the filmmaker.

Some of the sales agent's responsibilities to a filmmaker are:

- Determine the first markets they will try to sell your film to;
- Discuss the sales estimates and establish an approved high/low price range with the filmmaker;
- Track and collect royalties on behalf of the filmmaker;
- Have relationships with many buyers and distribution companies in each of the territories, not just one;
- Negotiate and draw up the contracts for each territory;
- Seek filmmaker's approval for sales that fall below the approved price;
- Set up screenings at the various film markets;
- Reasonable marketing, entertainment, and travel expenses;
- Have a decent slate of pictures they represent.

Filmmakers need to be honest with themselves and understand what they have to sell. A film may not be suited for a theatrical run and may be better suited to a straight to cable deal or DVD deal. In some cases, filmmakers will not see profits unless the DVD sales are strong. But a number of filmmakers make a good living selling VOD and Direct-to-DVD. This is nothing to be ashamed of, so don't discount this as a potential source of income.

BUYER'S REP

There is a third representative which is more of a niche than the other two types of agents. A *buyer's rep* represents the buyer. They have little contact with the filmmaker and act as an intermediary between the sales agent and the film buyers themselves. A sales agent will contact a buyer's rep in order to sell through to the companies the buyer's rep represents in foreign territories. They are paid by the buyers and help to get them the best product. As filmmakers, you don't need to concern yourself with a buyer's rep but it is important to know they are out there.

Most importantly, know the difference between a sales agent and a producer's rep, and then figure out what exactly you and your film needs to go beyond the film festival circuit. A film festival is only a step in the right direction. It doesn't end there!

CONCLUSION

There are other factors a producer and filmmaker need to consider while attending a festival. Some festivals have marketplaces in which their film can be promoted and sold in other territories. Attention must be paid as to whether the filmmakers will act on behalf of themselves or hire a sales agent and producer's rep to do their bidding. Whether

REPRESENTATION CHART

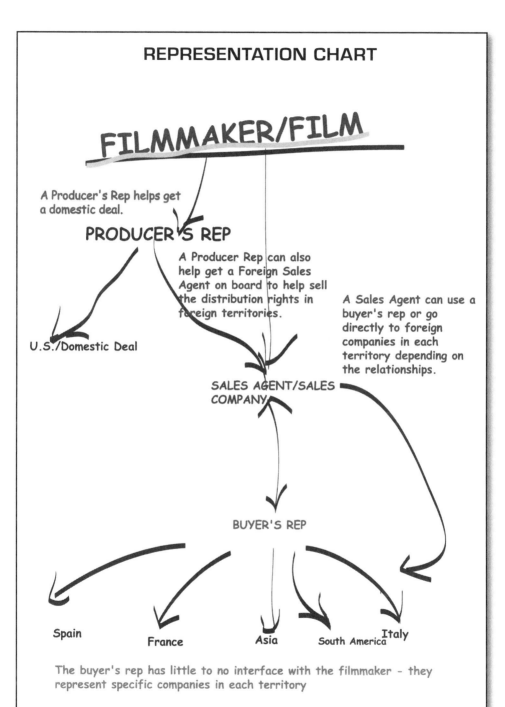

FILMMAKER/FILM

A Producer's Rep helps get a domestic deal.

PRODUCER'S REP

A Producer Rep can also help get a Foreign Sales Agent on board to help sell the distribution rights in foreign territories.

A Sales Agent can use a buyer's rep or go directly to foreign companies in each territory depending on the relationships.

U.S./Domestic Deal

SALES AGENT/SALES COMPANY

BUYER'S REP

Spain

France

Asia

South America

Italy

The buyer's rep has little to no interface with the filmmaker - they represent specific companies in each territory it's to raise money for another film by pre-selling territories or to make money on existing completed films, it would behoove the filmmakers to look for a sales agent that understands what their film is worth and how much it might bring in. But it also behooves the filmmakers to understand the costs involved in hiring a sales agent and producer's rep — though those expenses are usually recouped with the first sales.

In any case, having someone represent your film is necessary if you want to expand on the marketplace outside of film festivals. That being said, a film festival is the tipping point that can elevate a film into the international marketplace.

EXERCISES

1. Create a chart listing the different foreign territories you think your film will appeal to so you are prepared for a discussion with a sales rep.

2. What avenues domestically do you think your film is suitable for? (theatrical, broadcast, educational, etc.) List all possibilities.

DISTRIBUTION IN OUR MODERN WORLD

"You mean making the film isn't enough?"

WITH THE EVER-CHANGING TECHNOLOGICAL ACCOM-PLISHMENTS of our modern-day world offering multitudes of possibilities for artists to distribute and deliver their work outside the traditional formulas, it's hard to keep up with a myriad of choices available. We'll attempt to give you an overview of the environment today while offering some suggestions of alternative ways of getting your work out there and seen. If nothing else, you should be aware of the potential streams of income your film might bring in. Make a list of these possibilities; try and do some research as to the dollars a film like yours might garner and you may be able to not only make your output back, but also have a continuous stream of income from it. It's not just about a theatrical distribution, a television broadcast, and a home video sale anymore. Though it would be nice to have all three, with digital distribution, on demand and streaming, Pay-Per-View, library and educational sales, the filmmaker has to wear not just the hat of the creative force behind the film but also the salesman in front of the film. If you can't do that, then you need to include in your budget someone who can wear that hat or you will miss out on your film's true potential.

DISTRIBUTORS

Ultimately, everyone wants to get theatrical distribution for their film. It's the traditional way and it's probably still the most prestigious way of getting your film out there. But it's not the only way anymore. Filmmakers don't have to be at the beck and call of distributors and/or studios. There are alternatives that can still get your film seen by the masses.

However, let's begin with the way it was and still is today, and then identify those alternatives. A film needs a distributor to either:

- Release the film theatrically;
- Sell the film to different territories worldwide;
- Sell to other mediums (TV, DVD, etc.).

A film festival is not a sure-fire way to get distribution, but it is a sure way to get your film seen. You can invite distributors to view your film, create buzz, and ultimately give it your best shot. We've already mentioned numerous ways to achieve that buzz and promote your film and yourself in previous chapters.

Short films can also have a distribution life. Approximately 5% of the short films made get some form of distribution compared to at least five feature films that open each week.

Documentaries, too, are getting theatrical releases due to the success of Michael Moore, Morgan Spurlock, and others who have made a sound business of documentary filmmaking where it once wasn't profitable. Documentaries also perform well in educational and library distribution.

Do your research and know who the key players are at the distribution companies who acquire films. Write their name down on a list, along with their lower-level executives and assistants who help them search and acquire material. A lot of these executives are guest speakers on film festival panels. Use this as a great opportunity to capture their attention. Also, networking with other filmmakers, where you can share information and find out first-hand what other people have experienced, will help you to avoid the pitfalls of the distribution deal. Regardless, you should make sure you have proper representation to actually make those deals so you don't get the short end of the stick.

Top film festivals will attract the top acquisition executives, distributors, and buyers. The smaller festivals may get the junior executives and assistants covering the festival to scout films and talent that may not have been accepted into the top festivals. Don't discount film festivals like Rotterdam, Seattle, Mill Valley, Telluride, San Sebastian, Cinequest, and the Hamptons Film Festival, to name a few. These are great festivals to launch your film and create word of mouth.

A theatrical distributor will take a distribution fee from the profits and are responsible for the prints, marketing, and advertising that will more than likely go beyond the cost of making the film. Most advertising adds up to two thirds of the original budget of the film. When making a deal with a distribution company, the filmmaker is responsible for a number of items to deliver to that company. Seek out this information directly from these companies, but know you are responsible for the additional costs if you have not budgeted for them in your production or post production budget.

Some essential deliverables that could be requested are: the movie master (if on film) or other forms of transfers, signed talent agreements, credit blocks, a press kit that would include hi-res digital photos (some taken during the shoot), bios for both actors and talent behind the scenes, copyright registration, chain of title, and all clearances (music, likeness, and the lot). Some require a separate track for dubbing languages for different territories; some require closed captioning (especially in television). Check with the distributor for these deliverables as some may differ according to territory and needs while due to the changing technology, requirements may vary. Just be prepared for additional costs.

Understanding distribution deals is the responsibility of the sales agent and producer's rep. However, you should educate yourself on the various deal points. A good lawyer will also help and sometimes that lawyer might happen to be a producer's rep, as previously discussed. They negotiate the deals, but you need to have an understanding of what you expect from them in return.

But what do distribution companies expect from filmmakers? We'll be delving into this question more in Chapter 10 where we will interview prominent indie film distributors and get the lowdown directly from the horse's mouth.

NEW WAYS OF DISTRIBUTION

Filmmakers have a wide array of possibilities for distribution these days. They are not limited to a theatrical release or television broadcast. The Internet has changed all that. Some companies have set up arms that help self-distribute indie films so the filmmakers have access to the company's experience and contacts, charging them a fee for this service.

Most filmmakers dream of a theatrical release but the exhibitors are the ones preventing that. Ask yourself this question: Why would they book a small indie film into their theatre when they can have the next tentpole film from a major studio and make four times as much money? That's the reasoning they will use and, after all, they write the checks. However, it's not impossible for smaller films to get seen and build an audience either but that requires some strong word of mouth and buzz. Studio specialty arms pay attention to that strong hype.

One alternative to obtaining theatrical exhibition is Truly Indie, a company run by producers and entrepreneurs, Mark Cuban and Todd Wagner. They allow filmmakers to control the rights to their films and help them get their films screened in theatres for a flat fee. Their service includes publicity and marketing, which in turn helps garner attention and hopefully raises the film's profile. The cost for their service varies, but the average is $60,000 to $70,000. They're able to do this because Truly Indie is a subsidiary of 2929 and Magnolia Pictures. They own the Landmark theatres and have a ready-made network of theatres in 19 markets. Filmmakers submit their films to Truly Indie and then the company picks films that have artistic yet commercial potential for their theatres. This is one way of self-distributing your film with an end result guaranteed. Currently, there are 57 Landmark theatres in America and Truly Indie hopes to sign deals with affiliate theatres as well. All films are screened digitally, thus cutting down the cost of prints.

Other distribution houses, like Roadside Attractions, have also been known to work with filmmakers to distribute their films as a service and for a fee. It would be good to explore as many companies as you can that offer this kind of service.

DVD AND TELEVISION BROADCASTS

If you are lucky enough to get a distribution deal and a theatrical release, you may have a DVD and/or television broadcast deal as part of the overall distribution pact or keep each deal separate. DVD sales have been declining of late due to the onslaught of on demand, Pay-Per-View, and digital distribution platforms now available. However, you still want to include this potential stream of income in your overall business distribution plan. Most studios have Digital Distribution departments while some distribution houses do nothing but distribute DVDs or facilitate On Demand streaming. With Blu-ray technology, DVDs may still be a viable market, though you will also want to consider various forms of digital distribution after your window of DVD sales is exploited and if the distribution company (unless you're self-distributing) allows for this.

The same can be true of television broadcasts. Cable networks, in particular, acquire finished products all the time. Premium channels such as HBO and Showtime, along with IFC and Sundance, look for indie films as they have air time to fill and because it plays to their audience. Niche channels like Logo and Syfy offer opportunities for indie films that target very specific audiences. Documentaries find homes on the major premium channels, as well as the Discovery Channel, History Channel, National Geographic, IFC, PBS, and Sundance.

Know your outlets and where your film fits in.

INTERNET VIDEO SERVICES: ITUNES, NETFLIX, ETC.

More than ever before, filmmakers can self-distribute their work online without the middleman. Using online companies like iTunes and Netflix, indie film has found a way to gain an audience through alternative distribution. Even Blockbuster Video changed its infrastructure to add digital download to their in-store and by-mail rentals, forced into it by the success of Netflix, though they were a bit behind the curve and are now on the path of bankruptcy protection. It remains to be seen if they can salvage and re-organize the company. Redbox specializes in the vending of DVDs and games located at supermarket kiosks (vending machines) making it consumer convenient.

These video services have licensing agreements with the studios and independent distributors to provide a way for their customers to have access to the latest films released. But more importantly, companies like Netflix are on the cutting edge by offering VOD and streaming movies readily available for viewing with the click of a button. It won't be long until there will be no DVDs and everything will just be rented by downloading to a box directly to your television set.

Blu-ray, however, is about technology and less about the disc it comes on. Blu-ray is basically software, enabling content to be downloaded and updated whenever the studio and/ or filmmaker deems necessary. Trailers, behind the scenes updates, commentary with directors that happens live while you're watching the film are just the tip of the iceberg of what Blu-ray is capable of. This technology works perfectly with cyberspace and therefore will play an interesting role in the future of downloadable, VOD, and streaming movies.

Sometimes making a direct deal with a Walmart or Target, though difficult to accomplish and oftentimes time-consuming, will help propel a film into prominence. We know of one instance in which documentary filmmakers went directly to Walmart, pitched their film, and were accepted by the chain of low-cost department stores to sell their film, thus providing a steady stream of income for their movie. This takes perseverance and a bit of detective work, however. They contacted someone at Walmart who handed it up to the right person and the next thing you know they were in negotiations with the conglomerate. This is not the norm, however. But it just shows that having a little moxie can go a long way.

PAY-PER-VIEW AND VIDEO-ON-DEMAND

Satellite and cable companies have offered Video-On-Demand (VOD) and Pay-Per-View (PPV) for a while now. But with Netflix proving the model of easy accessibility and convenience for the consumer, more and more people are taking advantage of this mode of operation. Apple TV has gotten into the act and basically has connected everything media (from music to television to features) in one easy, manageable place. Google TV is not far behind. Therefore, filmmakers might consider selling directly to these companies if an overall distribution deal is not in place that encompasses this.

STREAMING AND DIGITAL DISTRIBUTION

IndieFlix is an online distribution network in which audiences can watch indie films and documentaries for a fee. Seventy percent of the profits go directly into the filmmakers pocket on a non-exclusive basis. Membership based, audiences can stream indie films hot off the festival circuit 24/7 for a monthly or yearly fee.

Film Baby, another online digital distribution network, is non-exclusive. They take 20% and give the filmmaker 80%. For a one time set up fee (around $40) they will set up a website for you. The only criteria is that you have your own barcode and if you don't, they can set that up for an additional $25. They also offer retail distribution and have partnerships with Super D (a wholesaler that distributes to directly to stores), Ryco Distribution, and Netflix.

CreateSpace, a subsidiary of Amazon, offers a self-distribution model akin to self-publishing books. CreateSpace allows filmmakers to distribute their movies on Amazon and thus utilize their vast search engine capabilities. Plus there's an air of legitimacy to having your product sold on Amazon.

Digital distribution, once the wave of the future, is now here to stay. There are countless other companies, whether established or up-and-comers, to also consider. There is an argument for and against whether you should allow your film to be on more than one website. Do your research. Just make sure you are not exclusive and that the cut is at least 70% or more. In addition, try to retain the rights to sell DVD copies of your film on your own website and at festivals.

A WORD ABOUT THE INTERNET

If you choose to stream your film on the Internet, whether on your own website or via Facebook, MySpace, Vimeo, or other networking sites, you must be aware that you are allowing anyone and everyone to view and embed your film into their websites (unless you password protect it). It sounds good, but there are still such issues as copyright to contend with. Copyright tries to protect creative content, but how do you protect your work on the web where people from all over the world can capture, embed, and link to your films, writing, and art? Information on the web is meant to be given away in order to gain the widest possible audience. Art is handed down through the ages and now with sampling and blogs, even more so. But there needs to be some form of license that allows this usage while still limiting consumers from changing it without permission. Or selling it when it's intended to be free. Or worse, claiming that they created it.

You may want to consider a Creative Commons license. Creative Commons licenses help you to publish your work online while letting others know exactly what they can and can't do with your work. When you choose a license, CreativeCommons.org will provide you with tools and tutorials that let you add licensing information to your site, or to one of several free hosting services that have incorporated Creative Commons into them. Technically, from the moment of creation, it is protected and copyrighted but sometimes it is good to have a stipulation posted on your site.

We as artistic individuals want to get the widest breadth of audience to view our work as possible, but we must also be responsible for this freedom. Creative Commons offers a way to protect your work on the web and still give it away, leaving you some semblance of control as to what you are allowing and licensing to the public.

That being said, note as we have said before, screening your film on the Internet could disqualify it from specific festivals and competitions, so it's best, if you plan to do this, to wait until you are through with your festival circuit run.

LIBRARIES AND EDUCATIONAL USES

Filmmakers should not underestimate the potential money-making opportunities for selling their films to libraries, film societies or organizations, and educational buyers.

Local bookstores that target the educational market or special niches may benefit from selling your film. For instance, if your film has a children's, spiritual or gay slant, there are many independent stores who just might be willing to give your DVD a spot on their shelf if you take the time to introduce them to your film. There are a few specific magazines and journals that list books and DVDs which libraries use to make their selections. Among them are Video Librarian (*www.videolibrarian.com*), Library Journal (*www.libraryjournal.com*), and School Library Journal (*www.schoollibraryjournal.com*). Send them a letter with your DVD and ask them to review your film. This is especially helpful with documentaries that have a social, historical, educational or scientific component to them.

Having a press kit available and lesson plans to help increase the educational interest could also enhance a sale to this market. Since some libraries and schools can only purchase films from a company and not individual filmmakers, you may need to hook up with a distributor who specializes in sales to the educational marketplace, but make sure it's a non-exclusive deal and that you maintain your right to sell the DVD yourself either at film festivals or on your website.

KEY PLAYERS IN INDEPENDENT FILM DISTRIBUTION

While the studios all have an indie film acquisition arm, there are also a number of other distribution companies that have helped propel and establish independent film to audiences worldwide. Below is a partial list of key studio specialty arms and independent film distribution companies who attend film festivals looking for product to distribute:

- 7th Art Releasing
- Focus Features
- Fortissimo Films
- Fox Searchlight
- Here Media
- IFC Films
- Lionsgate
- Magnolia Pictures
- Myriad Pictures
- National Geographic Films
- Roadside Attractions
- Samuel Goldwyn Films
- Sony Pictures Classics
- Strand Releasing
- Summit
- The Weinstein Company

FOUR-WALLING AND RENTING SCREENING ROOMS

Another choice filmmakers have is four-walling their film. Four-walling is when filmmakers rent a movie theatre for a flat fee to screen their film for a short length of time — possibly one or two weeks. Four–walling refers to the four walls in the movie theatre.

Many filmmakers do this in order to have a public screening so the film can become eligible for Academy Award consideration. Becoming eligible for an Academy Award means you have to have your film on public exhibition for a limited

amount of time (check the Academy website for exact qualifications). The theatre takes the concession (popcorn, candy,
drinks, etc.) money and the filmmakers gets to keep the box
office money. However, unless your film is sold out every
night, don't expect to make a profit, in fact you may not
make back your rental fee, but with the proper promotion
you just might break even or at least get back some money
for the theatre rental expense.

So if you don't have your premiere held at a film festival, a
great way to gain exposure for your film is to rent a screening
room and four-wall it. A lot of times, however, this is viewed
by distribution companies as a film that didn't get into festivals. So you must be careful how you present the film. Turn
it into a cast and crew screening and invite everyone on your
Rolodex, including agents, managers, studio executives,
producers, producer reps, sales reps, and distributors. Do
your homework and find out who the up-and-coming assistants are in town working on desks at literary agencies and
at studios. Send them an invitation. Don't forget to offer food
and wine — when there is food, people will come.

One rep confided to us that when she's invited distributors
to one of her films at a film festival, she might employ good-
looking interns to collect the distributor and escort him or
her to the screening, just to make sure they attend. No one
can resist a pretty face, and when that face also asks advice
of that person, well, no one can resist being a mentor either.
You have to think outside the box and entice people to come
to your screening whether at a film festival or if you set up
your own four-wall screening.

Some filmmakers share a block of time with another filmmaker so the cost is shared. If you have a feature film you
may consider teaming up with a shorts filmmaker and screen
their film before your film, or if you are a shorts filmmaker
consider going in with three or four other short films and

SCREENING ROOMS LOCATED AROUND LOS ANGELES

Screening Room	City	Website/Contact
ACADEMY OF MOTION PICTURE ARTS & SCIENCES		oscars.org
Linwood Dunn Theater (286 seats)	Hollywood	
Samuel L. Goldwyn Theater (1,012 seats)	Beverly Hills	
ACADEMY OF TELEVISION ARTS & SCIENCES (600 seats)	North Hollywood	emmys.tv/
CHARLES AIDIKOFF SCREENING ROOM (53 seats)	Beverly Hills	aidikoff.tv
THE CAHUENGA THEATER AT IO FILM (45 seats)	Hollywood	cahuengatheater.com
CLARITY SCREENING ROOM (114 seats)	Beverly Hills	claritypartners.net
CULVER STUDIOS	Culver City	theculverstudios.com/
De Mille Theater (70 seats)		
The Ince Theater (119 seats)		
ICM Screening Room MGM Tower	Century City	310-550-4310
(Screening Room 1: 127 seats; Screening Room 2: 46 seats)		
DIRECTORS GUILD THEATERS (600/155/38 seats)	Hollywood	dga.org
HARMONY GOLD THEATER (381 seats)	Hollywood	harmonygold.com/ theater/
LACMA-LA Museum of Art-Bing Theater (600 seats)	Los Angeles	lacma.org
LOS ANGELES FILM SCHOOL – LAFS Theater (345 seats)	Hollywood	lafilm.edu
MGM (127 seats/46 seats/16 seats)	Century City	mgm.com
NEW LINE SCREENING ROOM (48 seats)	Los Angeles	newline.com
OCEAN SCREENING ROOM (45 seats)	Santa Monica	oceanscreening.com/ facility/
PACIFIC DESIGN CENTER, SilverScreen Theater (388 seats)	West Hollywood	pacificdesigncenter.com
PARAMOUNT THEATER (528 seats/284 seats)	Hollywood	www.paramount.com
RALEIGH STUDIOS	Hollywood	raleighstudios.com
Chaplin Theater: 161 seats;		
Fairbanks Screening Rooms: 36 seats;		
Pickford Screening Room: 38 seats		
SONY STUDIOS (102 seats)	Culver City	sony.com
Jimmy Stewart Building Screening Rooms 23 and 24 (94 seats)		
Thalberg Bldg. Screening Rooms		
Screening Rooms A – F (various from 28 to 40 seats)		
20TH CENTURY FOX STUDIOS	Los Angeles	foxmovies.com
Darryl F. Zanuck Theater (476 seats)		
UNIVERSAL STUDIOS	Universal City	universalstudios.com
Screening Rooms (2 & 3:100 seats; Screening Room 488: 35 seats)		
WALT DISNEY STUDIOS	Burbank	studioservices.go.com/ postproduction/screening_rooms.html
Frank Wells Building Screening Room (116 seats)		
Old Animation Building Rooms 11 and 12 (54 seats)		
WARNER BROS. STUDIOS	Burbank	warnerbros.com
Steven J. Ross Theater (516 seats)		
Screening Room 5 (113 seats); Screening Room 12 (226 seats)		
WILSHIRE SCREENING ROOM – Screening Service Group (SSG) (43 seats)	Beverly Hills	studioscreenings.com/
WRITERS GUILD THEATER (541 seats)	Beverly Hills	wga.org

SCREENING ROOMS LOCATED IN NEW YORK

Screening Room	Website/Contact
57 SCREENING ROOM (55 seats)	57screeningroom.com
THE LIGHTHOUSE (236 seats)	
BROADWAY SCREENING ROOM (40 seats)	mybsr.com
BRYANT PARK HOTEL (70 seats)	bryantparkhotel.com
DGA THEATER (436 seats)	dga.org
DISNEY PARK AVENUE SCREENING ROOM (55 seats)	parkavenuescreening-room.com
DOLBY SCREENING ROOM (88/24 seats)	www.dolby.com/professional/services/cinema/at-dolby.html
FREDERICK P. ROSE HALL HOME OF JAZZ AT LINCOLN CENTER (1109 seats)	jalc.org/venues
GOLDCREST POST (50 seats)	goldcrestpost.com
MAGNO SOUND SCREENING ROOMS (68 seats/37 seats)	magnosound.com
MGM (88 seats)	(212) 708-0300
PARAMOUNT (72 seats)	(212) 846-4538
PLANET HOLLYWOOD (49 seats)	planethollywood.com
SONY (72 seats)	(212) 833-8000, Ext. 8500
SOUND ONE (50 seats)	(212) 765-4757
TRIBECA SCREENING ROOM (72 seats)	tribecafilmcenter.com
TRIBECA GRAND HOTEL (100 seats)	grandhospitality.com
UNIVERSAL (74 seats)	(212) 445-3833
HELEN MILLS THEATER (140 seats)	helenmills.com
MARK FORMAN PRODUCTIONS CORP (10 seats)	screeningroom.com
MUSEUM OF MOVING IMAGE (267 seats)	movingimage.us
NEW YORK FILM ACADEMY SCREENING ROOM (200 Seats)	nyfa.com
QUAD CINEMAS	quadcinema.com
STEINER STUDIOS (Brooklyn Navy Yard)	steinerstudios.com
TECHNICOLOR CREATIVE SERVICES	technicolor.com

make it a block of shorts with a reception before or a party afterwards. This is advantageous because it not only saves cost but will most likely garner a larger audience — after all, each filmmaker will be inviting cast and crew along with family and friends, let alone industry contacts. Just make sure that the film(s) you pair yourself with are respectable and that the film program makes sense.

Whatever you do, don't hold a screening in Los Angeles or New York the same time the Sundance Film Festival or Cannes Film Festival is happening. You won't get the audience you want since most of the industry is hobnobbin' in Park City or the South of France. Pay attention to when the major film festivals are happening and hold your screening when there are no distractions for the film industry. Try and get your screening listed in the trade papers such as *The Hollywood Reporter* and *Daily Variety*. All you need to do is send them your press release; just make sure to address it to the proper person.

Other cities such as New York also have screening rooms. You can find this out online or via different publications indigenous to those cities, such as *LA 411* and *New York 411*. Variety.com offers pricing and locations both in L.A. and in New York.

CONCLUSION

More than ever there are opportunities for filmmakers to be creative with their distribution models. They can have someone do it for them, like a sales rep, or they can DIY it. It takes hard work, determination, and a boundless amount of energy to accomplish a formidable release and use all possibilities available to them. With technology changing faster than anyone could have imagined, filmmakers should keep a keen eye toward those opportunities to get their work shown in many different platforms and avenues. Each can offer a

stream of income, but more than that, it might offer exposure and anticipation for the filmmaker's next project by
building a following.

Ask festival organizers to use their Twitter and Facebook
account to help announce the release. Generate publicity to
promote your film once you secure a distributor. Remember, you can't just sit back and hope they do the job; you
have to be proactive and try to generate sales on your own
to get people to attend the first-week opening, buy, rent, or
download the DVD. Take advantage of this new world of
technology and promotion. Above all, don't be discouraged
if you don't get the big distribution deal, because there are
still many avenues you can take to get your work seen and
make money. Put your nose to the grindstone and leave no
stone unturned.

FOLLOWING UP AFTER THE FESTIVAL

"Keeping the dream alive!"

SCHMOOZING OR NON-SCHMOOZING?

PLEASE WAIT TO BE SEATED

STEVE TATHAM '11

USING YOUR FILM AS A CALLING CARD

HAVING A FILM SELECTED TO screen at film festivals is an honor and filmmakers should be proud of that accomplishment and utilize this energy to create more networking and career opportunities. Your film is your calling card and you should use the momentum from the film festivals you attend to generate buzz even long after the festival is over.

All those business cards you received at the festival should have been added to your contact list. If you came home without any business cards, you need to ask yourself if you did a good job networking. Everyone you met at the film festival should have been given a postcard of your film and anyone who could open doors for you should have been given a DVD copy of your movie. In addition, if you said you were going to contact someone after the festival, do it. Don't wait six months.

When you return home, emails should be sent to the industry pros you met, letting them know that you enjoyed meeting them and that you might like to pitch your latest project or follow up with them on the DVD you sent or handed them at the festival. Try to open as many doors for your future work. Even though they might not be interested in your material at this time, you have their ear now, so make sure when you finish another screenplay or make another movie that they are aware of your accomplishments. You want them to recognize your name and remember you in the coming years. Send them periodic emails to let them know you've been accepted into another festival or that a screenplay was optioned, and anything else that is happening with your film or your career. You want to stay in touch and build a relationship.

SECURING MEETINGS WITH STUDIOS AND PRODUCTION COMPANIES

If you gave a studio executive or producer a copy of your film at a film festival, follow it up after a week or so with a phone call or email to their office offering to take them to lunch or requesting a meeting. Be nice to the assistant who answers the phone because they can help facilitate any meetings. You want to be pleasant yet not too aggressive. You never know, supporters can come from places you never would have thought. If you are requesting a meeting, be sure you have something to discuss, such as future projects, another film or screenplay. Let them know what you have in the pipeline. Don't get discouraged if you don't sell anything or get that three-picture deal. Building respect and friendships doesn't necessarily happen overnight.

When Monika was a studio executive, she would receive many invites to film school screenings and attended the Sundance Film Festival with an eye toward new talent making short films. Try to seek out specific agents and executives who have garnered reputations for finding new talent. IMDbPro.com or Baseline Studio System are great resources for filmmakers to target companies who might be interested in their films. In addition, the *Hollywood Creative Directory* and its offspring directories are also good resources, but as of this printing we understand they have been sold and have ceased production, according to their parent company, though you can still find hard copies available for purchase on various sites. Once considered the bible of the industry, we will just have to wait and see if someone is able to bring HCD back to life again.

GETTING AN AGENT OR MANAGER

Once you are accepted into a festival you should always target agents and managers and send them announcements of your film's screening at the festival. If they cannot attend, you want to try to get them to send their assistant or someone from the agency to see your film. It also doesn't hurt to go as far as letting them know you will add them to a reservation list so they don't have to pay to attend the screening. Talk to other filmmakers to find out which agents and managers are open to new talent and might be interested in seeing your work. Agents and managers are probably harder to get to attend than production company executives. But determination and persistence can pay off by casually reminding them, or their assistant, about you, your film, and attracting them with good reviews and festival acceptances. Sooner or later, someone from the agency will attend one of the screenings. Then it's up to you to follow up and get that meeting with the goal of representation for future works. If your film won awards at festivals, that's also a good time to get a rep's attention. You should put all your time and energy into finding representation while the iron is hot and you have some great reviews, recognition, and the buzz is positive.

FOLLOWING UP AFTER THE FESTIVAL

Not only is it important to follow up with all the people you met, but also with the festival itself. For example, if you have another festival coming up, you can request to have the current festival send your print or digital film (DVcam, Digi-Beta, BetaSP, HDcam, Blu-ray) directly to the next festival. A lot of festivals will return your film after the festival free of charge. Read the submission guidelines for more details on the festival's film return policy. If you contact them in advance and stay on top of the request, they will forward your film to the next festival and you get to save on the shipping cost.

If you haven't done so already, don't forget to get the festival's official "laurels" (the graphic icon festivals give out for official festival selections). You'll want to add this to your poster, website and/or DVD jacket as it looks prestigious to see multiple laurels showing your film as an official festival selection.

It is always nice to send the festival a "thank you" note for selecting your film to screen at the festival and telling them that you had a great time. Festivals like to hear that they have satisfied filmmakers and sometimes they will add your testimonial to their website, thus creating a circuitry of promotion for both.

CONCLUSION

Since you've put so much effort into making your film and money into submitting and attending film festivals, the follow-up is an important aspect of your film festival experience. You need to be clear on what you expect from each film festival and do your research on industry pros attending so you can meet them during the festival and develop a dialogue in which to follow-up with after the festival. Having a good contact list of producers, executives, agents, managers, and fellow filmmakers is important to help you as you navigate the waters of your career following the festivals. Don't just drop the ball here; continue carrying the banner forward into your next project. Nourish and develop these relationships into lifelong friendships.

Q&A WITH DISTRIBUTORS, PRODUCERS, ACQUISITIONS, AND REPS

"If ya gotta learn, learn from the best"

THE FOLLOWING INTERVIEWS ARE RATED FOR FILM FESTIVAL AUDIENCES ONLY

FFAO	FILM FESTIVAL AUDIENCES ONLY

S O YOU'VE MADE IT THIS FAR. You've been overloaded with information about how to prepare, target, and work the film festival circuit. You've even learned a bit about distribution and film markets. We realize this book is packed full of vital information, not only based upon our knowledge and investigation, but also by the countless interviews with distributors, buyer's reps, producer's reps, programmers, and filmmakers themselves, who have had successful runs on the festival circuit. While we've included some of that research in the previous chapters, we felt it was imperative that we let the filmmakers and industry pros speak to you directly about their experiences, good and bad, and offer what advice they would give others about to start what they've already finished. Though one could argue that you're never finished, you just begin again each time you make a film — hopefully a little bit wiser.

Let us introduce you to some of those industry folks we've talked with about their experiences in both the film festival circuit and film markets in the hopes that you will get an even better understanding of what it takes to promote your film and get noticed. These candid interviews with distribution companies, producers, a studio acquisition executive, and a buyer's rep will be an eye-opener for you.

MEET THE INDUSTRY PROS

Tony Safford is an Executive Vice President of Worldwide Acquisitions for 20th Century Fox which includes Fox Searchlight. Fox Searchlight releases approximately 12 pictures a year; about half of them are acquisitions and half of those are co-productions. Some of the films Tony has been responsible for are *Slumdog Millionaire, Little Miss Sunshine, Once,* and *The Tree of Life.* Prior to working at Fox, Tony worked at New Line Cinema and Miramax Films, and was the Program Director of the Sundance Film Festival from 1985 through 1990. *www.foxsearchlight.com*

Roadside Attractions has really made a name for themselves as a distribution company. The founders are **Howard Cohen**, who was an agent for UTA, where he packaged and put indie films together, and **Eric d'Arbeloff**, who produced the critically acclaimed *Trick* and *Lovely & Amazing*. They have a keen eye for unique and compelling films, having acquired *Winter's Bone*, *The Cove*, and *Biutiful* in recent years. We spoke with Eric and Howard who gave us their candid insight into the world of markets, acquisitions, and distribution of indie films. *www.roadsideattractions.com*

Kirk D'Amico owns Myriad Pictures, a company that has been acquiring films at the markets and festivals for more than ten years. Myriad is known for *The Good Girl*, *Kinsey*, and *Margin Call* starring Kevin Spacey, which had its international premiere at the Berlin Film Festival. Kirk has a long list of producing credits. He offered up an interesting take from his vantage point as to what he looks for when he or his staff attend festivals worldwide. *www.myriadpictures.com*

Harris Tulchin is an entertainment attorney, producer's rep, and producer. We met Harris at the Bangkok Film Festival in 2006. He is also the co-author of the widely popular *Independent Film Producer's Survival Guide: A Business and Legal Sourcebook*. He spoke to us at length about what filmmakers need to watch out for when it comes to hooking up with sales reps. *www.medialawyer.com*

Laurie Woodrow is a buyer's rep with over 20 years of experience specializing in acquisitions and worldwide distribution. She was President of Trans-Pacific Media from 1994 to 2009 when that company merged its business with Fierce Entertainment. She is currently Executive Vice President International for Fierce Entertainment, where she seeks out films for her clients to acquire and distribute in their territories. She frequents festivals and film markets all over the world, and has a great sensibility of the world in which filmmakers and film distributors live. *www.fierceentertainment.com*

Pamela Rosenberg is a producer who packages both talent and financing elements together. Her company, Hemisphere

Productions, sets up and assists with co-productions, recruits above-the line and below-the-line talent, and whatever other requirements are necessary for U.S., European, and Israeli indie production entities.

WHAT FILM FESTIVALS AND FILM MARKETS DO YOU ATTEND AND WHY?

Eric: There is a whole different hierarchy with film festivals and, essentially, there's the film festivals which the industry covers and the film festivals that get local audiences. There is some bleed in between, but the ones that we cover are Sundance, Cannes, Toronto, Los Angeles Film Festival, Berlin, South By Southwest, and Tribeca.

Howard: We pay a lot of attention to Sundance, Cannes, and Toronto.

Laurie: My primary business is done at the European Film Market (EFM) at the Berlin Film Festival in February, Marche du Film at the Cannes Film Festival in May, and the American Film Market (AFM) in November. The Toronto International Film Festival in September has become an increasingly important stop for international buyers, though technically it is a festival and not officially a film market. Sundance is an important festival primarily for domestic buyers. I also frequently attend the Telluride Film Festival and Tribeca Film Festival. I have attended events such as the Hong Kong Film Mart, Dubai Film Festival, and Busan (Pusan) Film Festival which have been interesting in terms of exploring new markets and searching for local filmmakers who might be of interest to my buyers.

Filmmakers should understand the difference between having their films screened in a festival versus a market — the former being a selection made by festival programmers for competitive or non-competitive screenings to be viewed by the public. Market screenings are arranged by sales companies and are primarily for viewing by buyers from individual territories, both domestic and international, for acquisition purposes.

Tony: We can go anywhere we need to go. Having said that, at least right now, we're in the fortunate position of being able to call in films we would like to see. But on a calendar basis, we will certainly go to Sundance, Berlin, Cannes, Tribeca, and Toronto, maybe Venice. The regional festivals, South By Southwest, for example, are still places where filmmakers can find an audience, generate word of mouth, and positive reviews. We may not attend but we do pay attention particularly to what's well-received there. The major festivals want premieres, which in some ways is counterproductive to filmmakers wanting exposure. I often think programmers should reconsider their notions of exclusivity.

In terms of the bigger ones — Sundance, Toronto, Cannes, Berlin — part of our job is to select from the selection. When the programs are announced, we then prioritize the pictures *for us*, essentially making educated guesses as to which films we think are the most likely acquisitions given our business, taste, and skills. Sometimes this is obvious. Going that year into Sundance, *Little Miss Sunshine* was not only a priority for us, it was a priority for *every* company. Other times, we go into Sundance not knowing much about, say, *Napoleon Dynamite*, which turned out to be a delightful surprise. By virtue of their profile (director, cast), some films are going to be obvious priorities; many others are absolute discoveries.

Kirk: We are becoming a U.S. distributor so we are more and more attuned beyond Sundance and even Telluride. For example, Palm Springs and Santa Barbara, Seattle, and the New York festivals are a whole other thing. The Hamptons and South By Southwest, Tribeca... those festivals are much more for domestic and also, quite frankly, a place for us to acquire films now... it used to be Sundance was the best place for us to acquire films. But then we've gotten a couple films out of Toronto and now we've gotten films out of Tribeca and, lately, we've been getting films out of South By Southwest. And Los Angeles is now becoming more important.

I love Toronto and I love the way it is organized. There are certain film festivals that take an active role and are really focused on having the industry... the buyers and sellers and sales companies and international distributors, so they create a great sales industry office and they create services, set up press, and industry screenings, have registration, badges, and create a marketing market that goes alongside the festival... Cannes is also great with that... there is even a party for the Cannes Market every year where buyers and sellers come together, mostly sellers show up there, and you feel, as a sales company, you feel wanted there. I think Venice is great in embracing the filmmakers and certainly out of necessity they pay attention to the Summits and Lionsgates of the world, but I think it isn't an easy festival for a sales company and it is a very expensive market. Also, there are certain ways in which film festivals will work with the sales companies, like Berlin, for example. Very early on — there is what's called the European Film Market that runs alongside the Berlinale and Beki Probst who runs it (I'm a big supporter of it), has worked really hard to help get companies hotel discounts making it accommodating, in terms of trying to make it affordable for sales companies to go there, while there are other festivals where you are on your own.

Harris: They all have their own personalities. You start out with Sundance, although Palm Springs is just before Sundance and, in fact, I like Palm Springs. I've had some films there and it is definitely a lot easier to maneuver and they get some great films. A lot of international films screen there and the weather is usually good. If you get your film in, it's not going to guarantee having all the distributors there, but it will get some. However, you can get a good review and an audience response, and I think it is quite good, actually.

Of course Sundance is the place if you are trying to sell films. It's really hard to get in and very political. A lot of films already have distribution. Or they're being tracked and they will have names and they won't be true, true, *true* indies, though John Cooper is trying to get back to that. Trevor and his crew are trying to get back to finding those undiscovered films. Maneuvering Sundance is a lot tougher than some of the other smaller festivals. But if you get in, it is fantastic and a great way to launch a film. Everybody is going to be there; the media is going to be there, the buyers are going to be there. I think it is real important, if you are going to be there, to have a team in place: a publicist, a producer's rep, and an attorney to get the broadest possible exposure. It's the best platform and venue to get a deal done.

Santa Barbara is like Palm Springs. You will get some distributors up there for that weekend. It's hard to come up during the week but people like to go to Santa Barbara. They do have incredible seminars up there and they have done a great job attracting the top, top talent of the world to be honored. I've seen films get sold there.

Then there's Berlin — I'm very fortunate I have a film out called *The Devil's Double* [AUTHOR'S NOTE: the film sold at Sundance] which I'm executive producer on and we were at Sundance and Berlin. Berlin is a very important festival for Europe and the world. The big four are Venice, Berlin, Cannes, and Toronto on the international scale. Sundance for domestic. You know, they do a great job in Berlin. I go every year because it is a market and they were very smart and strategic when AFM moved from February and Berlin plowed ahead and created a major festival at that time. If you want to sell a movie, go to Berlin. Another great thing about Berlin, from a producer's point of view, is they have this great co-production market there. I'm not going to say they copied, but they built it off of Rotterdam [CineMart] which created the whole idea of a co-production market, that a lot of other festivals mimic. They are very selective and invite experts from all over the world: finance, production and development, sales and marketing, and everybody meets these people and discusses their projects. I will say that my film would not have been made, I don't think, had it not been for the Berlin co-production market.

There are a few other festivals that are kinda cool. For example, Karlovy Vary stands out because they are in Eastern Europe [Czech Republic], a gorgeous town about three hours outside of Prague, but they celebrate American independent film there. Part of what they do is show American independent films that haven't necessarily been at a lot of the major festivals, and I kinda seek them out. That's a nice one. Locarno is also a good one. For South America, Rio is pretty neat. I actually went to the Singapore International Film Festival a couple times and had some films accepted there, and in a way it opens your eyes to Asia if you've never been. Plus they all speak English there.

Pamela: Berlin, Cannes, AFM. There are a lot of interesting things going on with Toronto and Venice. I think Rome is becoming very interesting. Telluride and Tribeca. London attracts the UK film community very strongly. So if you want to make inroads and connections with that community, it is the festival to go to. San Sebastian, if you're doing a picture with Europeans, is a good place to scout European talent. Survey what's going on in Europe. Rotterdam for documentaries; more artistic films with smaller budgets. You have to have a certain kind of product. These other festivals [outside of the top tier] are very specific, but what I love about them is that, if you do have product, they are perfect venues because they are manageable. People are very open, they don't have a certain kind of frenzy like Cannes does or the things that go on at AFM.

WHAT DO YOU DO TO PREPARE FOR A FILM FESTIVAL OR MARKET? WHAT ARE YOU LOOKING FOR AND HOW DO YOU PLAN YOUR DAYS AT THE FESTIVALS/MARKETS?

Howard: We try to prepare heavily for film festivals by looking at the lineup. You have a limited amount of time so you try to cover everything that looks on the surface like a possibility for distribution.

We have *Winter's Bone* out now. That was not one of the high-profile films going into the festival at all, except maybe because Debra Granik had done *Down to the Bone*. If you had said going into Sundance that *Winter's Bone* would be one of the three or four highest-grossing films of the film festival, no one would have believed that. *Cyrus* was there and, obviously, *The Kids Are All Right* was there, but its star rose incredibly in the trajectory from Sundance. Our head of acquisitions had targeted it because he had seen *Down to the Bone* and loved it. He was very much responsible for acquiring it. He went out of his way to get all of us to see it very quickly and one of the reasons why we got it is because we showered the filmmakers with love right after the first screening.

However, in thinking about how we approach film festivals and markets, there are several key elements. First, the art-house films or expanded art-house films where the typical audience member (whether we are right or not in our analysis) is a woman between the ages of 40 and 70, usually in urban environments. That's what the Landmark Theatre audience is, and obviously there are men in the audience, but we feel it's the women who drive the ticket-buying decisions and are more often willing to go to these movies on their own. What that means to us is asking ourselves this question: "What do we think a woman like *that* likes?" Movies aimed at teenagers are pretty tough for us. That's the studio's sweet spot but we've never had luck marketing art films to teenagers. We get out-spent by the studios. The other element we look at are the niche films. It is hard to make blanket statements about what sells and what doesn't, but I do think the things that defy categorization are often successful just because they are great.

Tony: Well, there is a group of us and we, frankly, sit around before the festival and go over our notes, prioritize the films, and make our schedule. And then life takes over. The challenge at the festival is that there are many things going on at once. Some films you may have high hopes for and leave after ten minutes. But then across town there is a film you've never heard of that is exploding with Tweets and blogs that was not on your radar.

Laurie: I prepare for the markets by tracking all the available titles from various sources (producers, sales companies, agencies) in all stages of production, from development to screening. Our clients have access to all of this information which is filtered through our database. We create reports for individual clients so they can see all the material presented at the market with project details, budget, asking prices, script coverage, everything they need to know to evaluate a project. We then help them navigate the market and assist in negotiations when necessary. It is important for me to be in tune with what each of my clients is looking for and what works in their individual territories in terms of material, genre, actors, censorship sensitivities, etc.

Kirk: Sundance had 5,000+ films submitted last year and of that they chose less than 400. So by virtue of the film being in that festival and having already gone through that filtering system and selection process, we then will look at all of those films to see, first of all, what is available for foreign. And since we've started doing some domestic distribution (as we have a deal with Paramount for DVD distribution), we are trying to find films that Paramount will want to distribute via DVD. We are looking all the time for both domestic and foreign, but ideally something that is available for both. So, we try and see those films to get a quick look before we go to the festival. We will get DVDs in here and go to screenings. Some sales reps will hold back the films until the festival to create a demand and we will go and cover those festival screenings. Festivals help to build profile for a film, but at the end of the day, a lot of the foreign distributors don't really care... they don't really care if a film has gone to Sundance. They care if the film has a recognizable cast and is well executed and a subject matter and story that appeals to their audiences.

When you walk down the Cannes Croisette and look up at those banners and see the Myriad Pictures banner, I'm stuck up there, having meetings every half hour from 9 a.m. to 6:30 or 7 p.m. I'm meeting with foreign distributors, as I am focused on selling to distributors, but Pam Rodi, our head of marketing, focuses on the festivals, especially the big festivals.

We took *The Good Girl* to Sundance and it was like an out-of-body experience.

Myriad Pictures company banner at Cannes.

Because you have Brad Pitt walking into the Eccles theatre and Robert Redford gets up and goes and gives him a hug and the place is completely quiet, looking at them, and no one is saying a word, you know... you can hear a pin drop... 1,500 to 1,700 people, and then the film played like gangbusters. Then, over the next sort of 48 to 72 hours, we ended up selling it to Fox for millions of dollars. So you have that kind of experience; you keep wanting to recreate it.

Pamela: What I always do and the way I start off is by asking myself why am I going? And what is the purpose? That is critical. I think most of the time I'm finding that I go for many, many different reasons. As any good producer or film-maker, you are doing your prep beforehand and identifying what those reasons are and what I need to do and what I need to accomplish at that film festival. If it is a festival I am not familiar with, then I find people who are and give them calls, whether I know them or not, and ask them to tell me what it is like — everything from housing, to places to go, where are the events to look for, where the screenings are... everything. If I know the festival then I know what I'm doing and how to do it, but I always identify what I need to do.

Generally, as of late, what I've been doing is I am putting together packages on pictures — which means putting together partners, elements, money. So a few months before, I am always collecting trade articles and filing them in ways so that I know that this is someone I want to meet at Cannes, Berlin, Toronto or wherever, and then I start booking appointments with people. Each festival has its own pattern in terms of booking appointments. I try to keep myself booked quite a bit but there is room for those spontaneous meetings that happen. I'm also watching what is being released and who is screening what, where, and when. Part of our job is to be aware of who is doing what as much as possible. Knowledge is critical and a full-time job keeping up with that stuff, but I want to make sure I get into the screenings to see the talent. I am interested in below-the-line as well as subject matter because that helps me put together my pictures in terms of international financing and in terms of talent and story.

HOW HAVE THE FILM MARKETS AND FESTIVALS CHANGED OVER THE YEARS?

Harris: Well, you know, first of all there is a proliferation of festivals. There is a lot of them and a lot of competition amongst them. There are a lot of sponsorship dollars involved. I think it is important to be very strategic about what film festival market you premiere your film at. You gotta look at your film and decide: is this an international film, domestic film? Every film is different.

Kirk: There is a seasonal way in which the industry organized itself. So the four main festivals for selling are: Toronto in September, AFM in November, Berlin in February, and Cannes in May. One thing that has really happened over the last, I would say, 20 years, is that festivals have become more important to the industry because they really do serve as launching pads for people's careers. I mean, when *Sex, Lies, and Videotape* premiered at Sundance, it was a shot fired around the world and reverberated. You still get it. It's just heard faster now. It is really hard to get your film heard above the noise that is out there. As a company sitting here with limited resources, when you tap into the festival you get all the journalists that are there; you get all the money and time, that people power that has gone into that festival to help profile your film. So it has become a regular part of our business.

Laurie: The access buyers have to information is one of the biggest changes I have seen. As a buyer's rep 20 years ago, we were an essential link to so-called Hollywood information. Pre-Internet, this information was a lot more difficult for international buyers to come by, so we were an important conduit in that process. Now, obviously, details are instantly

available to anyone who has a finger on a computer. Because of that, my job has shifted somewhat from information to service. Buyers can find fairly easily what is being sold, but the relationships and assistance with facilitating deals have become increasingly more valuable, as well as the ability to help them sort through the vast volume of projects in the pipeline to determine which ones are real and worth pursuing.

Another big change is the amount of business being done between film markets. Pre-sales used to take place primarily during the three major film markets, but more and more buyers are looking to close deals as soon as a film is packaged and ready to be sold to the marketplace. While the sales companies might benefit from the buzz and competitive environment that can be created by selling at a film market or festival, there may be financing requirements that may necessitate their selling projects between markets. Promoting films to buyers has become a lot more cost-effective for sales companies in recent years. In the past they would have to ship scripts, trailers, screeners to hundreds of buyers worldwide; now all of this can be provided online, which again helps to feed that between market activity. Still, meeting face to face at markets always helps to solidify the relationships between buyers and sellers, so I don't believe that markets will ever become completely obsolete.

Howard: The theatrical distribution traditional model can still work, but it can only work for a pretty small group of films. Here is the thing, I'm not sure it ever was working for hundreds and hundreds of movies... This idea that seems to be out there — that there was a Golden Age of Independent Film when tons of film festival films got distribution — is not really accurate. Not that many films ever came out of the festival circuit and had theatrical success. If anything, maybe a few more festival films have theatrical success now.

Tony: Well, I don't think markets have changed too much. The market dynamic is a fairly simple one: there are buyers and sellers. There are fewer independent distributors now and few independent movies theatrically released. Three or four years ago there were more, but the bigger distributors fell by the wayside. Warner Independent, Paramount Vantage, New Line, Miramax, have been replaced by micro-distributors driven by digital distribution. We are approaching the tipping point where this type of distribution can be monetized in a meaningful way.

Sundance has grown far beyond anything I could have imagined. It's big, sprawling, and influential. And it's become an acquisition-oriented event, at least as far as the press often reports it. A couple years ago, it was on the verge of being overwhelmed by signage, noise, and sponsorship, but they recognized this and pulled back. In my tenure as program director it started out to be an event dedicated to the filmmakers, the filmmaking community; a place to gather, cause reflection, and possibly have some influence. That's harder to do now and it's nearly become its antithesis: expensive, hard to attend, hard to navigate, overwhelming, a challenge for the public, industry, and press to navigate. But they wisely course-corrected. This is challenging. Nonprofits often start off struggling with certain aspirational goals. In the course of achieving those goals, you change from those founding principles or initial vision.

It's interesting to me that the one festival that has stayed true to its vision for over twenty years is Telluride, which had a slow-growth policy and, to the organizers' credit, kept a quality of experience consistent. I admire their dedication to a high-quality, low-impact experience surely in the face of opportunities to change, grow, and become different. They stuck to a vision that I think is singularly unique amongst worldwide festivals.

WHAT SHOULD FILMMAKERS UNDERSTAND ABOUT SALES REPS VS. PRODUCER'S REPS?

Tony: A rep can help get the attention of buyers, orient the structure of a sale, and drive a deal to completion. The best sales reps do just that — *represent* the interests of the film-maker, the producer, and the financiers. The trick is that they are usually paid a percentage basis of the sale, which means that it can be in their interest to drive a sale price up. There are other deals that are non-monetary, the term of license for example. Sales reps may care less about this because it is non-monetary for them but very important to the producer or financiers.

Harris: I have been doing this since 1990. We kinda created the job. I mean there were others out there... the Ira Deutchmans of the world. Producer's reps evolved, they used to be old distribution guys who were hired to book theatres and help people with their marketing campaigns. They would sorta interface with the studios. They didn't actually sell a film, it was already sold. Then it evolved into selling the films to the studios and major independents. Producer's reps, so you know, was a profession that evolved and I evolved with it. I think it is important to distinguish between a sales rep, sales agent, and producer's rep. A producer's rep is different from a sales rep. A sales agent sells films territory by territory. A producer's rep is more about marrying the producer with the right domestic distribution and international sales agents, and making sure those deals are done properly while making sure your client is protected and making sure you are in the right hands. There is a lot of hand-holding and a lot of terms and conditions that really need to be worked out. Another thing is that, especially with new producers — they will get into business with people — they have no idea who they are and will rob them blind... you have to be really careful and really know the personalities and have to know the history of the business, what happened in the past, you have to study the business and you have to know who to be in business with, and that's a lot of what a producer's rep does. You are going to advise and consult on how to put those deals together. A lot of times a producer's rep will handle domestic deals separately and then place the product with the best international sales company.

Laurie: A producer's rep can take the filmmaker through the steps of positioning their film and finding the best domestic and international representation and/or distribution for their film. A sales rep (or sales company) will actually sell the film directly to distributors in various territories. In selecting a sales company, a producer should do their research and find the best, most reputable sales company they can find. They should be looking for companies that already handle the type of film they are making so it will be marketed to the right buyers. If possible, they should talk to other producers who have worked with that sales company, see what their experience was like. They should fully understand their contact with the sales company, and have legal representation if possible.

Howard: I don't see a difference between a sales rep and a producer's rep. Either one needs to solicit and evaluate deals and present the options clearly and fairly to the filmmakers.

WHAT ARE SOME TOOLS AND TIPS FOR FILMMAKERS TO HELP PROMOTE THEMSELVES AT FESTIVALS?

Harris: You know, really be armed and have that army out there putting up posters to get people to show up. There is a lot of product and a lot of noise at these festivals. You want to make sure people show up at your screening. I can give you an interesting example. One year I was involved with a film that was not in the Cannes Film Festival, but there was a rep who was able to, because of his relationships, get Roger Ebert to show up at a market screening — and it was *not* in the festival, but a market screening at Cannes. Well, he absolutely loved the film and so in his daily festival article, because these guys do daily articles which are published everywhere, Roger Ebert writes, "perhaps the best film I've seen in Cannes thus far and this film isn't in the festival and I saw it at this little screening room in the market and there weren't that many people there and this performance and that performance..." of course — BOOM! The next thing is you have to be ready to have that quote on the Internet, make a new poster up, put the quote in there, and get it out as much as you possibly can so that you are taking maximum advantage of a lucky break that could happen. So when I'm talking about being prepared, really be prepared that if lightning strikes in a bottle, you are there to throw a Molotov cocktail all over the place to get your film noticed.

Kirk: My advice is have a recognizable cast; go out and canvas, get recognizable names because it is incredibly difficult to sell a film on any level... certainly for theatrical, television, DVD without recognizable names in the cast — that's really important. And choose your subject matter so it's not so limited. If you have a film that is a gay sex drug addict movie — Gus Van Sant — you're limited to pay television. That movie is not going to see the light of day on free television. You are limited to a typically small theatrical release... it has so much to do with how wide the potential is, and please don't get me wrong, we've handled gay sex drug addict films. You are really limiting the potential audience.

Tony: Well, it depends on the festival. Certainly at the major festivals, publicists organize and steer press and monitor reactions. I'm a believer in having a well thought through presentation to introduce the movie and the discussion points afterwards. Jokingly, we say sometimes we will walk out of a film based on the filmmaker's introduction.

Brief and articulate is good. I do believe that at the end of the day good films will out.

Pamela: Prep before going; keep focused or you can lose your way. Understand what your goals are; stay focused, but be open to hearing what is told to you. Do your follow-up afterwards; set up meetings, make phone calls, meet face to face. E-mail contact is very important. The phone call is better. Skype is better but meeting face-to-face is when things really get done however.

ANY ADVICE FOR FILMMAKERS ATTENDING A FILM FESTIVAL OR MARKET?

Harris: If you are at a major festival it is important to invest in your team so that it is not just you alone as a filmmaker — your team is gonna possibly include an agent, producer's rep, lawyer, publicist, and obviously your production team. You wanna have your stars, director, writer, cinematographer there, the key creative people who made the film. So that's number one: having your team there. And the second thing is being really strategic. We're in a process of preparing for a festival. We are making up a nice one-sheet ready to go with an image we want to help sell the film with, a good press kit that is available so that you have all the interviews and statements from the creative people, and bios, the director's take, all good stuff that will help any journalist write an article because that's what you want.

Also, sometimes I see filmmakers hook up with the wrong people and that is the number one problem. I think we in the film business kinda jump into bed together way too quickly and I think it is really important that you spend some time and do due diligence with people you feel comfortable with. Okay, we get into a festival, we gotta get a rep, gotta get an agent, we gotta get ... and boom! Then they are married... and it's hard to get out of it. The work really does start after

the film is made. You might be the greatest producer in the world, be organized, have budgets, production, logistics, get people to and from places on time and on budget, but distribution is a whole different animal. A completely different animal; and I think a lot of time people make a big mistake thinking that distribution will be easy and it is not. I mean, let's face it, if you don't have a bunch of P&A in your pocket, distribution is going to be real hard because there are very few buyers with any kind of clout. And then, you know, there are tons and tons of parasites out there, so you got to be super careful. You've invested two or three years of your life or more, and either your family's money, friend's money, colleague's money, your partner's money, investor's money, and you better make the right choices with the people you get involved with in distribution because that's where *all* the money is… it's not in production.

Tony: It concerns me when a filmmaker gets up in front of 500 people including critics and buyers and says, "I'm so excited to be showing my film. You're the *first* audience to see it." We moan to ourselves because we've seen so many films in need of further editing — editing which the audience, they're about to show to, will tell them is needed! It's a cruel and harsh world. You have one shot. It is very hard to re-interest us in a disappointing movie even when re-edited. That's the work a filmmaker needs to do prior to a festival and market. I strongly encourage pre-screenings to friends and family for candid feedback — not flattery, but candid feedback.

Kirk: I've handled, so far, over a hundred films. I'm always still amazed when relatively new filmmakers come in and they don't listen to us. It sounds so simple, but they literally don't listen to us. They know what is best. It is their film, their creation. I guess it's like raising a kid, kids have to learn for themselves no matter what you tell them, but I am always amazed at how little they actually listen to the people who have been doing it for so long. And we do know what works for audiences, not only here, but around the world, and we do know what works for particular festivals and have the knowledge not only for the overall festivals but even the sections within the festival. It must be like having sex for the first time... you think it's only happening to you... not every other person on the planet.

Howard: Most of the distributors acquiring films look for a film to be in one of the festivals that we mentioned and to create some kind of stir. Magnolia is buying from all those festivals pretty heavily. It's pretty hard to get distribution for real true indie filmmaking outside of that group of festivals. Occasionally, there is what the industry calls a "cold distribution screening," and that is what happens when films don't get into any of the festivals.

Eric: *Lovely & Amazing* screened in Telluride. We did a distributor screening afterwards because most people couldn't get to Telluride. I've seen that happen with the Aspen Comedy Festival and a few others. Anything that creates a buzz somewhere.

Howard: You are always looking for something that gives people a reason to believe the film is good. I'd say that, dealing with what's out there, 35 awards from tiny film festivals is not that convincing to most distributors — as painful and sad as that sounds. It might get us to watch it, but I've had enough bad experiences that it is not a guarantee that the movie is worth watching.

Eric: But it does help to get the word out if you're on the festival circuit. The Internet is also good for getting the word out about your film if you're on the festival circuit, but filmmakers should remember that whatever is on the Internet lives forever. It never goes away. A half-baked trailer is much worse than no trailer at all. A good teaser is valuable. Spend time working on whatever material you have and remember it stays online forever.

WHAT DO YOU THINK IS THE FUTURE FOR FILM MARKETS/FILM FESTIVALS? FOR DISTRIBUTION?

Tony: Well, that's a good question. No one quite knows. As we move into an increasingly digital age where so much can be consumed privately, we still have this need for public events. Festivals are great in this respect in that they can create a sense of community and shared experience. Even though some festivals will soon be an exclusively online experience, there is something about being out in public with others at a live event that is significant, almost encoded into our DNA. So in that sense, I think festivals are just that: *festive* occasions, reasons to celebrate cinema.

Harris: Obviously the business is going to evolve and continue to evolve. The digital media is just going to get bigger and more important. Get your film seen and put it up on the net and sell it... I don't think that's going to happen... there is a lot of personal contact that is important to buying and selling. VOD, Pay-Per-View, let's face it, the video/DVD market is going down but hey the digital buying is going up (thanks to iTunes) and just think how convenient this is. You're sitting in your house. You didn't get to the theatre to see the movie you wanted to see and all of a sudden, it is available for $5 and, instead of "this is like an important decision," a family of four or five has a choice: For $5, I can stay home, make my own popcorn, drink my own coke, and watch a theatrical movie on my nice big screen TV with surround sound or I can go park for $10, go buy dinner for another $50 or $60, pay $50 or $60 for the movie and $30 for popcorn and soda... is it really a decision anymore?

Kirk: I think historically we did an awful lot with the studios and now less so just because the studios are for the most part distributing films they are making themselves. Or they have these key financing partners from people like

Village Roadshow, Relativity, or Dune, financing a slate of films which for the pure independent is very hard to get. It is difficult for us to get the studios to look at our independent films. Therefore out of necessity we find ourselves selling to the IFCs of the world, Magnolias, and to even look at self-distributing films.

So, you know, that's where we are really... right now. We are still clearly in a transitional phase where the decline of DVD has not yet been offset by the financial liability of the VOD revenue. VOD is one of these terms that gets thrown around a lot and was originally traditional Pay-Per-View on cable. It is the nuances of the business. You have the technological changes but you also have the business terms that have evolved alongside them. It's all about access. Walmart, iTunes, even Comcast, Cox, and Time Warner and DirecTV, they really don't want to deal with one-off producers. They really want to deal with distributors who are going to be selling them packages of films. There just isn't enough time in the day to deal with every individual producer out there. You have to understand that just because there are more avenues doesn't mean that there is more revenue... it's just that the market has gotten fragmented. Those little pieces have actually added up to less and the people who ultimately benefit from the fragmented market are the studios who are able to maximize the fragmented revenue streams.

For the independents, you know, we are struggling... we are all definitely struggling. We are not able to get that initial broad-based release. We are kinda shut off from it by the way in which the studio system operates. Well I think that we, out of necessity, will do more and more self-distribution of our own product and look to do third-party distribution domestically. I think that we want to have our own VOD kind of virtual networks. Comcast, Cox, and Time Warner are the pre-imminent cable systems, and that's where most of the ad revenue is right now. They are like the Internet. They are the facilitators for the availability of content and it is now all about branding and consumer awareness. There is no reason why we couldn't have a Myriad network with our branded titles available and set up essentially a virtual network. If you go on these networks, you'll see like "mystery" or "action" channels. I think that you will find more companies like Summit and Lionsgate creating this branding and figure out packaging to get the consumers to download. I think, again, out of necessity, rather than letting third parties do that, we will be doing more of that ourselves.

Howard: More than ever there's a need for alternative voices. Studios have become conglomerates, and paradigms have changed. Studios briefly had indie divisions and then closed them, but the lasting effect was that the bar for quality got raised. On the plus side, it's easier to make an indie film that looks good. *Winter's Bone* had brilliant cinematography and was shot on the Red camera.

Eric: The future of distribution is more consolidation, multiplexes. Cable is fighting the valiant battle and is a successful part of the entertainment business. We hope the future will be some extensive on-demand system which would transport films to the consumer.

ADVICE FROM FILMMAKERS WHO'VE GONE THE FESTIVAL ROUTE

CHAPTER

11

"A Deal, A Deal! A Kingdom for a Deal!"

SO FAR WE'VE GIVEN YOU a road map that will put you on the right film festival path while furnishing you with considerations to be aware of, tools to publicize your film, and a creative approach to the film festival circuit. The one thing we want to make sure you never lose sight of is that this should be a fun experience. It takes hard work and perseverance but it should also be exciting, energizing, and the icing on the cake of your filmmaking experience. Seeing your film in a theatre filled with people who love movies, support filmmakers, and are of like mind are what we dream of. This isn't rocket science. Yet it is about strategy. This isn't taking a pragmatic math final or getting your law degree from Harvard. It is the culmination of the process you started when you either first put pen to paper, raised the financing, shot that first frame of film, locked your edit or mixed your sound. You've done all the hard work, so now is the time to benefit from that. Enjoy the experience. Be prepared but go with the flow. While there might be protocol, there are really no rules to it. Just ideas and creative thinking in the hopes of getting the most out of the exposure you will receive. But understanding what needs to be done and preparing ahead of time only allows you the freedom once you're at the festival to network, party, and enjoy the accolades you will hopefully receive.

This chapter is devoted to the filmmaker. We've interviewed filmmakers who have had varying degrees of success on the festival circuit. For some, the success was a happy accident while others used the festival to garner a reputation for their next film(s). Some found opportunities they wouldn't have found without getting their films into festivals — contacts that led to other stepping stones. This is what it's all about. We hope these examples will help to enlighten and inspire you, the filmmaker, to jump off the cliff and go for it.

JAY DUPLASS AND MARK DUPLASS: DO YOUR SHORTS

Jay Duplass and Mark Duplass are brothers who made a name for themselves for their award-winning short film, *This Is John,* which screened at the Sundance Film Festival in 2003. From there, they made such feature films as *The*

Puffy Chair, Baghead, and the crossover hit, *Cyrus.* Their latest project is *Jeff Who Lives at Home.* They got their start with low budget indie films, deemed "mumblecore," which describes a film made for a microbudget, that is character-driven about twentysomethings talking about their lives. Though that term is overused, and oftentimes dismissive, it helped propel them to the forefront as festival darlings and put them on the radar of the studios and distribution companies. With three shorts (*This Is John, Scrapple,* and *The Intervention*) and three features playing well over 300 festivals under their belts, the Duplass brothers are big believers in the festival circuit and in the short film genre as a launching pad for any filmmaker. All three of their initial shorts were purchased by Atom Films for Internet distribution. And two were bought out of Sundance while the third was purchased in Berlin.

However, their experience with their first feature, *The Puffy Chair,* was a different story.

It played over 50 film festivals and, in addition, they showed the film to as many distributors, before they finally sold the film a year later. The moral of this story is to not give up. It may take a while, but it's not impossible to sell your film a year after treading the festival path. Their next film, *Baghead,* sold within a few days of its premiere at Sundance. There is no real rhyme or reason. For the Duplass brothers it is all about making the best piece of art and then getting it into one of the major film festivals. They also feel having a sales agent is very important and have used different ones throughout the years (Cinetic Media for *The Puffy Chair* and Submarine Entertainment for *Baghead*) depending on the film. "It's important to find someone who has strong relationships with distributors, but at the same time is not so big in their britches that they won't give your film the personal attention it needs to sell if the distributors don't nab it right off the bat," they told us. So they did small domestic theatrical releases, DVD, and TV deals for all of their movies and sold the foreign rights via a foreign sales agent who represented the films' sale worldwide. You should note that for smaller American movies that aren't horror films, foreign sales can be a tough market. This is because horror films are all about the visual versus dialogue or scenarios that don't resonate with foreign audiences. With the feature *Cyrus*, however, it was all about having a big distributor and having movie stars. As they candidly shared, "Sometimes you need someone spending ad dollars on famous faces to get your movie out there."

DON'T LOSE THE FUN

The thing is sometimes you can lose the fun and excitement at a festival when filmmakers are obsessed with the sale. That's what happened to Jay and Mark at Sundance while trying to sell *Baghead*. There's ample opportunity to meet people and to just enjoy the experience. With the right people on your team pushing the film, hopefully you can take the time to meet industry and non-industry folks alike and enjoy the feedback and rewards, knowing that behind the scenes, your film is well repped. This doesn't mean you should put your head in the sand, but take the time to smell the roses.

DO THE SHORTS

Their first short, *This Is John*, was made for $3 and it was accepted into Sundance. "It's ugly and it sounds like shit. But, it connected with audiences and with the programmers," they said revealingly. "And, in many ways, it was our big break into the industry. We've been working steadily ever since."

Their advice is make a bunch of shorts! Once you feel like you have a great one, enter them into film festivals, then go and have fun. Meet people. Also, make sure you write a feature-length script that is cheap to make and is similar in tone and feel to your short in case a producer says, "I love your short. What's next?" That way, you can say "Here! This is similar to my short. I need X dollars to make it. Help!" Then, start trying to find the little money and the cast/crew you need to make it yourself. Emphatically they insist, "DON'T WAIT FOR THE STUDIOS! Make a great movie and everyone will come running to see it."

Jay and Mark's Memorable Festivals: Sometimes the best film festivals are the smaller ones. "We all had a blast at the Nantucket Film Festival. The Bend Film Festival in Oregon. And, of course, being at Sundance is kind of a dream come true."

ROSANNE KORENBERG: SO FEW BITES AT THE APPLE

Rosanne Korenberg is a producer, producer's rep, and film lawyer who has produced some festival favorites including *Half Nelson, Hard Candy,* and *Where God Left His Shoes.* She was previously Vice President of Acquisitions for 20th Century Fox, head of acquisitions for The Samuel Goldwyn Company, and Senior Vice President of Constantine Films. She started her entertainment career as a lawyer at Universal Pictures.

Her approach to film festivals is rooted in her knowledge of studio acquisitions. Though she's produced low budget indie films, she prefers that the pictures get picked up prior to screening for distribution or at least at the first screening. But as she will be the first to tell you, it doesn't always work that way. Some films take longer to get recognized. The process is customized since every film is different and each of the scenarios would be a book in itself. "Bottom line is to marshal all the assets that will show off the film to its best advantage. That may include: creating materials like a one-sheet or a website, hiring a publicist, enlisting the talent, and the various reps to speak positively about the film," she stresses. With some films it makes sense to have somebody present the film or to align with an applicable charity or not for-profit. It may make sense to get P&A funding in place. And these days, grass roots demographic support for a film is often helpful.

The main thing is to be prepared and don't wait until after the festival to sort out your goals and priorities. You need to think through the sales and marketing phase long before hitting the festival circuit!

While *Half Nelson*, starring Ryan Gosling, received Academy and Independent Spirit Award nominations, the film gained little recognition at Sundance, didn't win any awards, and was not picked up. It finally sold to Think Films, and in a carefully thought-through marketing and release strategy, and a total belief in the film, plus a cash infusion at a certain juncture, Think Films managed to nurture the film into a critical, award-winning, and financial success. It doesn't often happen that way.

Rosanne agrees with most producers that content is primary. You've got to start with a good movie and then it's kismet — the right audience, etc., falling into place; and no catastrophe getting in the way. Sometimes it's just luck and timing. "So many things can go wrong at a festival and there are so few bites at the apple," she warns. "You must be prepared for the problems but also realize it goes with the territory." She encourages filmmakers to have their next project ready to go or at least discuss when enthusiastic film producers and execs ask, "What's next?" Your film is your calling card but they're going to want to know what else you're working on.

Rosanne's Memorable Festivals: "Taking *Y Tu Mamá También* to its world premiere in Venice and then finding an audience at Toronto was pretty great. Flying Al Pacino and *Chinese Coffee* to Telluride was also very scenic and memorable. On a personal level, standing in the snow outside the Egyptian Theatre (Sundance) at midnight before the first screening of *Hard Candy* trying to keep everyone (i.e., distributors) waiting while our post production guy fixed the sound problems."

MARY JO GODGES & RENEE SOTILE: REACH FOR THE STARS AND GET WALMART!

Mary Jo Godges and Renee Sotile are documentary film producers who have produced shorts and feature documentaries that have won audience and jury awards at various festivals. They have had a lot of success selling their movies in the educational market and even had Walmart selling their award-winning documentary, *Christa McAuliffe: Reach for the Stars*.

They are strong believers in the film festival circuit. "Right off the bat, your film gets publicity in the festival film guide, website, and it may get some local media coverage. If you're able to attend the festival — networking is a must." In fact, networking is something that they excel at quite well. And it doesn't have to be at one of the top five festivals or even some of the more prominent festivals. In fact, sometimes, the smaller festivals can surprise you the most.

In their case, the Harlem International Film Festival turned out to be a pretty awesome experience for them. They had a short film screened titled, *Bessie, Billie & Ruth* in which actress Sweet Baby J'ai became Bessie Smith, Billie Holiday, and Ruth Brown in one take! At the festival opening night party, Susan Sarandon was in attendance and, long story short, she ended up narrating their feature documentary, *Christa McAuliffe: Reach for the Stars*. The timing was incredible because they were in final production on it. They believe film festivals give you a chance to hobnob with people that you would never have access to anywhere else, and Sarandon even donated her time.

It doesn't stop there. After the film was completed, they screened it at numerous festivals. And while screening it at the Big Bear Lake International Film Festival, they met a filmmaker from Arkansas who connected them with the buyers at Walmart. Kismet! They ended up making a direct deal with the department store for the feature documentary, something unheard of, but it happened. And it didn't take a Sundance to accomplish that.

DIY — DO IT YOURSELF

Renee and Mary Jo have pretty much stuck to self distribution, although they do have a couple of non-exclusive deals which they've been happy with. They further explain that the "exclusive" offers are tempting because by the time you finish your film you are so exhausted and want someone else to take over, but they encourage filmmakers to really think it over. "You are pretty much giving up all the rights to all the hard work you just created and are very unlikely to see the kind of money that would make it worth it for you to do that. Don't give away your film." They warn that there are opportunistic distributors trolling the circuit. However, if a distributor is what you absolutely want, then at least RETAIN the rights to sell your film off your website and at screenings. "This is small potatoes to a distribution company but the cash in your pocket is huge."

If you truly are an "independent" filmmaker as they are — be realistic with your film and pursue options that may not be the norm. Get creative in charting your own course. Making short films can show off your talents and there are more slots at festivals for shorts. Keep in mind, with your feature film, unless it is a niche film, you are competing with the masses. Also, film festival programmers have an easier time programming shorter films in blocks then full-length features because they can include more films on the festival slate.

In addition, short docs are great for the educational market. Renee and Mary Jo's documentary, *Astronaut Pam: Countdown to Commander* is 39 minutes and *Samuel Goldwasser* is 26 minutes. They kept them under 40 minutes on purpose so they would be good lengths for teachers to play in the classroom. You can't discount the educational marketplace as a place to create a stream of income for your films.

RENEE AND MARY JO'S TIPS FOR DOCUMENTARY FILMMAKERS

1. Make short films so that your films will be more attractive for programmers to slot into their blocks;

2. Don't give your film away. Beware of signing an exclusive agreement unless you're being paid handsomely for it. Retain some rights;

3. Always have DVDs to sell. Get them made as soon as you finish the film;

4. Don't waste a captive audience ever with thinking that selling your DVDs at your screening will hurt distribution chances later. Sometimes the cash you make from sales will help pay for the expenses to attend the festival;

5. Request t-shirts and programs from the film festivals you can't attend;

6. Pinpoint and outreach to the community that might embrace the film due to its subject matter;

7. Don't discount the educational market. You can find the names of reputable companies online. Get your film reviewed by library journals in order to get schools and libraries to buy your documentary for their bookshelves;

8. Documentary filmmakers do not underestimate the beauty of a TV broadcast.

OSCAR TIME

As members of the International Documentary Association, Renee and Mary Jo submitted *Christa McAuliffe* for Academy consideration but didn't make the final pick, which turned out to be a blessing. They ended up getting broadcast on CNN, so instead of paying to have their film screen in theatres for Academy qualification (which would have required renting a theatre), they actually *got* paid to have their film on TV and seen by many more people.

The two disclosed that it's hard getting your film into the very first festival but once you do, others usually follow and that's fun! However, festival entry fees add up! They encourage filmmakers to research festivals to see if their film is a good fit before randomly submitting everywhere. "And if you're thinking of attending a festival, find out if the festival has a built-in audience," Renee advises. "There's nothing worse than traveling all the way to a festival just to sit in the theatre with yourself and five other people. However, if you have unlimited funds, then ignore the above and go to all the festivals you get into and just have a blast!"

Renee and Mary Jo's Memorable Festivals: Renee and Mary Jo recommend the Hot Springs Documentary Festival (in Arkansas) because the whole town is supportive and fills the theatres. "Big Bear is a great festival for networking with professionals. The big surprise was The Harlem International Film Festival — without attending that one we wouldn't have gotten Susan Sarandon."

BETH MCELHENNY: BRING YOUR POSSE

Beth McElhenny took her own stroke experience and created an award-winning short called *Still Me*. She was able to use her film festival experience to market the film to educational organizations for stroke victims and self distributed it using her website *www.brookwoodfilms.com*.

In her effort to get the most out of her experience, Beth researched prior winning films to determine if the festival and attendees would be a good match for her film's content. "Putting butts in the seats for the screening was imperative," she divulges. So she canvassed the local community, spoke one-on-one, requested local shops to allow a display of the film's poster and postcards, and made sure all materials contained updated local screening info. Then she sought out VIPs at the festival to extend a personal request to attend the screening (if not, she provided them with a DVD and contact info). She also verified that the screening quality was acceptable prior to the actual screening time and she carried an alternative backup copy in case of technical difficulties. A few tidbits of advice from Beth include:

- DO get enough rest, wear comfortable shoes, and stay positive;
- DO NOT annoy the projectionist with perfectionism outside of the festival's capabilities;
- Respect the other filmmakers and their work;
- DO bring one or more people to *help* you promote the film;
- Ensure your "posse" has tickets to your screening (even if they have to be bought by you or by them) but also request that they respect the other filmmakers (save the partying for the party).

SPUDFEST DID NOT SPUDDER

Beth told us about a smaller festival with which she was amazed at how well the filmmakers were treated. SpudFest. Located in Idaho and founded by *Gilligan's Island* star Dawn Wells, it was a family film and music festival. They provided housing for filmmakers where they were kept all together, encouraging them to interact in one location. "From this *Big Brother* house we were away from the glitz, and everyone relaxed, allowing open communication. Filmmakers shared the experiences of their art and talked about what filmmakers love most: films!" she recounts excitedly. Unfortunately, Spudfest has been discontinued for now. It takes a lot to keep a festival going and in hard economic times, budgets get cut. It also takes a lot to put on a festival, which we'll go into at length in the next chapter as it will be helpful for filmmakers to understand the ins and outs from the other side of the table.

TARGETED ORGANIZATIONS

In addition to festivals, Beth contacted national associations that would have a connection to stroke victims in order to obtain exposure. She sought out opportunities for promotion through pre-established channels already in use by these national organizations — *Stroke Smart* magazine and mass email mailings. Lastly, she scheduled special screenings for established stroke-focused local groups and national hospital systems. While she wanted to qualify for the Oscar, she ran up against the submission deadlines and opted for local theatrical qualification rather than to wait another year to qualify at a designated Academy qualifying festival. But she emphatically suggests checking the Academy website for the rules and details on how to do that as qualification rules can change annually — so be sure and check the requirements periodically through your entire filmmaking process.

Above all, Beth wanted to impart that you must plan your festivals. Plan your festival fees. Know your film's audience. Plan your festivals to determine which ones will be a good match for your intended audience. If your film is a heartfelt drama, don't submit it to a festival that routinely screens horror films. Attend targeted film festivals the year before. Talk to the programming director to let them know why you are looking forward to submitting your film — be honest!

"Remember the festival has expenses just like you had a budget to produce your film," she reminds. "It's not a free-for-all — so don't be cheap — do pay your fees (submit EARLY for the discounts). Go to all the festivals local to you, your cast and crew, and be sure to let your local connections be known — this means butts in the seats, and that means ticket sales, which means the festival can continue to meet their budgets to bring you better festival services! (You don't think those VIPs pay for their hotel stay, do you?)"

Beth's Memorable Festivals: Aside from Spudfest, Beth enjoys going to film festivals because of the opportunity for filmmakers and VIP industry people to get together, exchange experiences, and to learn from peers and pros. She believes providing the filmmakers with opportunities for professional growth through educational seminars and organized networking gatherings, helps attract great filmmakers and makes for a successful festival.

LORETTE BAYLE:
THE AUDIENCE REACTION IS KEY

Lorette Bayle has always been a friend to the indie filmmaker, having worked at Kodak for many years as a liaison. She herself is an accomplished filmmaker having directed an award-winning feature documentary, *Conversations With Nickle*, and the more recent children's short, *The Bake Shop Ghost*, based upon the bestselling children's short story by Jacqueline Ogburn, which has played at 40–45 festivals all over the world in less than a year. As an executive working at Kodak, she's had many opportunities to attend festivals worldwide. She created an Excel file over the years of all the festivals she thought were important and because her film was a children's film which adults would still enjoy, she knew from her experience that the film would most likely be programmed at night rather than during an afternoon.

And she was right, as it became part of the opening night at five different festivals. It's also a numbers game. With the first forty submissions, she only got into half of those she submitted her film to. She also knew that some of the major festivals harkened to darker, edgier films, so that was also a consideration for her submissions.

One of the mistakes she sees filmmakers make in not only the festivals she's attended but also from working at Kodak, is they make their films too long. "You want to keep it simple and tell a story well," she explains. "You want to be familiar with what the festival needs. They need shorter shorts so they can program more. They might program a film before a feature because it is short and a nice thing." In addition, you have to have several different formats available for film festivals: 35mm, HD, many of the fests will have HDCam or some festivals that are more technology-savvy will take whatever format you have and transfer it to a hard drive. Then they screen from the hard drive. Sometimes you can put a film on a festival website server and they can then pull it down onto a hard drive. The important thing is to check the festival guidelines and be prepared for what is requested.

Another issue for filmmakers is not checking on the guidelines each time you submit to a festival. Lorette knew she wanted to submit to the Berlin Film Festival, but her film was too long for the competition itself. She found out later that the festival has a second tier where they show longer films, but by then the short had already screened at Festroia Film Festival in Portugal, taking away the European Premiere status. So her film didn't qualify for Berlin or some of the other significant European festivals due to the premiere status. She warns, "It wasn't until after Portugal that I realized what I could have done. I had read all the rules, but I read them the year before and not that year."

She also believes there is an emotional hit for her as a film-maker when the film has a technical problem of some sort — projectors for both film and digital screenings are not tested prior to the screenings. By arriving ahead of time and with some simple adjustments to correct aspect ratios, sound issues, dim images or color misalignments, you can resolve a lot without the headache or pain of watching your film in front of a live audience and seeing things go wrong. "As a filmmaker you spend a huge amount of time and money making good images and sound for that story so you want to make sure it's as perfect as it can be when it screens at festivals," she points out.

Because, after all, "the audience reaction is the key. As a filmmaker, you make films for other people to watch and how they respond is the joy of the craft," she declares. She believes it's really less important *where* the film is programmed and the venue in which it is screened. "It was a nice surprise when the film was programmed on the opening night at its first two festivals: Seattle and Rhode Island. Usually those screenings are for award-winning films."

PRE-QUALIFYING FOR OSCAR

The Bake Shop Ghost won several Audience and Jury Awards, but only won Audience Awards at the Academy pre-qualifying festivals, which meant that she needed to screen the film in Los Angeles or New York in order to qualify it for submission to AMPAS (Academy of Motion Pictures Arts & Sciences). Lorette opted for the Laemmle Theatre in Los Angeles which is available for special Academy qualifying screenings for shorts and charges about $750 for the screenings. In the end, her film did not make the short list, but she did receive a nice note from a juror who said he was surprised by it not making the list. He was touched by the film and had a tear in his eye at one point. If you're going to get a rejection notice, Lorette feels at least that was a nice way to get the news that the film did not move to the final round.

In the end, Lorette reveals, "Do your research by reading about the festival, seeing the type of films that they give awards to, and talking to filmmakers about their experiences at a festival." You can discover some wonderful film festivals that really attend to the filmmaker through the comments of other filmmakers. And remember programmers are looking for short shorts so that they can program more films into their presentation blocks.

Lorette's Memorable Festivals: Seattle Film Festival — opening night world premiere with over 400 people in a packed room. "I don't know if you know this, but Seattle's per capita has more screens than in any city in the USA. I guess because of its cold weather and people go to the movies when it rains. Everyone in the audience laughed at all the right places in the movie. It was the very first screening of the film. This was good because they were savvy people. Seattle is great and a very well organized film festival. I really truly enjoyed my experience." The most significant festivals the film played at following Seattle were: Rhode Island, Austin, Florida Film Festival, Short Shorts in Tokyo. Big Bear Lake was also cool. "The jurors were most impressive and the panelists were as well. Perhaps because it is close to Los Angeles and is at a time of year when the really cool people are not off to another festival."

JEN MCGOWAN:
NOT COMING UP SHORT IN SHORTS

Jen McGowan's thesis short film, *Confessions of a Late Bloomer*, was honored with a grant from The Caucus Foundation and a scholarship from Women in Film. *Late Bloomer* premiered at the Tribeca Film Festival and played at the Cannes Short Film Corner where it was chosen for a special Palais screening by film critic Michel Coulombe. It went on to showcase at over 50 festivals worldwide, earning awards and positive reviews. Jen's recent short film, *Touch*, premiered and won at the Academy qualifying Florida Film Festival. She's still in the throes of screening it but so far it's had 34 screenings and eight wins. She's also managed to get distribution for her shorts. And that's a tall order for a short film. *Late Bloomer* was picked up by Mini Movies and Shorts International after it finished its festival run. *Touch* was just picked up by Network Ireland TV (distributor), KQED (TV station), and Spiritual Cinema (DVD subscription).

DON'T BE "SHORT" CHANGED: *TOUCH*

Distribution companies, whether for features, documentaries or shorts, tend to send out programmers to the various festivals to scout for potential product to distribute. That's why it's important to investigate each festival and who attends them. You never know who you might meet and who might be interested in helping you get your film out there, albeit a distribution deal, a connection to Walmart, and/or a broadcast.

While *Late Bloomer* was picked up after Jen had completed its festival run, with her next movie, *Touch*, it was a different experience and so far the film has closed a few deals. The first contact came from KQED for broadcast. Their programmer saw *Touch* at Palm Springs and contacted Jen in June of 2010. He then reached out to them again in December expressing an interest to program the film. Six months later, after the first contact, they completed the contract and deliverable requirements. That was January, 2011.

Just prior to that, in December, however, Jen reached out to Spiritual Cinema on a suggestion from the programmer at the Breckenridge Film Festival. At the same time she also reached out to Network Ireland TV (NITV), but you have to understand that she had a great pitch to sell her product: she had already won eight festivals. That, in addition to the accolades for her previous short, provided a good track record. She found NITV was very open to working with them on the European festivals and willing to wait on making the sale until the end of the festival run — that was a condition that made them sign the agreement so early. Having a great trailer, website, and supporting materials didn't hurt either, as it helps to persuade people to watch the film and respond quickly. What also aided in her quest to have her film acquired, and one that she thinks is very important, is that she kept the film off the Internet and did not allow any festivals to screen it in its entirety anywhere other than at the festival. Once the film gets around for free, why would any buyer want to pay you for it? "Of course, that doesn't apply to films that traditional distribution won't work for, but if you think you'll get bought, keep it offline," she further offers.

However, Jen feels she still hasn't cracked the international festival circuit properly, which is frustrating to her. She points out, "There are some I should have applied to sooner and others I should have waited on. Many require certain types of premieres and it's a challenge to keep track of it all."

Regarding technical issues, there was one time she did get upset at a festival. It was a packed house in a huge theatre and the festival would not allow her to do a tech check before the screening. The film ended up playing almost entirely in extreme close up because it was zoomed in and the sound was so low you could barely hear the dialogue. "I should have dealt with it better but I was very embarrassed to show the film that way and I could have easily prevented that from happening. I didn't yell at anyone or anything, but I certainly took aside the guy in charge and made my complaint very clearly known. I basically said I wasn't going to allow them to screen it again unless I could tech it. Needless to say, I got to before my next screening that week."

Tech issues always come up at festivals, even when people do their best to get it right, and you just have to know which ones to worry about and which ones to let slide. Sometimes something goes wrong and, although you know it's not right, the audience couldn't care less. Her advice is to just "let it go. If the audience is happy I'm certainly not going to point something out to mess it up for them."

Let's face it, no one festival can do everything and each one has a different agenda so, it's not entirely fair to judge them. Jen's pretty self-sufficient but there are some things she's appreciated along the way. For example, when there's a packed house and a good moderator for Q&A. When a festival is able to pay for travel, that's a huge help. A central hangout for the filmmakers with WiFi can also be really useful. One festival she attended assigned a personal liaison for each filmmaker who made sure they were introduced to whomever they wanted to meet. Some festivals make an effort to put you in touch with local media, while others give tickets for free meals at many of the local restaurants. There are a ton of great festivals out there that she's enjoyed for various reasons: "Some smaller fests are great because you get 'real' audiences. Some are good for networking, some pack their houses in high-tech cinemas, some have great seminars, some are purely about caché or winning or about traveling to a place you've always wanted to go."

GOING THE OSCAR ROUTE

For non-student short films, you can qualify for the Oscar in two ways. You either win a specific award at a certain festival on a list designated yearly by the Academy or you have your film publicly exhibited for paid admission in a commercial theatre in L.A. or New York for at least three consecutive days with at least two screenings a day. *Touch* qualified by winning the jury award at the Florida Film Festival, a festival that is on that qualifier list. Once you meet one of those qualifications you then have to complete the entry form and supply a screener that meets their very precise specifications. Jen explains, "In our case, we delivered a DCP file with a 5.1 mix. And then you wait. One thing that's interesting is that no matter how many producers a film has, the Academy will not give more than two statues per film, so you have to designate who those one or two people will be that were most responsible for the concept and creative execution of the film." Also, anyone credited as producer, director, and the copyright holder of the film must sign the application form, and in doing so will agree about the one or two people who will receive the statue in case the film wins. "Looking back, I very much regret not lobbying the few people I could have figured out would have been voting. I think it could have made the difference in *Touch* making the short list. But what can you do? You learn as you go."

JEN MCGOWAN'S FESTIVAL TIPS
FOR SHORT FILM FILMMAKERS

After interviewing Jen McGowan, we realized she had some strong, valuable opinions and tips for filmmakers who embark on the film festival experience. These DOs and DON'Ts will help you avoid some of the pitfalls she and others like her have encountered, saving you in time and mistakes.

■ The clock starts ticking once you make your first screening, so make sure it's a good one. Once you screen you cannot update your completion date and that can disqualify you from important festivals.

■ The shorter your short is, the better chance it has to get programmed. Think about it this way — why would a festival program your good 30-minute "short" when they can program three equally good 10-minute shorts and get three times the audience? This is especially true in the American market. Though it changes a bit for distribution where you get paid a certain rate per minute.

■ At the moment, the best you can ever expect a short film to make in distribution is between $5,000 and $30,000. And we're talking $5K for an award-winning strong festival short to $30K for an Oscar winner.

■ Have good artwork that pulls people in. With both *Late Bloomer* and *Touch*, doors opened just because of the artwork.

■ Get to know the programmers and the people at the festival. These people work very hard and they love movies. And, if you're lucky, you'll make another film that both you and they will want to have back at their festival.

- Always get to the theatre before your screening and do a tech check. Get there early so the projectionist isn't too busy and do it fast so they can get back to work, but definitely make sure the aspect ratio is correct and your sound levels are good.

- Learn through practice how to do a good Q&A and interviews. You'll see some filmmakers come off like complete jerks and others win over huge audiences.

- This is just good manners, but if you don't have something nice to say, keep your mouth shut. It is really bad form to talk poorly about another film, filmmaker, or anything about the festival. If you find yourself at a shitty one, make a note not to go back, have a few drinks and smile a lot.

- Something I seem to always mess up is my credits. A lot of people help me on my films so I make sure everyone is properly credited and thanked, but at festivals they need to move quickly. Mine have always played too long.

- Shorts programming is an art and some programmers are great and others not so much. I've seen my films killed because of the films that were shown before them. Other times I've known from the first film that we're going to play brilliantly.

IN THE END — JUST HAVE FUN!

If you have a good film, that will make all the difference in the world in order for you to have a good festival experience. Not to say that some good films aren't successful on the circuit, but it's rare that you see a film that audiences enjoy and not get why.

Jen's mantra is to tell a good story, make people laugh, make people cry, whatever. Just connect with your audience and you'll be fine. Once you get in, promote the film so that you get the right audience in the seats. Enjoy yourself and keep your expectations low but work hard. Jen concludes, "When I go to festivals, I really see it as a part of my job as a filmmaker. I do my best to get the word out, represent the film well, and help it be a success. Also, it's important to keep in mind that the festival world is always changing and there's a ton to know so you're not going to get everything right."

Jen's Memorable Festivals: "Unfortunately, I don't get to go to all the ones we get in to, so I'm sure I'm leaving some great ones out, but some I've really enjoyed are DC Shorts, Florida, St. John's Women's, Palm Springs, Big Bear Lake, Luna Fest, Tribeca, Palm Beach, Breckenridge, Boulder, Petaluma, Munich Int'l Fest of Film Schools."

CREATING A FILM FESTIVAL?

"Does your hometown have one?"

WHAT IT TAKES TO CREATE A FILM FESTIVAL

WHY CREATE A FILM FESTIVAL when just about every town in the U.S., and big cities worldwide, already has at least one? Slamdance cropped up after the success of Sundance in Park City. In Los Angeles, you can throw a stone and hit a festival just about every week.

While not necessarily money-making ventures, a film festival might take years before seeing a minimal profit. But with good films, a respect for the filmmaker's craft, and an organized staff, a festival has the chance to flourish, bring business and tourism to small communities, and celebrate the art of filmmaking. The more years committed to their festival's vision, the more it will eventually see a break-even or profit stance.

Cities like to support film festivals because they provide an outlet for community arts programs and they are a great way to bring communities together that have an interest in movies. In addition, having so many places to submit a film offers filmmakers an opportunity to travel and showcase their films in places they haven't been to and meet people from all over the world.

Those creating a film festival must know how to run an organization and have a lot of patience to get it started. There are many details that need to be worked out and a lot of footwork required. Securing a dedicated group of volunteers and creating a team is one of the most challenging efforts a festival has to face... a festival is only as good as its volunteers.

Because many festivals are created for tourism and a way to bring money into the community, it is important for festival organizers to have the city, chamber of commerce, county and local community support. Cannes Film Festival moved its festival dates years ago to accommodate a time of year that would capture more tourism to help keep the festival flourishing. A festival like Tribeca Film Festival in New York was an overnight success after 9/11 because it brought the city together. However, festivals located in a mountain community or off the beaten path have more of a struggle to gain attendees and will need to work harder to promote their festival. If they don't have the industry or sponsor support that festivals like Sundance, and other high-profile festivals have, they will have a tougher time staying afloat. Getting sponsors is challenging, especially in today's economic times, and takes a great deal of schmoozing. In addition, one needs to be able to back up the community demographics and attendance numbers, making a sponsorship worth their time and money. Being able to write convincing proposals will go a long way toward securing sponsors.

Most small towns have local theatre groups and organizations that encourage the arts and they can be used to help each other. More and more cities are creating their own film societies to meet once a month and charge a small membership fee to network and watch films. The proceeds from a film society may be part of a festival's fundraising efforts.

Some towns still have vintage classic movie theatres that are utilized for film events and serve as a focal point for festivals. Each small town brings their own hometown uniqueness and charm to welcome filmmakers and support independent filmmaking. Look at your town and see what it has to offer. Exploit the positive so that it's inviting to not only filmmakers, but industry pros and audiences alike.

GETTING STARTED — THE BUSINESS

The first thing a U.S. festival organizer must do is to apply for a nonprofit 501(c)(3) tax status if the organization plans to apply for grants and sponsorships. In foreign countries, there might be an equivalent. However, securing an attorney to help guide the festival through the legal process should be considered. If you plan to approach any of the government agencies like the city, county, state or private foundations to request financial assistance, you will need to incorporate with a nonprofit status and apply for a Tax Identification Number (TIN) or your country's equivalent.

The National Endowment for the Arts will support certain film festivals that meet their criteria, while the Academy of Motion Picture Arts and Science (AMPAS) offers grants to festivals that have a nonprofit status. A festival can apply to AMPAS if they have held five consecutive festivals in five years. The grants are awarded to festivals that advance the arts and sciences of motion pictures for cultural, educational, and technical progress. They are not easy to obtain due to the competition amongst all the festivals, but after you've reached your fifth year you should keep on applying and don't get too discouraged if you are not awarded a grant immediately. To apply for the grant, the festival must submit a proposal, festival budget information, and fill out the application found on their website: http://www.oscars.org/education-outreach/grants/filmfestival/apply.html.

Having a tax-exempt status from state and federal income taxes will save the festival from having to pay taxes on income generated from the festival events and it will provide sponsors who donate services (hotel rooms, prizes for filmmakers, free food, etc.) a tax deduction for what they contribute. It qualifies the festival to be eligible to receive charitable gifts that are tax-deductable from private sources, as well as organizational grants.

Net profits earned from the festival event go right back into its coffers for next year's festival or for outreach programs developed throughout the year leading up to the festival. There are strict rules as to how money can be spent from the net receipts, so be sure and read those guidelines or have your attorney advise your organization on those stipulations.

OPENING A BANK ACCOUNT

Once you have secured your festival non-profit status and you have the appropriate information, you can open a bank account with your Tax Identification Number or your country's equivalent. Make sure the bank you use handles nonprofits so you can try to get lower monthly and transaction fees. Remember, you want to save as much money as you possibly can in running the organization so that the money you spend is on the festival itself. You will also want to investigate a merchant credit card account so you can accept Visa, MasterCard, and American Express for the film entry fees, ticket sales, and merchandise sold.

You don't need a physical office space to create a film festival. Your computer, email, website, designated phone line with voicemail as well as having software programs like Microsoft Excel or FileMaker Pro is all you need. If you don't have a physical office, open a local post office box where all the films and mail can be sent. However, you will need a physical address for FedEx and UPS courier deliveries, as they only deliver to a street address, so it might behoove you to get a board member's office for those kinds of deliveries that require a physical office.

A laptop computer should be designated only for film festival business. The database of emails, sponsors, city contact personnel, county contact information, and volunteer information should all be kept on the computer and backed up on an external drive for safekeeping. In addition, you should secure a place for the board members to meet on a regular basis.

MANAGEMENT

Most festivals are run by a board of directors assembled to carry out the day-to-day policy and bylaws of the festival. The bylaws are the rules set forth that the board of directors must abide by and serve as a structure and blueprint for the organization.

The amount of board members will be determined by how big your organization and budget is. Having a smaller board allows decisions to be made quicker so things can get done faster. Some festivals have honorary board members who are "names" in the entertainment industry helping to attract and generate sponsor interest, talent, and donations.

A majority of board members constitutes a quorum and a passage of a motion is required by the majority to make any significant decisions. The success of the festival relies on the commitment of the board of directors' ability to organize and steer the festival in a successful direction each year. In addition to the board officers, some board members oversee various areas of the festival referred to as committees. For instance, individual board members will oversee committee heads, who help in the areas of securing volunteers, handling ticket sales, the website, local and corporate sponsors, the media, advertising and marketing, and overseeing various events.

CREATING A MISSION STATEMENT

Creating a mission statement will help define the festival's goals and how it plans to connect audiences and filmmakers. It is a brief paragraph that clearly states the purpose of the film festival, what it wants to achieve, and what makes it different from other festivals. The mission statement should be placed on the website under a category labeled *About Us* or *Mission*. It should also be listed in the festival program and on various advertising. A one-sentence mission statement can be added to letterhead and emails. For example, the Big Bear Lake International Film Festival's mission statement is:

Dedicated to showcasing independent films and emerging filmmakers.

You can think of this as a way to focus and attract submissions which, like a logline, entices people to see your film. So, too, would this draw audiences and filmmakers to attend the festival.

EXAMPLES OF MISSION STATEMENTS

Sundance Institute & Film Festival — *Sundance Institute is a nonprofit organization dedicated to the discovery and development of independent artists and audiences. Through its programs, the Institute seeks to discover, support, and inspire independent film and theatre artists from the United States and around the world, and to introduce audiences to their new work.*

Tribeca Film Festival — *The Festival's mission is to help filmmakers reach the broadest possible audience, enable the international film community and general public to experience the power of cinema and promote New York City as a major filmmaking center. Tribeca Film Festival is well known for being a diverse international film festival that supports emerging and established directors.*

South by Southwest (SXSW) — *The South by Southwest (SXSW) Conferences & Festivals offer the unique convergence of original music, independent films, and emerging technologies. Fostering creative and professional growth alike, SXSW is the premier destination for discovery.*

Big Bear Lake International Film Festival — *The Big Bear Lake International Film Festival is a non-profit organization dedicated to showcasing the emerging talent of screenwriters and independent filmmakers within the idyllic setting of Big Bear Lake. Our goal is to nurture a festival, which is highly creative, filmmaker friendly, and which provides an educational experience for those people interested in all aspects of the film industry.*

Maui Film Festival — *Maui Film Festival is built on the belief that great filmmaking is pure alchemy. When filmmakers choose to tell compassionate life-affirming stories they can turn darkness into light. It is this belief in the power of creativity to enlighten, as well as entertain, that is the guiding principle that gives the Maui Film Festival its character, its energy and its soul.*

Seattle International Film Festival — *SIFF's mission is to create experiences that bring people together to discover extraordinary films from around the world. It is through the art of cinema that we foster a community that is more informed, aware, and alive.*

Click around the various film festival websites, which we list in the back of this book, so you can see how they describe their mission and see how you can create your own statement.

CREATING A BUDGET

A budget must be prepared for the current year and the following year, listing anticipated expenses and income. Good recordkeeping is important so you have a comparison from the prior year. When you begin to submit proposals for grants, a profit and loss statement from the prior year and the budget for the upcoming year will need to be provided.

GETTING SUPPORT — CITY, COUNTY, LOCAL COMMUNITY

The city and county in most cases will provide financial assistance for local nonprofits. Some cities and counties have film commissions that are under the government umbrella that may provide some assistance. Some local government (city hall or civic center) organizations may have a venue large enough to hold screenings and events. You will want to investigate each local government opportunity in your area.

It is important to gather all the support you can when creating a film festival. Put your budget, mission statement, and a proposal together. Present it to the city for their approval. It is wise to do preliminary footwork with the chamber of commerce, business merchants, and screening venues to secure their interest so you have more ammunition when you present your proposal to the city. A city can provide local in-kind-trade services like the use of a city venue, office space, and installing street banners. You must apply for permits to promote the film festival around town. A date must be determined for the following year's festival and placed on the city events calendar so another event doesn't conflict with the festival's dates. It is essential to have festival board members or staff members participate in community activities to help bring awareness of the festival to city officials and locals.

For instance, the Big Bear Lake International Film Festival spent years trying to get the local community to realize there is a film festival in town and that locals *are* allowed to attend. For whatever reason, the locals felt the festival was an event only for people working in the entertainment industry. After many years of advertising and participating in other local events like the Old Miners Day Parade, Doo Dah Parade, providing festival passes to use as raffle prizes at local organizational functions, and hosting a community Academy Award viewing party at a community restaurant, the locals now understand what a film festival means to a small community and supports it.

Most cities have a chamber of commerce, resort associations, events office, community arts organizations, television station(s), radio station(s), and newspaper(s) who help promote and generate community support for the town's film festival. Some countries and cities have government money set aside to encourage such events.

SECURING VENUES

If there is a local movie theatre in town then you will want to make a deal with the owner to secure a rental contract for the dates of the festival. A rental agreement details what the theatre will make available and what the festival will provide. For instance, the contract should indicate the length of time the festival plans to rent the theatre and how many screens it will use. The venue will retain the concession stand profits and their own staff sells the popcorn and drinks. If a projectionist is needed for running 35mm prints, then a fee might be negotiated for screening prints and the use of the theatre's projectionist. However, it is most likely the festival's technical staff that is responsible to set-up and run any digital projection. They are responsible for the film-makers' screenings.

There are many other venues a festival could use to screen films. Local convention centers, theatre playhouses, recreation centers, churches, Elks lodges, hotels, and libraries, all can be used as festival venues.

SECURING INSURANCE

Insurance must be secured for each venue location and possibly a separate policy is needed for the rented projection equipment used to screen the films. If you rent equipment like BetaSP, DigiBeta, HDCam, HiDef or Blu-ray decks, or projection equipment from equipment rental companies, they will require an insurance rider before releasing any rental equipment. Shop around and get a few insurance quotes. Make sure you understand what is covered and the length of the coverage. In addition, festivals should have a limited liability of responsibility for technical damage to films as well as loss or theft for the period of time that the film is in the festival's possession. You never know what could happen so you need to be covered and protect the festival from lawsuits.

Alcohol insurance is required if you plan on selling hard liquor. However, if you are serving alcoholic beverages at no charge, then the Certificate of Insurance must indicate having secured Host Liquor Liability Coverage with a minimum liability limit of one million dollars. If you have wine or beer served that is donated by sponsors, it is the law, in some states, that representatives of the wine or beer company serve the alcohol not festival volunteers or staff. For other countries, please check your local requirements.

CREATING A WEBSITE

Your website is the face of the festival, so you want to have as much information available for filmmakers about what the festival provides. Use the site to raise awareness to attract audiences and filmmakers to take part and encourage them to come to the festival. Also, potential sponsors will check the website to view current and past festival archives. It is important to get a couple of quotes from entertainment industry professionals to add to the website. If you are giving honorary awards to industry pros, you will want to get their information up on the website immediately and begin promoting the event.

Ask around for recommendations for the best Internet hosting providers. Secure your domain name immediately and start the ball rolling.

Poke around other film festival websites so you get a feel of what you want your site to look like. It should be easy to find information and be attractive. If your site is in a language other than English, make sure the pages translate and/or has a clickable button that translates into English. The website should also have these suggested buttons to help people navigate the festival site:

- HOME
- ABOUT US
- ARCHIVES (or PAST FESTIVALS)
- SPONSORS (financial, lodging, restaurant, media, etc.)
- FILMMAKER ENTRY FORM (or HOW TO SUBMIT A FILM)
- FILMS
- FILM SCREENING TIMES (or SCHEDULE)
- EVENTS
- TICKET SALES

- PRESS RELEASES
- DIRECTIONS/MAP
- LINKS TO FACEBOOK, TWITTER & YOUTUBE

CALL FOR ENTRIES

By now you have the administrative basics down to start promoting your festival. Your next step is to determine what type of films you want to screen so filmmakers can decide if your festival is a good fit for their film. A "call for entry" form needs to be created so you can track film submissions outlining the fees they need to pay. Remember, filmmakers want to get the most bang for their buck and they'll ask the question, "Why *your* festival?" So make the entry fees reasonable.

Even if you use one of the Internet submission systems like Withoutabox.com, it is good to have a hard copy of the submission form on file just in case. There are usually three or possibly four phases for the call for entries:

1. Early bird deadline;
2. Regular deadline;
3. Late deadline;
4. And maybe an extended late deadline that Withoutabox allows.

The entry fees begin at a discounted rate and then bump up for each deadline, making the last (and late) deadline the most expensive entry fee for last minute submissions. This is done to encourage early submissions.

As already discussed in previous chapters, Withoutabox is the best way for film festivals to promote their event to filmmakers. Festivals have an opportunity to purchase a marketing package which includes email blasts promoting their festival entry deadlines during the call for entry period. Festivals can also purchase a banner ad to promote their film festival on the Withoutabox system. But even without paying those additional fees, Withoutabox offers festivals a connection to the filmmakers and visa versa with just the click of a few buttons.

Publications like *MovieMaker* and *Indie Slate* magazines have a section listing call for entries and have yearly issues devoted to film festivals. They also provide special rates for film festivals to advertise. It is beneficial to get your call for entry listed in as many publications, film organizations, and websites available.

STAFF AND VOLUNTEERS

The festival is dependent on the volunteers who support their efforts and want to help see the festival succeed. Finding a committed group of volunteers that will stick with the festival and donate their time is not an easy task. A volunteer can sign up for various duties before the festival begins to help procure local sponsors, oversee event organization, become a film screener and help watch the hundreds or thousands of films submitted, become a reader and read screenplays for the screenwriting competition if the festival has one, and become involved in the myriad of activities leading up to and during the event itself. During the festival, they can help oversee hospitality, venues, taking tickets, and handing out audience award ballots or assist the technical staff with running the projection of the films in each venue and troubleshoot any issues that come to pass. Volunteers will be expected to attend meetings as the festival gets closer to its date where they will be trained by the board members or committee heads on how to accomplish their tasks. When a volunteer displays strong enthusiasm and enjoys the preparation process, they may become more committed to helping out as a staff member year-round or seasonally and eventually become part of the board of directors.

The best way to find volunteers is to place an ad in the local newspaper or announce it on the local radio and/or TV station. It also helps to advertise on the festival website: *How to become a volunteer.* Volunteers are the backbone of the festival organization. Treat them well and they will keep coming back to help out every year.

FILM PROGRAMMING

Film programming is the most important function of the festival since the festival exists because of the films and the filmmakers. A *programming director* oversees the slate of festival films starting with all the films submitted to the festival. *Programmers* attend other film festivals to scout for films and bring the festival to the filmmakers' attention.

As the films are received, they are logged into a database or checked off as received on Withoutabox and given to *screeners* who watch the films and evaluate them based on their content, storytelling, how creative they are, and last but not least, their filmmaking skills. Some festivals rate films on a numerical system: one to five. One is poor, two is bad, three is average, four is good, and five is excellent. Films that receive a three or above might have a shot at being screened, but the fours and fives are scheduled first. Films that receive a consistent five rating by screeners will definitely be seen by *industry jurors.* A *screener sheet* is given to the screeners which includes information like the title, tracking number, a section for the screener's rating as well as a section for comments. It is up to the festival programmer to determine what information they want from the screener.

Jurors should be professionals who work in the entertainment industry. They are given a certain amount of films to review and bestow the *Jury Award* winners. The programmer may give the jurors a few of the highest-rated films in each film competition jury category including Best Feature

Film, Best Short Film, Best Student Film, Best Animation, Best Family Film, and Best Documentary. They'll then rate it much like the screeners did on the preliminary entries. When the votes are tallied, there emerges a winner in each Jury Award category. But in order to have credibility, it is important to enlist industry professionals to become part of the jury, whether from Hollywood or from the local film/TV industry in your town.

Once the films have gone through the screening process with the screeners, the film ratings are evaluated and the highest-rated films will be targeted to screen at the festival. If there is a sidebar showcase, meaning if the festival is going to put the spotlight on a handful of films in a specific area (e.g., Latino films, African American films, Asian films, gay films, German films, Jewish films, sports films, films dealing with animals/pets, etc.), the programming director needs to make sure there are enough sidebar films or niche films to make a showcase.

Once all the films are targeted, a screening timeslot is prepared on a schedule. The schedule should list all the venues along with a seat count for each theatre and the screening times for each film.

Normally, feature-length films should fit into a two-hour time-slot — 85 to 100 minutes in length, allowing at least ten minutes of questions and answers with the filmmaker, plus time to clear the theatre for the next screening. Short films should run in a two-hour time block with other programmed shorts.

TECHNICAL DIRECTOR AND TECHNICAL ISSUES

The technical director is crucial to a film festival. They are the ones who are the nuts and bolts of the event, making sure that everything is running smoothly from a technical standpoint. They should be familiar with filmmaking and, more importantly, the range of video projection equipment needed to successfully screen all the films programmed. They must be savvy to the changing digital technology.

The technical staff on the ground not only runs the mechanics of the festival but also must deal with confrontational filmmakers who get angry if their film loses sound or the ratio isn't right. All festivals have experienced these types of horror stories. Be prepared. It will take a strong personality to handle irate directors or producers.

You never know what kind of situation arises, so you want to make sure you have a technical staff who can troubleshoot as well as volunteers who are helpful to everyone. Filmmakers need to know they're being taken care of and that their work matters.

GALAS, OPENING NIGHT, WRAP

In order to create a unique film festival experience you need to have additional events surrounding the screenings of films. The Palm Springs International Film Festival is known for its glamorous star-studded Black Tie Awards Gala sponsored by big-name corporations such as Cartier, Audi, and Mercedes Benz to name a few. These companies help roll out the red carpet and bring in honorees and presenters like Tom Cruise, Clint Eastwood, Nicole Kidman, Ron Howard, and major industry professionals. Other festivals might be less formal and have a BBQ Picnic or a simple awards presentation held in a hotel ballroom or a theatre.

Many film festivals have sponsors supporting individual events and specific film screenings. For instance, the galas might be sponsored or hosted by a corporate or

industry organization, while others might be sponsored by local businesses.

The opening night is the kickoff of the festival. You want attendees to be excited about the weekend of films, upcoming events, and panels. The opening night might have a reception, honorary awards, and an opening night film that could be a premiere of a studio film before its release date in your town.

The best way to secure a top-notch opening night film, if you don't have a contact person to help you, is to write to the production company who made the film or distribution company releasing the film and ask them if you can screen the film at the festival. Finding honorary award recipients, you need to contact their production company (if they have one), manager or agent. This information can be found on many websites or in the *Hollywood Creative Directory*, IMDbPro.com or Baseline Studio System.

Organizers need to make sure that there is plenty of food and booze exciting attendees as to what's in store in the days ahead. They need to think about what type of food and drinks to serve that's within their budget. Hiring a local catering company or restaurant to provide the food as a designated sponsor might cut down the cost.

The Cannes Film Festival has two or three star-studded, red-carpet premieres a day, each followed by a party at one of the local restaurants, hotels or bars.

Some festivals hold the opening night event and premiere screening at the same time as a regular film screening in competition at a different venue. The reasoning is so that attendees who cannot afford to pay for the opening night gala will have an alternative. This is usually done at larger film festivals, however.

The wrap party, sometimes called the filmmaker awards ceremony, will sum up the week or weekend of events.

Filmmakers and festival attendees have an opportunity to mingle and discuss what they saw, learned, and who they networked with. Like the opening night, all effort should be made to have a successful wrap party with plenty of food and drinks. Guests will remember this as they head home and share amongst their friends. Attendees need to leave the events with a positive feeling toward the festival so they'll continue to submit films in the future and encourage their friends to come the next year.

The wrap party and filmmaker awards ceremony at the Big Bear Lake International Film Festival is stocked with food because they invite local restaurants to provide a certain amount of food for an agreed upon price. This allows these restaurant sponsors to promote their restaurant to locals and visiting filmmakers. In return, the festival is able to put on the event at a lower cost and thus stay within their budget. This is an event that is looked forward to by the festival goers and helps highlight the eateries, providing them with mostly free advertising.

Lastly, it's a good idea to have some *after parties* when all the movies have screened for the day so that filmmakers have a place to go to unwind, network, and celebrate. These parties can be at the local watering hole or restaurants and are usually a no-host bar.

FILMMAKER AWARDS CEREMONY, HONORARY AWARDS, TRIBUTES, RETROSPECTIVES

Most festivals have a filmmaker's award ceremony. There are two types of awards: Jury Awards and Audience Awards in the categories of Best Feature Film, Short Film, Student Film, Documentary, etc. The jury should be made up of industry professionals or those with a cinematic background.

Most people involved in festivals probably know someone in the film industry. Get them to ask their contacts to be jurors. Some festivals only offer a few awards while others offer a wide variety of them. The Palm Springs International Film Festival has about a dozen honorary awards that are presented to winners at their Black Tie Awards Gala. Some of those include the Break-through Performance Award, Career Achievement Award, Chairman's Award, Desert Palm Achievement Award, Ensemble Performance Award, the Frederick Loewe Award for Film Composing, Lifetime Achievement Award in Directing, Rising Star Award, Sonny Bono Visionary Award, and Spotlight Award. By giving a Rising Star or Breakthrough Performance Award, it might attract those celebrities to attend the event in order to accept the award, and thus create more publicity for the festival.

Poppy Jasper Film Festival Award.

Photo Courtesy of Kim Noonan

Honorary awards or tributes offer a great opportunity to meet distinguished and seasoned filmmakers. A festival may screen one of their films during the festival and call it a trib-ute screening. A retrospective pays tribute to a filmmaker's career by screening a few of their films and then awards the filmmaker with a plaque commemorating their contribu-tion to cinema. They are always a crowd-pleaser and a great opportunity to see older films on the big screen as well as meet the filmmaker or talent. It is also another way to bring in more of an audience from the local environs.

A WORD ABOUT NETWORKING AT FILM FESTIVALS

Filmmakers want to party and talk about their films. A small festival can score big if industry professionals are in attendance and they have enough audience members attending their screenings. Having plenty of opportunity for filmmakers to mingle with agents, managers, executives, producers, and honorary guests will help make the festival a success.

SIDEBAR SHOWCASE

As previously mentioned, a sidebar showcase is when the film festival curates approximately a dozen films that connect with a certain audience, demographic, ethnic community, culture, etc. These sidebars screen alongside the other films in the festival. Depending on the amount of sidebar films submitted and accepted it could range from a two-hour block of short films to a few documentaries or even a couple of feature films that would be showcased. This offers a festival more variety of films that are specifically focused.

Sidebars can also provide sponsorships not otherwise thought of for the festival. For example, if you have a mountain activities sidebar showcase it might behoove you to contact companies like Jeep, Range Rover, Luna Bars, Patagonia, Northface, a local ski resort or sporting goods store to try to get them to sponsor the event. Another example is if you have an animal or pet sidebar, you can get the local zoo involved, seek sponsors from pet stores, create family events and have the public bring their animals, and give out prizes for the best pet costume or pet tricks. This might bring the locals out and create even more awareness of the festival. Other potential sidebars might be: Native American, Asian American, Latino, African American, German, Italian, Greek, Australian, outdoor activities, Jewish, Gay/Lesbian,

vintage cars, etc. Can you think of more sidebars that would work for your film festival?

SEMINARS AND PANELS

Most festivals have a couple of educational seminars or panels pertaining to film and filmmaking. Rona and Monika present many seminars and lectures on topics like "Maneuvering Film Festivals," "Finding & Developing New Ideas," "Creating A Production Company," or "What Happens to a Screenplay When It's Submitted to Studios and Production Companies." They also sit on panels discussing film festivals, getting an agent or manager, the best ways to pitch ideas, etc. These are usually highly popular and offer something more for the filmmakers in attendance.

Seminars and panels are a great way to get industry professionals to attend the film festival. If you can provide them with complimentary lodging, transportation, and a few free meals, they are likely to attend. This helps the credibility of the festival and encourages filmmakers to attend as they know they'll have the opportunity to network with pros.

SCREENPLAY COMPETITION

Not every festival has a screenwriting competition held in conjunction with a film festival. There is a lot of work involved to keep it running smoothly. It's another way of enticing more than just films and filmmakers, the festival could attract screenwriters, too. A screenwriting or screenplay competition requires a strong organizer to oversee the submission of screenplays and log each one into a database. The screenplays are then given to readers who evaluate the scripts and provide feedback on what they feel worked or didn't work in the script. Their evaluations can kick the screenplay into the Jury Awards where their screenplay should be read by agents, managers, and producers. It helps if the organizer has a background in writing to help readers and be a deciding voice in the selection process.

In addition, festivals could provide written feedback to the writers who submit their screenplays, another great incentive in attracting more people to submit their work and attend the festival.

MUSIC AND MUSIC VIDEO COMPETITON

Some festivals like South By Southwest (SXSW) in Texas provide musical acts the opportunity to connect with companies involved in music. SXSW showcases close to 2,000 newcomers hoping to be discovered. They also have a trade show for registrants to meet managers, promoters, media outlets, and recording labels. This is in addition to the film festival.

Other festivals like Temecula Valley Film & Music Festival in California also simultaneously showcase music and films. They present new and unsigned musical talent to music industry professionals and music fans attending the festival. There are many ways for you, the organizer of the festival, to promote more than just film if the environment is enticing enough. For example, a film festival starting up in Kentucky might also highlight bluegrass music in addition to films or emphasize films with a country flavor to them.

HOSPITALITY

Many festivals have an area dedicated for filmmakers. Sometimes called hospitality suite, filmmaker's lounge, VIP room, or green room, where all can nosh on pizza, drinks or sandwiches for lunch with all the food sponsored by local businesses. Some festivals have special areas with sponsored beer, vodka or wine. As it is on the set of a film, so should it be at a festival; good food keeps a crew happy. Good food is the surest way to a filmmaker's stomach and heart. Film-makers appreciate having complimentary snacks available and festivals that are generous with their food are remem-bered by filmmakers. Sponsors who provide the snacks have an opportunity to promote their goods and restaurants in exchange for this exposure.

SPONSORS AND FUNDRAISING

Securing sponsors is one of the most difficult tasks a film festival must handle in order to stay in the black. There are many different types of sponsor opportunities that can benefit a film festival financially in addition to providing the sponsor with benefits for their donation. Some of these sponsors are recognized and acknowledged in film programs as *Presenting Sponsors, Partners, Premiere Sponsors, Festival Supporters, Festival Affiliates, Promotional Supporters, Friends of the Festival*, etc.

Other sponsors are:

- City Sponsor — cash funds donation and donated city services;
- County Sponsor — cash funds donation;
- Film Commissions — assistance in getting the word out;
- Tribute Ad Sponsors — financial donation;
- In-Kind-Trade Sponsor — food, drinks, etc.;
- Prize Award Sponsor — film competition prizes;
- Film Sponsors, Venue Sponsors, Event Sponsors — financial donation;
- Media Sponsors — exposure for the festival.

Many film festivals have a sponsor for a block of short films, feature films or documentaries. There could even be a venue sponsor.

The festival attendance numbers is key to all sponsors. They want to make sure they get the most people and the right demographic to see their product or services.

With the lean economic times festivals have become more creative with their fundraising. Recently one film festival challenged audience members to open their pocketbooks further and make donations right there at the screening — begging the audience to give them a few bucks in a popcorn box that was handed out at each row... just like church tithing. Or better yet, using their mobile phones to text donations right at the screening. However, this could backfire because audiences might resent being asked to give money when they've paid for a pass already.

A festival program is created about four weeks before the festival with ads from local sponsors and a listing of all the films screening at the festival, tribute award recipients, and all information pertaining to the festival's weekend of events. Ads sold in the program usually end up paying for it; that should be the goal anyway. The thing to know is there are many kinds of sponsorships and the program is a cornerstone of the event itself. Sponsors like seeing their names in print and a program offers that opportunity.

PUBLICITY, MARKETING, PROMOTION, TICKET SALES

By now you should have a good understanding of what it takes to create a festival. Now you need to begin promoting it. Postcards should be created with your festival name and an eye-catching logo, festival dates, website, call for entry deadline dates, and if you have a special niche outside of independent films, i.e., a genre or sidebar to focus on, it should be noted. These need to be created at least six months before your final call for entry deadline. They should be placed at other film festivals so filmmakers recognize that you have a festival in your area, and dropped off at local coffee houses, movie theatres, and any social places where people gather. As you get closer to the festival, a poster should be created with the dates, venues, and website listed. They should be placed at supermarkets, store fronts, and restaurant windows.

Some towns have a rack card program through their chamber of commerce which distributes rack cards to various shopping centers, cinemas, hotels, and restaurants. Rack cards are similar to a large postcard, 4" × 9" with information on both sides. You will also want to deliver postcards to various organizations like the Elks Lodges, Rotary Clubs, churches, and senior centers.

Artwork courtesy of Eric Yamamoto

Rack card example (front and back).

Advertising will take a big chunk of your festival dollars. You want to be careful how you spend the money and where you advertise. For instance, an ad in *The Hollywood Reporter* or *Daily Variety* runs over a $1,000 dollars. This is unaffordable for a festival just starting out, let alone one reliant on sponsorships. First, think of your local audience and target the local town newspaper. Branch out to the surrounding areas and contact the county newspapers that are delivered to your area and make sure any free newspapers with a section for local events carries your festival with the dates and website listed. You want your local town to know about the festival, but you also want to bring in tourists and reach out to potential audience patrons in surrounding areas as well. You also want filmmakers to submit their films, so you'll need to promote this aspect early or you won't get any films to screen in the festival itself. You should also advertise at film schools.

Another way to advertise your festival is to create a slide or trailer for the local movie theatre to screen a couple months before the festival. While audience members are waiting for their film festival to start, they will have an opportunity to see the advertisement on the screen promoting the festival dates.

Most small towns have a radio station and public access television station. Schedule frequent interviews with them to promote the festival. If you have filmmakers or known talent willing to go on the radio or television, get them to promote their films with a one- or two-minute trailer and this will promote the festival at the same time. It's a win-win for both filmmakers and the festival.

Once you are ready to rock and roll, it's time to create a press release. You might begin by sending out a general release about the film festival so people will mark it on their calendars and also provide a phone number and email address for people to volunteer or become involved as a sponsor. Other press releases could address the deadlines for submissions and announce when tributes, retrospectives or honorary awards are secured. The press release should go out as a newsfeed to all the newspapers and Internet news sites in your area.

A Facebook page should be created to share and update information. In addition, sending out Tweets via a festival Twitter account, announcing more up-to-the-minute news

about the panels, lectures, premiere films, special events, and honorary awards will also help get the word out and create buzz.

Ticket sales can be a tough nut to crack. You can sell tickets via your website, use an outside ticket service or team with a local organization who already has a ticket system in place. You should sell individual tickets in addition to general all-access passes, so people can attend all events with one pass or have a less expensive option and buy one or two movies if they wish.

Badges are then created by a printer. But it doesn't stop there. You need to have plastic holders and lanyards (the rope from which you hang your plastic badge holder) for the badge itself. You can purchase lanyards for around 18¢ each in a box of 500 and plastic badges for around 26¢ each in a box of 100. They can both be purchased from local venders just by doing an Internet search in your local area. A good suggestion would be to secure a lanyard sponsor whose name or logo would appear alongside the festival's logo on the lanyard itself.

Some festivals might have a free film screening for the community during the festival that will also bring awareness and possibly generate stronger audience participation.

THE FESTIVAL — ALL HANDS ON DECK!

It's time. The festival is about to begin. The volunteers are in place, having been trained to cope with the pressure of the fast-paced event about to unfold. Some festivals utilize a couple of different venues so it is important that everyone at the venues have a cell phone, two-way radio or some form of communication device to get assistance quickly.

Festival staff must troubleshoot any issues that arise in a timely manner, whether it's a problem with projection, not having enough audience ballots or any other unknown possibilities. Volunteers and staff working with the filmmakers should be knowledgeable about the various screening formats, projection equipment, and sound systems. Having a filmmaker on your staff to help run the projection of the films could be an advantage as they may be able to troubleshoot when things go wrong — and they always do.

POST-FESTIVAL

Once the final film is screened, movie-watching finished, and the last party presented, heave a big sigh of relief for a job well done. We advise you to assign a few volunteers to function as a strike crew to take down posters, fold up tables, stack away chairs, clean any food areas, and take out the trash.

If you accepted certain exhibition screener copies of films (DigiBeta, BetaSP, Blu-ray, DVcam, HDcam or even a film print), then they need to be sent back to the filmmakers. This task should be assigned to a staff member, deemed film traffic, who sends the film(s) back the following day via courier services.

Even though the festival is over, there is still more press to be gained. Send out a press release to your initial list of newspapers, radio, and television outlets, listing all the winning films as well as touting how successful the festival was and thanking the sponsors for their participation.

A week or so following the festival there should be a meeting of the staff to recap the event and share their thoughts about the festival and address any problematic situations in order to come up with ways to make the festival better for next year... in addition to addressing what worked well. This is invaluable as it will help work out the kinks for next year's festival.

Thank You notes should be sent to all the VIP guests, speakers, jurors, presenters, and sponsors. A couple of weeks after things have settled down, a volunteer appreciation party to thank all the volunteers for their hard work in making the festival a success is something to consider as a final wrap-up and to encourage them to volunteer again next year.

And then it begins again... planning for next year's festival.

CONCLUSION

Film festivals are about making choices, so creating various events gives filmmakers and guests an opportunity to see more than just films, but also to partake and network in a weekend of film and cinematic events. Some attendees will spend their time only attending the panels and seminars while others will try to see as many films as they can. There are those who only attend the parties to network or see celebrities. The more you have to offer, the more attractive it is for your audience members and filmmaking talent participating in the festival. Having something for everyone makes for a good festival experience.

You can't please everyone at a film festival, but you want to make sure you give audiences a good time and keep each event moving at a brisk pace.

The key to a successful film festival is having the volunteer manpower and dedicated organizational staff to keep the festival on track and become a yearly success. There's a lot of work in creating a film festival, and this is just the beginning. But it will help you to jump start the event. You can add your own touches to the festival effort, adding themes and more programs each year. You can begin with a short festival and then add on days when you get more support from sponsors or your city. Above all, if you have a passion, if you have perseverance and drive, a good team with the same vision and goals, producing a film festival can be a very satisfactory and satisfying experience.

THAT'S A WRAP!

CHAPTER
13

"That wasn't so hard, was it?
Now let's do it all over again next year!"

THE FUTURE OF FILM FESTIVALS

AS LONG AS THERE ARE people who want to see movies, film festivals will thrive and play an important part for filmmakers to expose their work in places they may have only dreamed of going. Audiences will flock to theatres or venues to discover new talent, films from around the world, and mingle with entertainment professionals. Let's face it, there's nothing like sitting in a darkened theatre watching a film. Festivals offer the festival goers an opportunity to hobnob with the creators, experience new worlds, and make lifelong friendships — all in the name of art. Like one big happy family, you run into people you know, catch up with old friends, and have that heightened, intensive few days (or weeks as the case may be) of immersing yourself in what you love most: film and filmmaking.

So what does the future hold? Well, to start, there are new ways of projecting films with the advancement in digital technology. More festivals are moving toward requesting a digital media file of accepted films so the festival can download the films onto a hard drive for exhibition and forego the constant switching of BetaSP, DigiBeta, DVCam, HDCam, Blu-ray, and DVD screening formats. Companies like Vimeo also give festivals a way to view films.

With the latest technology available, influential film festivals like Sundance and Tribeca are leading the way in helping filmmakers with their distribution efforts while catering to general audiences who cannot attend their festivals by streaming some films online or via Video-On-Demand for viewers to watch simultaneously during the festival days.

We'll be seeing more of virtual film festivals in the future. In the past, a film would go through a festival circuit run for a year or two before landing at one of the streaming Internet sites. But, now, with the help of some of the top festivals' relationships with distribution companies, they are providing new ways to help films reach audiences. There are more and more innovative ways for independent filmmakers to get their films seen, and as distribution platforms change rapidly, film festivals will play an important role in that effort.

With the closure of many art house theatres, film festivals bring more thought-provoking, diverse, and independently made films right to the collective moviegoer who would rather be entertained by watching a film on a big screen versus renting a DVD or downloading a film onto a computer or TV. It is also important to educate the general moviegoing public about film festivals in their community and give them access to an array of independent films and documentaries with fascinating subject matters that they may not have an opportunity to see in their local theatres.

Educational outreach will continue to play an important role for festivals, especially since sponsors like supporting festivals with an educational mission. Festivals have the opportunity to help emerging filmmakers and can bridge the gap between school and working as a professional in the industry by providing workshops, seminars, and panels with professionals, displaying the latest technology, and teaching the skills necessary to stay current as filmmaking and the business side of making movies continue to evolve.

While some festivals are experiencing financial difficulties in these tough economic times and therefore have to scale back their schedules or cut down on their venues due to loss of sponsorships or grants, others are evolving into more complex, comprehensive, and robust institutions for their cities and towns. Toronto Film Festival has incorporated the Bell Lightbox as a new festival venue and the New York Film Festival's Film Society of Lincoln Center has built a state-of-the-art screening venue for the New York Film Festival. In addition, the 2011 Busan (Pusan) International Film Festival inaugurated the brand new Busan Cinema Centre, a 9-story building with three indoor theatres, a multipurpose venue accommodating 841 seats, and boasts an outdoor performance hall with a 4000 seating capacity, all next to the equally large BEXCO convention center. With this expansion, it only proves there is a viable future for film festivals in the years to come.

Festivals will continue to be used as part of the film's marketing campaign to get the word out about the film.

More filmmakers are using the high-profile festivals as their Premiere event. More festivals are adding the film's trailer to the film title listing on the website and utilize social networking like Twitter, Facebook, MySpace, and YouTube to connect to the festival website in order to help filmmakers expose the film at the festival and reach more audiences. Some filmmakers who cannot attend a festival may conduct their Q&A via Skype or one of the live video face-to-face systems, or ask questions via Twitter.

The way films are exhibited during a festival is also changing with the transition of digital technology. As 16mm and 35mm print screenings become less and less prevalent, BetaSP, DigiBeta, DVCam, HDCam, DVD, and Blu-ray formats are also being replaced with digital media files that are downloaded onto hard-drives and projected via laptop computers.

Even the festival programming staff is adjusting to new ways of watching films now that Withoutabox has a *secure online screeners* section to view films uploaded to the site. Festival programming staff will no longer need to have DVDs duplicated and shared with each other. Instead, they will be able to watch the films submitted via a click of a button in their individual festival database site.

These are just some of the changes in store. Who knows what tomorrow will bring? The one thing that remains constant is the insatiable need for entertainment. As long as audiences have that desire, filmmakers will always have an outlet to share their work and expose their stories to the masses. We are eager to see where the next chapter leads us and hope that all of you will stay on top of the ever-changing world of moviemaking and distribution. We live in exciting times. We are all one big global village. We all have stories to tell and audiences who want to hear them. Film festivals are a way for you, the individual, to help curate a path and cultivate a wide breadth of filmgoers. Not only are you giving to them, but their response to your film will influence you for years to come.

THAT'S A WRAP!

When we began this book, we wanted to write the quintessential book on film festivals. Our goal was to give filmmakers about to embark on a year or two of the festival circuit a handbook, a tool, which would be their "go to" wiki for all things festival. The more we wrote, the more we wanted to write. In these times, despite technology changing as fast as ever, the future of film festivals seems not to be diminishing any time soon. In fact, they are flourishing. The way we access our information and connect to each other worldwide might change, but the bottom line is that as long as there is storytelling (which has been around since the beginning of man), there will always be a place for the exhibition of films; for strangers to come together in a movie theatre and experience that one-time phenomenon of shared encounters. Human beings want to laugh, cry, and feel the joy that comes with moviemaking. They want to be taken on journeys and become enlightened by messages that transcend from the silver screen right to their heart. It has been a joy for us learning and relearning this festival path for filmmakers; a path that has also made the general public more aware of wonderful and varied types of filmmaking, open to all levels of expertise and budgets, and more accepting of a wide range of genres across borders.

This is the end of our book. You might say it's an intensive crash course, much like our ESE Film Workshops Online course, "Maneuvering Film Festivals," a four-week intensive online class where we help filmmakers from all over the world create their press kits and strategies for the festival circuit. While that's a hands-on class, you have the tools you need right here at your fingertips, all in one book. While you may not have our mentorship for the length of the course (though we welcome you anytime to take our courses), you are nevertheless now equipped with the information necessary to help you succeed, although you still have a lot of work to do.

You now know about targeting the festivals that are right for you and you have Internet resources to help you submit to those festivals. You know what a call for entry form looks like and how to fill it out so your film is presented in the best light. You know how to pitch your film with a good logline and you've put together a cohesive plan for both a marketing and publicity strategy.

You also know it is important to include monies in your production budget for film festivals and the expenses it may incur. It can be costly, but it can be money well spent if you are prepared to exploit it to your advantage. In addition, following this chapter is a comprehensive list of festivals and resources. We will keep them updated on our website for our readers and ESE Film Workshops Alumni.

Monika and Rona with festival badges.

We've given you many tools between these covers to begin your journey into the festival circuit. Nothing is absolute, however things change, and you must adapt what you've learned to whatever circumstances arise. However, you are many steps ahead of where you were when you first opened this book. It may seem overwhelming, but put one foot in front of the other and just begin. That's all it takes. Be smart, be strategic, and above all, have fun!

We look forward to hearing from all of you about your experiences and how the book has helped you prepare for the countless festivals you attend. We wish you all great success with your films and all your creative endeavors — and remember, as you work hard to put into motion all the steps we outlined in this book, absorb as much as you can on your journey, make new and wonderful friends, and enjoy the experience. The next one to two years on the festival circuit could change your life! And then, with your next film, you'll start all over again, but this time you'll have the tools necessary, and now the experience, to put your best foot forward and benefit from your own wisdom as you journey the path once more, increasing your visibility, and heightening your relationships along the way. Good luck and have a great screening!

RESOURCES

CHAPTER
14

"Here's your safety net!"

N OUR OPINION YOU CAN'T get enough reference books, sites, and knowledge at your fingertips. We have been collecting these useful resources since the beginning of our careers. We want to share them with you in the hopes that you will also use them as we have. They help make your life easier by showering you with pertinent information in your daily lives as filmmakers.

Some of the resources we've cited have basic service and some have additional services for a fee. Some have a great resource page of links to other useful sites, which is quite helpful. We can't possibly list every website, what with all the new sites popping up all the time, while others listed may not be updated or maintained. But we've given you our choices for the ones we use often or have heard other industry pros use to their benefit. We also want to point out that we are not endorsing or advocating one over the other. If we've missed any, feel free to drop us a line, and we'll include them in the next edition.

INDUSTRY SITES

ACADEMY PLAYERS DIRECTORY
(www.playersdirectory.com)
Contact information for actors and actresses. Fee based.

BASELINE STUDIO SYSTEM
(www.studiosystem.com)
Database for contacts, in-production and tracking. Fee based. Sign up for the free *First Look* newsletter.

BASELINE INTELLIGENCE
(www.baselineintel.com)
Site for entertainment research with an emphasis on Indie Film. It's fee based, however, you can sign up for their free *Research Wrap* newsletter.

BOX OFFICE MOJO
(www.boxofficemojo.com)
Offers comprehensive Box Office data, etc.

CINANDO
(www.cinando.com)
A database dedicated for industry professionals buying, selling, and attending major film festivals and markets. The site provides film and contact information on films for sale and in development, along with schedules of film screenings. Industry Pros only and there's a yearly fee.

EUROPA DISTRIBUTION
(www.europa-distribution.org)
This site serves as a voice for leading independent film distributors around the world but more European-centric.

HOLLYWOOD CREATIVE DIRECTORY
(www.hcdonline.com)
Once the bible of the business that offered contact information, addresses, and phone numbers for industry companies, they also published a *Representation Directory*, *Distribution Directory*, and even a *Music Industry Directory*. On their website, you can download a version of the *Blu-Book Production Directory* for free which lists a comprehensive list of production services, etc. However, as of this printing, its parent company has ceased all work on HCD and its future is uncertain at this point. We still wanted to list it because you can still buy copies of the latest versions which would be helpful. In addition, we hope that someone will have the foresight to take the reins once again because what made this company special is that their information was extremely reliable and less expensive than the other reliable industry resources.

IndieWIRE
(www.indiewire.com)
A quintessential leading source for independent films and film festival news. Major film journalists e.g., Anne Thompson and Leonard Maltin contribute regularly as do indie players, Sydney Levine (*SydneysBuzz*) and Ted Hope (*Hope for Film*), and includes the award-winning daily *indieWIRE* email newsletter.

INTERNET MOVIE DATABASE PRO
(www.imdbpro.com)
Fee based, more in-depth version of the free IMDb.com

NIKKI FINKE'S DEADLINE HOLLYWOOD
(www.deadline.com/hollywood)
Since launching her Deadline Hollywood site in March 2006, Nikki Finke has become the best connected journalist on the industry scene. Covering everything from television and film, Finke seems to find out the information faster than even the heads of studios and networks. Sign up for a free newsletter or breaking news alerts and stay connected to the behind-the-scenes world of show biz!

SHOWBIZ DATA
(www.showbizdata.com)
Cool info on Box office stats, development, production, reviews in addition to industry search engines, some of which offer free info, others may be fee based.

SYDNEY'S BUZZ
(blogs.indiewire.com/sydneylevine)
Sydney Levine blogs on international film industry developments and international film markets related to buyers, sales agents, filmmakers, film festivals, and distribution, "pulling back the curtain on the international movie biz."

THE NUMBERS
(www.the-numbers.com)
The Numbers offers a database to track business information and box office numbers on movies. Good source for business plans as it also lists comparison charts for different years.

THE WRAP
(www.theWrap.com)
The Wrap offers business analysis and news, articles, tweets, invites to industry events and screenings to those who sign up for their free newsletter.

PUBLICATIONS & MAGAZINES

DAILY VARIETY
(www.Variety.com)
One of the two major daily trade papers available as a hard copy and online, recapping film festivals and slates, along with the deals that are made at the various festivals and markets.

THE HOLLYWOOD REPORTER
(www.TheHollywoodreporter.com)
One of the two major daily trade papers also highlighting film festivals and their slates along with what deals are being made at the markets and festivals. Available online and in digital form for your mobile devices.

SCREEN INTERNATIONAL
(www.screendaily.com)
An international publication that offers free newsletters including Asian Pacific, UK & European, U.S., and tech news in both daily and weekly formats. Though to read the full articles you must buy a subscription for either the online version or magazine.

FILM BUSINESS ASIA
(www.filmbiz.asia)
Film Business Asia, run by Patrick Frater and Stephen Cremin, is based in Hong Kong, has a reach across the Asia-Pacific region, and is considered the next-generation film trade publication that is less magazine and more market intelligence platform. Their database is akin to Studio System but for Asia and costs $240 a year. But check out their website for all kinds of news articles. Subscribe to their free digital newsletters.

MOVIEMAKER MAGAZINE
(www.moviemaker.com)
The art and business of making movies is their tagline. This is a print magazine and online site with inspiring articles on the art and business of moviemaking, film education and festivals. Free newsletter.

FILMMAKER MAGAZINE
(www.filmmakermagazine.com)
This is a print magazine and online site specifically for independent film and filmmakers. It is an IFP (See Below) publication and offers fantastic articles on the indie film-making scene.

INDIE-SLATE MAGAZINE
(www.indieslate.com)
This is a print magazine and online site for the indie filmmakers.

ORGANIZATIONS & GUILDS

ACADEMY OF MOTION PICTURE ARTS AND SCIENCE

(www.oscars.org)

(www.oscars.org/awards/academyawards/rules/ shortsfestivals.html)

Here is the link that will get you to the link to the Academy Award qualifying film festivals. Each year the festivals change, as does the regulations, so make sure you check for the latest information on the Academy's website. Click on the Rules and scroll down to the Short Film Awards.

AMERICAN FEDERATION OF TELEVISION AND RADIO ARTISTS (AFTRA)

(www.aftra.org)

Since a number of films are shot on video or digitally today, the actors used might be covered under an AFTRA contract versus a SAG agreement. Check out the latest minimum wages under AFTRA's contracts.

DIRECTORS GUILD OF AMERICA (DGA)

(www.dga.org)

The union for directors of motion pictures and television; including the directing team. Look up members and their contact info, read up on the up-to-the-minute news, find out about the basic minimum agreement. Membership and dues in addition to guild professional requirements are necessary to join the guild.

FILM INDEPENDENT

(www.filmindependent.org)

Was originally called IFP West until it split with its east coast counterpart, Film Independent (FIND) sponsors the Los Angeles Film Festival as well as the Independent Spirit Awards. Anyone can join for a yearly fee and then you're eligible to vote for the Spirit Awards.

FILMMAKERS ALLIANCE
(www.filmmakersalliance.org)
Filmmakers Alliance has been around since 1993 and offers filmmakers support via their non-profit 501(c) 3 fiscal sponsorships, equipment, expertise, and creative support from concept through distribution. They also offer international as well as U.S. filmmakers support though U.S. members pay dues. Good links on their site as well.

IFP
(www.ifp.org)
Based in New York, IFP encourages emerging and experienced indie film talent with workshops, events, seminars in addition to the Gotham Independent Film Awards, film labs, independent film week, film conferences, fiscal sponsorships, and, depending on the membership you choose, either online access to the digital version or the print version of *Filmmaker* magazine. No requirements to join just a yearly fee.

INTERNATIONAL DOCUMENTARY ORGANIZATION (IDA)
(www.documentary.org)
IDA promotes nonfiction film and video around the world. The IDA also offers fiscal sponsorships for member's approved projects along with the prestigious Doc Week in Los Angeles. No requirements to join just a yearly fee.

PRODUCERS GUILD OF AMERICA (PGA)
(www.producersguild.org)
A professional guild (not a union) for the producer and the producing team. In addition to monthly seminars and workshops, including a highly active New Media Counsel, the PGA produces the annual Producers Guild Awards which kicks off Oscar season and the *Produced By Conference* in June. Membership fee/dues with requirements to join. Though anyone can partake in the Produced By Conference.

SCREEN ACTORS GUILD (SAG)

(www.sag.org)

Professional actors union. Find out contact info for actors, basic minimums contracts and general info on the union. Pretty much all professional actors are members of this union if they act on the screen.

SAGIndie

(www.sagindie.org)

Under the umbrella of SAG above, SAGIndie is an alliance between actors and passionate filmmaking mavericks who buck the system. Encouraging the use of professional talent onscreen, it offers low budget, micro budget and experimental budget agreements to help save money for the indie film-maker and still be a SAG signatory production. They offer free monthly workshops on how to make your film SAG compliant.

WRITERS GUILD OF AMERICA (WGA)

(www.wga.org)

The professional union for screen and television writing talent. Here you can look up members and their contact info, search the Basic Minimum Agreements as well as check out some great screenwriting resource links. However, to be a member there are requirements and membership dues and fees just like SAG, AFTRA, DGA, and PGA.

HELPFUL LEGAL SITES

HARRIS TULCHIN & ASSOCIATES

(www.medialawyer.com)

Harris Tulchin is an entertainment attorney with expertise in all phases of the industry with an emphasis on indie film. He's co-writer of *The Independent Film Producers Survival Guide: A Business and Legal Sourcebook* by Gunner Erickson, Harris Tulchin, Mark Halloran. There's some cool articles to help filmmakers on his site.

MARK LITWAK'S ENTERTAINMENT LAW RESOURCES

(www.marklitwak.com)

Litwak is an entertainment lawyer. His website has some very helpful articles and suggestions for filmmakers to protect themselves, fair use, etc. Plus his past blogs and articles are archived.

MICHAEL C. DONALDSON

(www.michaelcdonaldson.com)

Michael C. Donaldson is an entertainment attorney who has served as Legal counsel to the International Documentary Association and is an author of several books on clearances and copyrights as well as fair use.

RESEARCH SITES

FILMMAKERS

(www.filmmakers.com)

The art and showbiz of filmmaking. News and resources for indie filmmakers.

FILM STEW

(www.filmstew.com)

Film Stew tracks the offbeat side of indie film, shorts and docs in a blog format.

MANDY.COM

(www.mandy.com)

International film and TV production resources including job listings, film markets, production services, sales and distribution on a global scale for almost every country you can think of.

MOVIE REVIEW QUERY ENGINE

(www.mrqe.com)

Search engine listing movie reviews from different papers for over 40,000 film titles.

WHO REPRESENTS
(www.whorepresents.com)
Find the agent and/or manager that represents specific talent for a small monthly fee. Also has an iPhone app and you can receive a free newsletter.

FILM FESTIVAL RESOURCES

FESTIVAL GENIUS
(www.festivalgenius.com)
Formerly B-Side, Festival Genius is a scheduling and ticketing platform film festivals use in order to organize film screenings and events. Also has an iPhone app associated with this part of their business. It is about to launch a film finance online marketplace in the hopes of bringing qualified producers, financiers, and film investment opportunities.

FILM FESTIVAL TODAY
(www.filmfestivaltoday.com)
The business of film and entertainment. Free *Reel Fast Daily News* newsletter. Good site listing festivals, deals, interviews and finance info.

FILM FESTIVALS
(www.filmfestivals.com) (Fest21.com) (filmfestivalspro.com)
A list of worldwide festivals by month, date, etc., as well as having great resources. Fest21 and the pro site have an extensive database and social network, reviews, and news for indie films.

FESTIVAL FOCUS
(www.festivalfocus.org)
An online directory of films festivals, short and independent film with some extensive resources for indie filmmakers including an extensive festival directory, database of cast and crew, and films. In addition, you can list your film, be alerted to festival deadlines, etc.

FILM THREAT
(www.filmthreat.com)
Website that covers independent films. Created by Chris Gore, the author of *The Ultimate Film Festival Survival Guide.*

MOVIES BY MARVIN
(www.moviesbymartin.com/EZLeaves/index.htm)
A free application for download to create festival laurel leaves to be placed on your website, posters, and postcards.

SHORT FILM DEPOT
(www.shortfilmdepot.com)
Like Withoutabox, this is a short film registration system geared towards the International marketplace especially Europe. Most, if not all, festivals on the Short Film Depot site have no submission fees.

WITHOUTABOX FILM SUBMISSION SYSTEM (WAB)
(www.withoutabox.com)
There are other submission registration sites but Withoutabox is the number one website used by over 300,000 filmmakers for submissions to festivals worldwide. A subsidiary of IMDB and Amazon, Withoutabox can be integrated into Amazon's distribution platform (CreateSpace) and IMDB's database of credits.

RAISING FINANCING THE OLD FASHIONED WAY

INDIEGOGO
(www.indiegogo.com)
Crowd sourcing is a bona fide way of financing indie films these days. IndieGoGo provides the tools to effectively build a funding campaign to raise money. They take a percentage of the money you raise on their site.

KICKSTARTER
(www.kickstarter.com)
Fund and follow creativity is their tagline. Another crowd sourcing site to raise funds for your film. However, it must be fully funded before the expiration date or no money will exchange hands. They take a percentage of the funds raised if it's funded.

FILM EDUCATION & LABS

AMERICAN FILM INSTITUTE
(www.afi.com)
World-renowned AFI offers two-year graduate degree programs in screenwriting, directing, producing, cinematography, editing, and production design. They also offer the prestigious Directing Workshop for Women.

ESE FILM WORKSHOPS ONLINE
(www.ESEFilmWorkshopsOnline.com)
ESE Film Workshops Online provides a unique opportunity to learn the ins and outs of today's Hollywood from working industry professionals via online workshops. Provides professional online instruction without leaving your home. Click, Type, Download and Read. Today's world of feature films and television is more complex than ever. Learn from people who work in Hollywood every day. Courses offered: Creating A Production Company; Maneuvering Film Festivals; Finding & Developing New Ideas and Screenplay Development From the Inside Out.

FILM INDEPENDENT (FIND)
(www.filmindependent.org)
The filmmaker's labs include directors, producers, screenwriters, documentary as well as Project: Involve which helps cultivate careers of underrepresented filmmakers. They also have a program called Fast Track, a film finance market that takes place during the Los Angeles Film Festival.

IFP
(www.ifp.org)
IFP's Independent Filmmaker labs are the only programs in the world currently supporting first-time directors with low budget features under a million dollars in post production to completion including marketing and distribution. Some of the labs include: Documentary and Narrative Finishing Lab, Networking and Marketing Lab, Distribution Lab and ongoing mentorship support. In addition they sponsor a five-days film-maker conference and independent film week in New York.

LOS ANGELES FILM SCHOOL
(www.lafilm.com)
L.A. Film School (LAFS) was started by industry profession-als and offers a one year intensive filmmaking workshop in the heart of Hollywood with concentration on writing, directing, producing, cinematography, editing, sound design, production design. They also have animation and computer gaming programs.

SUNDANCE INSTITUTE
(www.sundance.org)
With so many labs and workshops held throughout the year in Park City, Utah, it's difficult to list all of them. On the feature side there are directing, screenwriting, film composing, and creative producing labs in addition to a three-day producing summit. There is also a documentary lab and programs for Native Americans. Just go to the website and click programs.

THE ENTERTAINMENT STUDIES PROGRAM – UCLA EXTENSION
(www.uclaextension.edu)
The Entertainment Studies program at UCLA Extension offers comprehensive courses on the art and business of entertainment with several certificate programs in film, tele-vision, development, producing, and digital entertainment media.

MAINE MEDIA WORKSHOPS
(www.mainemedia.edu)
Located in picturesque Rockport, Maine, this conservatory for photography, filmmaking, video, and new media offers both certificate and degree programs with concentrations in cinematography, directing, digital media, documentary, editing, post production, producing, sound, and writing.

PRODUCED BY CONFERENCE
(www.producedbyconference.com)
Presented by the Producers Guild of America and taking place in Los Angeles on a major studio lot, the Produced By Conference is an intensive three day conference where producers come together to hobnob with each other and attend financing, co-production, television showrunners, feature film producing, and distribution panels to name a few. The networking opportunities are endless and are targeted at the producer and their team.

EDUCATIONAL LIBRARY JOURNALS & RESOURCES

VIDEO LIBRARIAN
(www.videolibrarian.com)
A video review site for the public, schools, academics, and special libraries, Filmmakers with films geared towards the educational market should definitely try and submit their films for review.

LIBRARY JOURNAL
(www.LibraryJournal.com)
Library Journal is the oldest publication covering the library field. Read by over 100,000 library directors, administrators, and staff in public, academic, and special libraries, it is the single-most comprehensive publication for librarians, and evaluates nearly 7,000 books annually, along with hundreds of audiobooks, videos, and DVDs which libraries buy.

SCHOOL LIBRARY JOURNAL
(www.schoolLibraryJournal.com)
Considered the world's largest multimedia reviewer for libraries focusing on children and teens.

MIDWEST TAPES
(www.Midwesttapes.com)
A full service DVD, music CD, and audiobook distributor exclusively dealing with public libraries.

DIGITAL FILM AND FILE SHARING SITES

The following sites are used to share movies, images, and information. They can be password protected as you don't want them to have a public viewing especially if you are not through with your film festival circuit. Some are free up to a certain amount of megabytes/gigabytes of storage, then most have tiered pricing.

VIMEO
(www.vimeo.com)

YOU SEND IT
(www.yousendit.com)

BOX
(www.box.net)

DROPBOX
(www.dropbox.com)

DISTRIBUTION SOURCES

Check out the following as potential distribution platforms for your films.

AMAZON / CREATESPACE
(www.createspace.com)
A manufacturing and on-demand publisher/distributor for books, music, and film. A great way to sell your product and

keep most of the profit while using Amazon's multi-faceted distribution model.

NETFLIX

(www.netflix.com)

The largest Internet subscription based service for film and television with 25 million subscribers. Though there are no specific requirements for picking up an indie film without distribution in place, it has been noted that they most likely would base that opinion on queue demand, critical appeal, audience appeal, and film festival premieres. If you want your film considered for Netflix, make sure you present a good package to them and check out any guidelines to do so.

iTUNES

(www.itunes.com)

You can submit films to iTunes using an application which can be found on their website. They consider feature-length motion pictures or documentaries that were initially released either in theatres or directly to video, as well as short films of theatrical or DVD quality.

DIGITAL DOWNLOADS & STREAMING SITES

BABELGUM

(www.babelgum.com)

A free Internet TV platform supported by advertising, Babelgum combines the full-screen video quality of traditional television with the interactive capabilities of the Internet, offering professionally produced programming on demand to a global audience. They also have Babelgum Go for iPhone, iPad, iPod Touch.

CINEMANOW

(www.cinemanow.com)

CinemaNow is a service that offers instant access to films to rent or purchase using Internet-connected devices. Owned by Best Buy.

FILM BABY
(www.filmbaby.com)
Indie Filmmaker site with over 2,000 film titles for downloads and sale.

HULU
(www.hulu.com)
Hulu offers television movies, episodes, trailers, and movies for Internet viewing. However, you may not be allowed to view them if you're not in the U.S. It's free though there's an upgrade for a monthly fee.

INDIEFLIX
(www.indieflix.com)
IndieFlix is kind of a Netflix for festival films. Fee based to buy or stream downloadable films.

MUBI
(www.mubi.com)

Mubi is an online destination to watch independent, foreign, and classic films from anywhere at any time in high quality streaming, no players to download. Calling themselves an online cinema, they also encourage discussion about the film in real time. Fee based with tiered pricing depending on if you watch shorts or full-length features.

SNAGFILMS
(www.snagfilms.com)
SnagFilms offers a free website to view documentaries. They're also a platform that lets you "snag" a film and put it anywhere on the Internet by shining a light on a cause that you care about and thereby open a virtual movie theatre on any website. Soon they will be expanding to narrative fictional films. They have an iPad app as well.

VUDU

(www.vudu.com)

Vudu provides a site to download films on demand instantly the same day it is released on DVD. Fee based though they have a free trial.

APPS & MOBILE PHONE APPS

FILMFEST: A festival in your pocket

(www.filmfest.me)

Provides an app to review films screening at select film festivals sharing their festival guides with a separate app for each festival. It's free on iTunes.

TOKBOX.COM

(www.tokbox.com)

TokBox offers video conferencing for multiple people on the web as well as video chat on your website.

STONEHENGE PRODUCTIONS

(www.stonehengeproductions.com)

Builds apps for filmmakers to promote films, engage audiences, etc., on iTunes and other platforms.

DVD REPLICATION & DUPLICATION

DUPLITECH

(www.duplitech.com)

Provides Blu-ray, DVD, and CD duplication at a reasonable cost. They provide DVD and Blu-ray authoring services.

DISC MAKERS

(www.discmakers.com)

Disc Makers is a CD / DVD Duplicator, Replicator, and Printer. They provide DVD Authoring services and custom DVD Menu Design.

INDUSTRY FILM FESTIVAL
BOOKS & RESOURCES

Academy of Motion Picture Arts and Sciences, Margaret Herrick Library.

Adelman, Kim. *Making it Big in Shorts: The Ultimate Filmmaker's Guide to Short Films.* Michael Wiese Productions, 2nd edition, 2009.

Beauchamp, Cari & Behar, Henri. *Hollywood on the Riviera: Inside Story Cannes Film Festival.* W. Morrow & Co., 1992.

Bedal, Sharon. Swimming Upstream: A Lifesaving Guide to Short Film Distribution. Focal Press, 2008.

British Film Institute. *Directory of International Film & Video Festivals BFI 1987-88.* British Council in association with the British Film Institute. 4th edition, 1987.

Castello, Giulio Cesane & Bertieri, Claudio. *Venezia 1932-1939: Filmografia Critica.* Bianco E Nero, 1959.

Gaydos, Steven. *The Variety guide to film festivals: the ultimate insider's guide to film festivals around the world.* Berkley Pub./Perigee Trade, 1998.

Gore, Chris. *Ultimate Film Festival Survival Guide.* Lone Eagle, 4th Edition, 2009.

Hagener, Malte. *Moving forward, looking back: The European avant-garde and the invention of film culture, 1919-1939.* Amsterdam University Press, 2007.

Langer, Adam. *The film festival guide: for filmmakers, film buffs, and industry professionals.* Chicago Review Press,1998 and Independent Publishers Group, 2000.

Munroe, Roberta. *How Not to Make a Short Film: Secrets from a Sundance Programmer.* Hyperion, 2009.

Petrucci, Antonio. *Twenty years of cinema in Venice Mostra internazionale d'arte cinematografica* (12th: 1952: Venice, Italy) Biennale di Venezia. International Exhibition of Cinematographic Art, Ateneo, 1952.

Stolberg, Shael. *International Film Festival Guide, 1998.* Festival Products, 1998.

Tulchin, Harris, Gunnar Erickson, and Mark Halloran. *The Independent Film Producers Survival Guide: A Business and Legal Sourcebook.* Omnibus Press, 3rd edition, 2010.

Turan, Kenneth. *Sundance to Sarajevo: film festivals and the world they made.* University of California Press, 2002.

Valck, Marijke De. *Film Festivals From European Geopolitics to Global Cinephilia.* Amsterdam University Press, 2007.

APPENDIX
A COMPREHENSIVE LIST OF FILM FESTIVALS
BY REGION WITH WEBSITES

FILM FESTIVAL RESOURCE GUIDE
BY COUNTRY

Please note while we've vetted each of these websites, sometimes festivals change, are on hiatus or cease to exist. Some links require typing "www," while others do not. We've tried to note those for you. In addition, for non-English film festivals, there is usually an option to click on an English version link.

Academy Qualifying for Short Films (check www.oscars.org for current list)

REGION	CITY	WEBSITE
EUROPE		
AUSTRIA		
International Film Festival Innsbruck	Innsbruck	iffi.at
Crossing Europe Film Festival	Linz	crossingeurope.at
Vienna International Film Festival	Vienna	viennale.at
BOSNIA-HERZEGOVINA		
Neum Animated Film Festival	Neum	naff.ba
Kid's Festival	Sarajevo	kidsfest.ba
Sarajevo Film Festival	Sarajevo	sff.ba
BELGIUM		
Brussels International Fantastic Film Festival	Brussels	bifff.org
Brussels Short Film Festival	Brussels	courtmetrage.be
Ghent International Film Festival	Ghent	filmfestival.be
Namur International Film Festival	Namur	fiff.be
CROATIA		
*Zagreb World Festival of Animated Films	Zagreb	animafest.hr
Libertas Film Festival Forum	Dubrovnik	libertasfilmfestival.com
Pula Film Festival	Hrvatsk	www.pulafilmfestival.hr
Croatia One Minute Film Festival	Pozega	crominute.hr
25 FPS Festival	Zagreb	25fps.hr
CZECH REPUBLIC		
Karlovy Vary International Film Festival	Karlovy Vary	kviff.com
Mezipatra Queer Film Festival	Mezipatra	mezipatra.cz
Academic Film Olomouc	Olomouc	afo.cz
European Student Film Festival	Prague	esff.org
Fresh Film Festival	Prague	freshfilmfest.net
International Film Festival Prague	Prague	febiofest.cz
International Film Festival For Children & Youth	Zlin	zlinfest.cz
DENMARK		
Buster Copenhagen Int'l Film Festival for Children and Youth	Copenhagen	buster.dk
CPH: DOX Copenhagen Int'l Documentary Film Festival	Copenhagen	cphpix.dk
Odense International Film Festival Short Films	Odense	filmfestival.dk
ESTONIA		
Parnu Int'l Documentary and Anthropology Film Festival	Parnu	chaplin.ee/filmfestival
Animated Dreams Animation Film Festival	Tallinn	anima.poff.ee
DocPoint Tallin Documenatry Film Festival	Tallinn	tallinn.docpoint.info
Sleepwalkers Student & Short Film Festival	Tallinn	swff.ee

REGION	CITY	WEBSITE
Tallinn Black Nights Film Festival	Tallinn	poff.ee

FINLAND

*Tampere International Short Film Festival	Tampere	tamperefilmfestival.fi
Animatricks Animation Festival	Helsinki	animatricks.net
DocPoint Helsinki Documentary Film Festival	Helsinki	docpoint.info
Helsinki International Film Festival	Helsinki	hiff.fi
Helsinki Woman Film Festival	Helsinki	artisokka.info
Midnight Sun Film Festival	Helsinki	www.msfilmfestival.fi
Oulu International Children's and Youth Festival	Oulu	www.oulunelokuvakeskus.fi
Rock Film Festival	Joensuu	rokumentti.com

FRANCE

*Cannes Festival Int'l Du Film	Cannes	festival-cannes.com
*L'académie des Arts et Techniques du Cinéma	Paris	lescesarducinema.com
*Annecy Festival Int'l Du Cinema	Annecy	annecy.org
*Clermont-Ferrand International Short Film	Clermont-Ferrand	clermont-filmfest.com
Albert International Wildlife Film Festival	Albert	fifa.com.fr
Brest European Short Film Festival	Brest	filmcourt.fr
The American Pavilion Emerging Filmmaker Showcase at Cannes Film Festival	Cannes	ampav.com
Cannes Film Festival Short Film Corner	Cannes	shortfilmcorner.com
Cannes Independent Film Festival	Cannes	cannesfest.org
Fantastique Semaine du Cinéma	Fréjus	cinenasty.blogspot.com
FIDMarseille Int'l Documentary Festival of Marseille	Marseille	fidmarseille.org
European Film Festival	Paris	film-festival.eu
European Spiritual Film Festival	Paris	festival-esff.com
Paris Cinema International Film Festival	Paris	pariscinema.org
ECU European Independent Film Festival	Paris	ecufilmfestival.com
Sexy International Paris Film Festival	Paris	sexyfilmfestparis.fr
Strasbourg International Film Festival	Strasbourg	strasbourgfilmfest.com

GERMANY

*Berlin International Film Festival	Berlin	berlinale.de
*International Kurzfilmtage Oberhausen Short Film Festival	Oberhausen	kurzfilmtage.de
*Stuttgart International Animation Festival	Stuttgart	itfs.de
European Film Awards	Berlin/Traveling Festival	europeanfilmacademy.org
Globians Doc Fest	Berlin	globians.com
Interfilm Festival	Berlin	interfilm.de
Kuki International Short Film Festival	Berlin	interfilm.de/kuki2011
Lucas International Children's Film Festival	Frankfurt	lucas-filmfestival.de
Hamburg International Short Film Festival	Hamburg	festival.shortfilm.com
Hamburg International Queer Film Festival	Hamburg	lsf-hamburg.de
DOK Leipzig	Leipzig	dok-leipzig.de
Nordic Film Days Lubeck	Lübeck	filmtage.luebeck.de
International Filmfestival Mannheim-Heidelberg	Mannheim-Heidelberg	iffmh.de
CrankCookieShortFilmdays	Passau	crankcookiekurzfilmtage.de
Go East Festival of Central and Eastern European Film	Wiesbaden	filmfestival-goeast.de

GREECE

Athens Animfest	Athens	animationcenter.gr
Athens International Film Festival	Athens	www.aiff.gr
Athens International Sci-Fi and Fantasy Short Film Festival	Athens	sffrated.wordpress.com
Athens International Short Film Festival	Athens	psarokokalo.gr
Cyprus International Film Festival	Cyprus	cyprusfilmfestival.org
Short Film Festival in Drama	Drama	www.dramafilmfestival.gr/en/index.html
Naoussa International Film Festival	Naoussa	naoussafilmfestival.gr
International Film Festival of Patras City	Patras	independent.gr
Rodos EcoFilms International Film & Visual Arts Festival	Rodos Island	ecofilms.gr

REGION	CITY	WEBSITE
Thess International Short Film Festival	Thessaloniki	azafestival.com
Thessaloniki Documentary Film Festival	Thessaloniki	www.filmfestival.gr
Thessaloniki International Film Festival	Thessaloniki	www.filmfestival.gr

ITALY
*David Di Donatello Award (Accademia Del Cinema Italiano)	Rome	daviddidonatello.it
*Venice Film Festival	Venice	labiennale.org/en/cinema
Biografilm Festival International Celebration of Lives	Bologna	biografilm.it
Capri Hollywood Film Festival	Capri	caprihollywood.com
Festival dei Popoli Documentaries	Florence	festivaldeipopoli.org
Genova Film Festival	Genova	genovafilmfestival.org
MIFF - Milano Int'l Film Festival Awards	Milan	miff.it
Montecatini Terme Short Film Festival	Montecatini Terme	filmvideomontecatini.com
Concorto Film Festival	Pontenuere	concorto.com
Courmayeur Noir in Festival	Rome	noirfest.com
International Rome Film Festival	Rome	www.romacinemafest.org
Taormina FilmFest	Taormina	taorminafilmfest.it
CinemAmbiente Environmental Film Festival	Torino	cinemambiente.it
Torino Film Festival	Torino	torinofilmfest.org
Trento Film Festival	Trento	trentofestival.it

LATVIA
Riga International Film Forum "Arsenals"	Riga	arsenals.lv
Riga International Children Film Festival	Riga	festivali.arsenals.lv/berimors/en

MONACO
Monaco Charity Film Festival	Monte-Carlo	monacofilmfestival.org
Monaco International Film Festival & Angel Film Awards	Monte-Carlo	monacofilmfest.com
Monte-Carlo Film Festival	Monte-Carlo	montecarlofilmfestival.com

NETHERLANDS
Africa in the Picture	Amsterdam/Netherlands	africainthepicture.nl
Imagine Amsterdam Fantastic Film Festival	Amsterdam	imaginefilmfestival.nl
Int'l Documentary Film Festival Amsterdam	Amsterdam	idfa.nl
International Film Festival Breda	Breda	filmfestivalbreda.com
Leids Film Festival	Leids	leidsfilmfestival.nl
Go Short International Short Film Festival	Nijmegen	goshort.nl
Architecture Film Festival	Rotterdam	affrblog.nl
International Film Festival Rotterdam	Rotterdam	filmfestivalrotterdam.com
Holland Animation Film Festival	Utrecht	www.haff.nl
Netherlands Film Festival	Utrecht	filmfestival.nl
Film By The Sea	Vlissingen	filmbythesea.nl

NORWAY
Bergen International Film Festival	Bergen	biff.no
The Norwegian International Film Festival	Haugesund	filmweb.no/filmfestivalen
Bollywood Fest Indian Dance & Film Festival	Oslo	bollywoodfest.com
Films from the South Festival	Oslo	filmfrasor.no

POLAND
*Krakow Film Festival	Krakow	kff.com.pl
Camerimage Film Festival	Bydgoszcz	pluscamerimage.pl
Off Plus Camera Int'l Festival of Independent Cinema	Krakow	offpluscamera.com
Tofifest International Film Festival	Torun	tofifest.pl
Warsaw Film Festival	Warsaw	wff.pl
Amateur and Independent Film Festival KAN	Wroclaw	kan.art.pl
American Film Festival	Wroclaw	americanfilmfestival.pl
New Horizons International Film Festival	Wroclaw	nowehoryzonty.pl

PORTUGAL
*Cinanima International Animation Film Festival	Espinho	cinanima.pt

REGION	CITY	WEBSITE
Avanca International Meeting of Cinema, TV, Video & Cinema	Avanca	avanca.com
Algarve International Film Festival	Lisboa	algarvefilmfest.com
Doclisboa International Film Festival	Lisboa	doclisboa.org
IndieLisboa Int'l Independent Film Festival	Lisboa	indielisboa.com
Queer Lisboa	Lisboa	queerlisboa.pt
Funchal International Film Festival	Madeira	funchalfilmfest.com
Black & White Audio Visual Festival	Porto	artes.ucp.pt/b&w
Fantasporto Festival International De Cinema	Porto	fantasporto.com
Oporto International Short Film Festival	Porto	porto7.com
Festroia International Film Festival	Setúbal	festroia.pt
Curtas Vila do Conde Shorts	Vila do Conde	curtasmetragens.pt

ROMANIA

Anim'est International Animation Film Festival	Bucharest	animest.ro
Bucharest International Film Festival	Bucharest	bieff.ro
NexT International Film Festival	Bucharest	nextfilmfestival.ro
Transilvania International Film Festival	Bucharest	tiff.ro
Anonimul International Indepdendent Film Festival	Delta	festival-anonimul.ro
Timishort Film Festival	Timisoara	timishort.ro

RUSSIA

Moscow International Film Festival	Moscow	moscowfilmfestival.ru
Eurasia International Film Festival	Kazakhstan	eurasiaiff.kz
Festival of Festivals International Film Festival In St. Petersburg	St. Petersburg	filmfest.ru
Message to Man Int'l Documentary, Short & Animated Film Festival	St. Petersburg	m2m.iffc.ru
Open Saint Petersburg Student film Festival	St. Petersburg	festival-nachalo.ru

SPAIN

*Academia De Las Artes Y Ciencias Cinematograficas de Espana		academiadecine.com
*Bilbao Int'l Festival of Documentary & Short Films	Bilbao	zinebi.com
*Gijon International Film Festival For Young People	Gijon	gijonfilmfestival.com
*Festival De Cine De Huesca	Huesca	huesca-filmfestival.com
Sitges International Fantastic Film Festival of Catalonia	Cantalonia	sitgesfilmfestival.com
The Inigo Film Festival	Madrid	tiffestival.org
Shots: Festival Int'l Fantastic Short Film Fest	Madrid	scifiworld.es/shots.php
San Sebastian Horror & Fantasy Film Festival	San Sebastian	donostiakultura.com/terror
San Sebastian Int'l Film Festival	San Sebastian	sansebastianfestival.com
Curtocircuito International Short Film Festival	Santiago	curtocircuito.org
Cinema Jove International Film Festival	Valencia	cinemajove.com
Mostra de Valencia Action & Adventure Film Festival	Valencia	mostravalencia.com
Valladolid Int'l Film Festival	Valladolid	seminci.es

SWEDEN

*Nordisk Panorama – 5 Cities Film Festival	Sweden, Iceland, Norway, Denmark, Finland	nordiskpanorama.com
*Uppsala International Short Film Festival	Uppsala	shortfilmfestival.com
Lund international Fantastic Film Festival	Lund	fff.se
Stockholm International Film Festival	Stockholm	stockholmfilmfestival.se/en/

SWITZERLAND

*Locarno International Film Festival	Locarno	pardo.ch
Fribourg International Film Festival	Fribourg	fiff.ch
Time Film Festival	Lausanne	timefilmfestival.ch
Zurich International Film Festival	Zurich	zurichfilmfestival.org

TURKEY

International Golden Boll Film Festival	Adana	altinkoza.org
Ankara International Film Festival	Ankara	filmfestankara.org.tr
Antalya Golden Orange Film Festival	Antalya	aksav.org.tr

REGION	CITY	WEBSITE
Eskisehir International Film Festival	Eskisehir	eskfilmfest.anadolu.edu.tr
Art By Chance Ultra Short Film Festival	Istanbul	artbychance.org
IF Istanbul AFM Int'l Independent Film Festival	Istanbul	ifistanbul.com
International 1001 Documentary Film Festival	Istanbul	1001belgesel.net
International Istanbul Short Film Festival	Istanbul	istanbulfilmfestival.com
Istanbul Animation Festival	Istanbul	iafistanbul.com
Istanbul Film Festival	Istanbul	iksv.org/film
Festival on Wheels	Traveling Festival	festivalonwheels.org

UKRAINE
Irpen Film Festival	Irpen	kinofest.g-2b.com
STEPS International Rights Film Festival	Kharkov	cetalife.com.ua
Kyiv International Film Festival Molodist	Kyiv	molodist.com

UNITED KINGDOM
*Encounters International Film Festival	Bristol	encounters-festival.org.uk
*British Academy of Film & TV Arts (BAFTA) Awards	London	bafta.org
Bradford International Film Festival	Bradford	www.nationalmediamuseum.org.uk
Cambridge Film Festival	Cambridge	cambridgefilmfestival.org.uk
Dover Film Festival	Dover	dover-film.com
Minghella Film Festival	Isle of Wight	minghellafilmfestival.com
Leeds International Film Festival	Leeds	leedsfilm.com
Raindance Film Festival	London	raindance.co.uk
London Independent Film Festival	London	londonindependent.org
London Film Festival	London	lff.org.uk
London Lesbian & Gay Film Festival	London	bfi.org.uk/llgff
London Young Film Festival	London	lyff.org.uk
Open City London Documentary Film Festival	London	opencitylondon.com
SCI-FI-LONDON: London Int'l Festival of Sci-Fi & Fantastic Film	London	sci-fi-london.com
Branchage Film Festival	London	branchagefestival.com
Sheffield Doc/Fest	Sheffield	sheffdocfest.com
Wimbledon Shorts Film Festival	Wimbledon	wimbledonshorts.com

IRELAND
*Foyle Film Festival	Derry/Londonderry	foylefilmfestival.org
Cinemagic Int'l Film & TV Festival for Young People	Belfast	cinemagic.org.uk
Corona Cork Film Festival	Cork	corkfilmfest.org
Darklight Festival	Dublin	darklight.ie
Jameson Dublin International Film Festival	Dublin	jdiff.com
Galway Film Fleadh	Galway	galwayfilmfleadh.com
Kerry Film Festival	Kerry	kerryfilmfestival.com
Fresh Film Festival	Limerick	freshfilmfestival.net
Fastnet Short Film Festival	Schull	fastnetshortfilmfestival.com

SCOTLAND
Dead By Dawn Scotland's Int'l Horror Film Festival	Edinburgh	deadbydawn.co.uk
Edinburgh Int'l Film Festival	Edinburgh	edfilmfest.org.uk
Edinburgh Mountain Film Festival	Edinburgh	edinburghmountainff.com
Glasgow Film Festival	Glasgow	glasgowfilm.org
Celtic Media Festival	Western Isles	celticmediafestival.co.uk

CANADA
*Academy of Canadian Cinema & Television (GENIE)	Ottawa	academy.ca
*Ottawa International Animation Festival	Ottawa	animationfestival.ca
*Canadian Film Centre's Worldwide Short Film Festival	Toronto	worldwideshortfilmfest.com
*Montreal Festival Du Nouveau Cinema	Montreal	nouveaucinema.ca
*Montreal World Film Festival	Montreal	ffm-montreal.org
Int'l Festival of Animated Objects	Calgary	animatedobjects.ca
Edmonton Int'l Film Festival	Edmonton	edmontonfilmfest.com
Reel Shorts Film Festival	Grand Prairie	reelshortsfilmfest.ca

REGION	CITY	WEBSITE
SharpCuts Indie Film and Music Festival	Guelph	sharpcuts.ca
Atlantic International Film Festival	Halifax	atlanticfilm.com
ViewFinders International Film Festival for Youth	Halifax	atlanticfilm.com/festivals/ viewfinders
Mississauga Independent Film Festival	Mississauga	miff.ca
Carrousel International Du Film De Rimouski	Rimouski	festivalcinemarimouski.com
Nickel Independent Film Festival	St. John's	nickelfestival.com
Hot Docs Canadian International Documentary Festival	Toronto	hotdocs.ca
COMMFFEST (Global) Community Film Festival	Toronto	commffest.com
North by Northeast Film & Music Festival	Toronto	nxne.com
Lakeshorts Int'l Short Film Festival	Toronto	lakeshorts.ca
Moving Image Film Festival	Toronto	miffest.com
Giggleshorts Int'l Comedy Short Film Festival	Toronto	giggleshorts.com
Toronto International Film Festival	Toronto	tiff.net
ReelWorld Film Festival	Toronto	reelworld.ca
Toronto Jewish Film Festival	Toronto	tjff.com
Vancouver International Film Festival	Vancouver	viff.org
Vancouver Woman in Film Festival	Vancouver	womeninfilm.ca
Your Indiefilm Online Short Film Festival	Vancouver	yourindiefilm.com
Victoria Film Festival	Victoria	victoriafilmfestival.com
NSI Online Short Film Festival	Winnipeg	nsi-canada.ca
Winnipeg Real to Reel Film Festival	Winnipeg	winnipegfilmfestival.com
Female Eye Film Festival	Woodbridge	femaleeyefilmfestival.com
Yellowknife Film Festival	Yellowknife	wamp.ca
Yorktown Film Festival	Yorkton	goldensheafawards.com
Dawson City International Short Film Festival	Yukon	dawsonfilmfest.com

MEXICO

*Morelia International Film Festival	Michoacán	moreliafilmfest.com
International Documentary Film Festival of Mexico	Colonia Centro	docsdf.com
Guadalajara International Film Festival	Guadalajara	ficg.org
Kinoki Int'l College Film Festival	Mexico City	festivalkinoki.com
Monterrey International Film Festival	Monterrey	monterreyfilmfestival.com
Oaxaca International Film & Video Festival	Oaxaca	oaxacafilmfest.com
Guanajuato International Film Festival	San Miguel de Allende	guanajuatofilmfestival.com

CENTRAL AMERICA / CARIBBEAN / ATLANTIC

BELIZE

Belize International Film Festival	Belize	belizefilmfestival.com

BERMUDA

*Bermuda International Film Festival	Bermuda	biff.bm

CARIBBEAN ISLANDS

St. Barth Film Festival: Cinema	Caraibe	stbarthff.org

CUBA

Habana International Festival of New Latin Cinema	La Habana	habanafilmfestival.com

PUERTO RICO

Rincon International Film Festival	Rincon	rinconfilm.com
Puerto Rico Int'l Film Festival	Vieques Island	priff.org

SOUTH AMERICA

ARGENTINA

Buenos Aires Int'l Festival of Independent Film	Buenos Aires	bafici.gov.ar
Buenos Aires Rojo Sangre Festival of Terror & Fantasy	Buenos Aires	rojosangre.quintadimension.com
Festlatino Buenos Aires	Buenos Aires	festlatinoba.com.ar
Mar del Plata Film Festival	Mar del Plata	mardelplatafilmfest.com

REGION	CITY	WEBSITE
BRAZIL		
*Rio De Janeiro International Short Film Festival	Rio De Janeiro	curtacinema.com.br
Belo Horizonte International Short Film Festival	Belo Horizonte	festivaldecurtasbh.com.br
Anima Mundi Int'l Animation Festival	Rio De Janeiro/Sao Paulo	animamundi.com.br
It's All True Int'l Documentary Film Festival	Rio De Janeiro/Sao Paulo	itsalltrue.com.br
Sao Paulo International Film Festival	Sao Paulo	en.mostra.org
Sao Paulo International Short Film Festival	Sao Paulo	kinoforum.org.br/curtas
Sao Paulo Jewish Film Festival	Sao Paulo	fcjsp.com.br
COLOMBIA		
*Cartagena International Film Festival	Cartagena	festicinecartagena.org
Film Festival of Bogota	Bogota	bogocine.com
International Image Festival	Manizales	festivaldelaimagen.com
ASIA		
CAMBODIA		
Cambofest Film & Video Festival of Cambodia	Phnom Penh	cambofest.com
Cambodia International Film Festival	Phnom Penh	cambodia-iff.com
CHINA		
Beijing International Movie Festival	Beijing	beijingfilmfest.org
Hong Kong Int'l Film Festival	Hong Kong	hkiff.org.hk
Hong Kong Independent Short Film & Video Awards	Hong Kong	ifva.com
Shanghai International Film Festival	Shanghai	siff.com
INDIA		
Dhaka International Film Festival	Dhaka, Bangladesh	dhakafilmfest.org
International Film Festival of India	Goa	iffi.gov.in
Jaipur International Film Festival	Jaipur Rajasthan	jiffindia.org
Kerala International Film Festival	Kerala	keralafilm.com
WorldKids Int'l Film Festival	Mumbai	worldkidsfoundation.com/filmfestival
Golden Elephant Int'l Children's Film Festival	Mumbai	efsindia.org
Mumbai International Film Festival	Mumbai	mumbaifilmfest.com
Chinh India Kids Film Festival	New Delhi	chinh.in
JAPAN		
*Hiroshima International Animation Festival	Hiroshima	hiroanim.org
Short Shorts Film Festival & Asia	Japan/Korea	shortshorts.org
Skip City International D-Cinema Festival	Kawaguchi City	skipcity-dcf.jp
Okinawa International Movie Festival	Okinawa	oimf.jp
Con-Can Movie Festival	Tokyo	con-can.com
Tokyo International Film Festival	Tokyo	tiff-jp.net
PAKISTAN		
FiLUMS International LUMS Film Festival	Lahore	filums.com.pk
Lahore International Children's Film Festival	Lahore	lahorechildrenfilm.com
PHILIPPINES		
Cinemalaya Philippine International Film Festival	Pasay City	culturalcenter.gov.ph
Cinemanila International Film Festival	Quezon City	cinemanila.org.ph
SINGAPORE		
Singapore International Film Festival	Singapore	www.siff.sg
SOUTH KOREA		
Jeonju International Film Festival	Jeonju	eng.jiff.or.kr
Busan International Film Festival & Asian Film Market	Busan	biff.kr
Green Film Festival in Seoul	Seoul	en.gffis.org
Seoul International Youth Film Festival	Seoul	siyff.com

REGION	CITY	WEBSITE
TAIWAN		
Taipei Golden Horse Film Festival	Taipei	www.goldenhorse.org.tw
Taiwan International Children's Film Festival	Taipei	www.ticff.org.tw
Taiwan International Documentary Festival	Taipei	www.tidf.org.tw
Taiwan International Ethnographic Film Festival	Taipei	www.tieff.sinica.edu.tw
THAILAND		
World Film Festival of Bangkok	Bangkok	www.worldfilmbkk.com
Pattaya International Film Festival	Pattaya	pattayafilmfestival.asia
Phangan Film Festival	Thongsala	phanganfilmfestival.com

AUSTRALIA/NEW ZEALAND

REGION	CITY	WEBSITE
AUSTRALIA		
*Melbourne Int'l Film Festival	Melbourne, VIC	miff.com.au
*Sydney Film Festival	Sydney, NSW	sff.org.au
*Flickerfest International Short Films Festival	Sydney, NSW	flickerfest.com.au
Canberra International Film Festival	Canberra, ACT	canberrafilmfestival.com.au
Canberra International Short Film Festival	Canberra, ACT	csff.com.au
Scinema Festival of Science Film	Canberra, ACT	csiro.au/scinema
Brisbane International Film Festival	Brisbane, QLD	biff.com.au
Redland Spring Festival	Cleveland, QLD	redlandspringfestival.com.au
Heart of Gold International Film Festival	Gympie, QLD	heartofgold.com.au
Shorts Film Festival	Norwood, QLD	shortsfilmfestival.com
Port Shorts Film Festival	Port Douglas, QLD	portshorts.com
Shorts on the Green	Surfers paradise, QLD	shortsonthegreen.com
Byron Bay Film Festival	Byron Bay, NSW	bbff.com.au
Mardi Gras Film Festival	Darlinghurst, NSW	queerscreen.com.au
Mudfest International Short Film Festival	Mudgee, NSW	mudfest.com.au
Newcastle National Video Festival	Newcastle, NSW	nvm.org.au
Nimbin Film Festival	Nimbin, NSW	nimbinfilms.co.cc
A Night of Horror International Film Festival	Sydney, NSW	anightofhorror.com
Bondi Film Festival	Sydney, NSW	bondishortfilmfestival.com
Spanish Film Festival	Sydney, NSW	spanishfilmfestival.com
Sydney Underground Film Festival	Sydney, NSW	sydneyundergroundfilmfestival.com
World of Women International Film Festival	Sydney, NSW	wift.org/wow
Atom Awards	Altona, VIC	atomawards.org
Little Big Shots International Film Festival For Kids	Melbourne, VIC	littlebigshots.com.au
MuVifest International Music Video Festival	Melbourne, VIC	muvifest.com
Melbourne Queer Film Festival	Melbourne, VIC	mqff.com.au
Melbourne Underground Film Festival	Melbourne, VIC	muff.com.au
The Other Film Festival	Melbourne, VIC	otherfilmfestival.com
Shepparton Shorts Film Festival	Shepparton, VIC	sheppartonshorts.com
St Kilda Film Festival	St Kilda, VIC	stkildafilmfestival.com.au
Hillside Film Festival	Upwey, VIC	hillsidefilmfestival.com
Adelaide Film Festival	Adelaide, SA	adelaidefilmfestival.org
Shorts Film Festival	Adelaide, SA	shortsfilmfestival.com
Int'l Film Festival of Australasia	Tanunda, SA	amritsa.com/oz/one.htm
Australian International Documentary Conference	Unley, SA	aidc.com.au
Margaret River Shorts	Margaret River, WA	mrshorts.com
Revelation Perth International Film Festival	Mt Lawley, WA	revelationfilmfest.org
Rottofest Film & Music Festival	Rottnest Island, WA	rottofest.com.au
NEW ZEALAND		
Auckland International Film Festival	Auckland	nzff.co.nz
New Zealand Film Festival	Auckland/Wellington	nzff.co.nz
Show Me Shorts Film Festival	Auckland	showmeshorts.co.nz
Canterbury Short Film Festival	Christchurch	belladonna.org.nz
Big Mountain Short Film Festival	Ohakune	bigmountain.co.nz
Reel Earth	Palmerston North	reelearth.org.nz
Magma Film Festival	Rotorua-Aotearoa	magmafilm.org.nz
Moviefest	Trentham	moviefest.org.nz

REGION	CITY	WEBSITE
Wairoa Maori Film Festival	Wairoa	manawairoa.com
New Zealand Mountain Film Festival	Wanaka	mountainfilm.net.nz
Documentary Edge Festival	Wellington	documentaryedge.org.nz
Out Takes A Reel Queer Film Festival	Wellington	outtakes.org.nz
Wellington Film Festival	Wellington	nzff.co.nz

MIDDLE EAST

Abu Dhabi Film Festival	Abu Dhabi	abudhabifilmfestival.ae
Dubai International Film Festival	Dubai	dubaifilmfest.com
Cairo International Film Festival	Egypt	cairofilmfest.org
Cinema Verite Iran Int'l Documentary Film Festival	Iran	defc.ir/en
Fajr International Film Festival	Iran	fajrfestival.ir
Tehran International Animation Festival	Iran	tehran-animafest.ir
Tehran International Short Film Festival	Iran	iycs.ir/Persian
Jordan Short Film Festival	Jordan	jordanfilmfestival.com
Beruit International Documentary Festival	Lebanon	docudays.com
Carthage Film Festival	Tunisia	jccarthage.org

ISRAEL
Cinema South International Film Festival	Ashkelon	csf.sapir.ac.il
Haifa International Film Festival	Haifa	haifaff.co.il
Jerusalem Film Festival	Jerusalem	jff.org.il
International Women's Film Festival	Rehovot	iwff.net
Doc Aviv International Documentary Film Festival	Tel Aviv	docaviv.co.il
Tel Aviv Spirit Film Festival	Tel Aviv	spiritfestival.co.il

AFRICA

SOUTH AFRICA
Durban International Film Festival	Durban	cca.ukzn.ac.za
Fespaco Pan African Film Festival	Ouagadougou	fespaco.bf
International Film Festival South Africa	Howick Kwa-Zulu Nat	amritsa.com/eiff/2010/home.htm
Encounters South African Int'l Documentary Film Festival	Johannesburg	encounters.co.za
Tricontinental Human Rights Film Festival	Johannesburg	3continentsfestival.co.za
Out In Africa – South Africa Gay & Lesbian Film Festival	Johannesburg	oia.co.za
Cape Winelands Film Festival	Stellenbosch	films-for-africa.co.za

TANZANIA
Zanzibar International Film Festival	Zanzibar	ziff.or.tz

UNITED STATES FILM FESTIVALS

(*Academy Qualifying Film Festivals for short films. For a current listing of Academy Qualifying Film Festivals visit: www.oscars.org)

Alabama
Sidewalk Moving Picture Festival	Birmingham	sidewalkfest.com
Alabama International Film Festival	Troy	alafilm.org

Alaska
Alaska Film Festival	Anchorage	alaskafilmfestival.com
Anchorage International Film Festival	Anchorage	anchoragefilmfestival.org

Arizona
Phoenix Film Festival	Phoenix	phoenixfilmfestival.org
Prescott Film Festival	Prescott	prescottfilmfestival.com
International Horror & Sci-Fi Film Festival	Scottsdale	horrorscifi.com
Scottsdale International Film Festival	Scottsdale	ScottsdaleFilmFestival.com
Sedona International Film Festival	Sedona	sedonafilmfestival.com
Arizona International Film Festival	Tucson	filmfestivalarizona.com
Loft Film Fest	Tucson	loftfilmfest.com
Arizona State University Short Film and Video Festival	Tempe	asuartmuseum.asu.edu/filmfest

REGION	CITY	WEBSITE
Arkansas		
Hot Springs Documentary Film Festival	Hot Springs	hsdfi.org
Little Rock Film Festival	Little Rock	littlerockfilmfestival.org
California		
*Los Angeles Film Festival	Los Angeles	lafilmfest.com
*Los Angeles Int'l. Short Film Festival	Los Angeles	lashortsfest.com
*Los Angeles Latino International Film Festival	Los Angeles	latinofilm.org
*Short Shorts Film Festival	Los Angeles	shortshorts.org/ssff
*Palm Springs Int'l Festival Of Short Films	Palm Springs	psfilmfest.org
*Siggraph (USA)	various cities	siggraph.org
*San Francisco Int'l Film Festival	San Francisco	sffs.org
*Cinequest Film Festival	San Jose	cinequest.org
*Santa Barbara Int'l Film Festival	Santa Barbara	sbfilmfestival.org
Bel Air Film Festival	Bel-Air	belairfilmfestival.com
Beverly Hills Film Festival	Beverly Hills	beverlyhillsfilmfestival.com
Beverly Hills Shorts Festival	Beverly Hills	beverlyhillsshortsfestival.com
La Femme Film Festival	Beverly Hills	lafemme.com
Big Bear Lake International Film Festival	Big Bear Lake	Bigbearlakefilmfestival.com
Big Sur International Short Film Screenings	Big Sur	bigsurfilm.org
Burbank International Film Festival	Burbank	burbankfilm.org
International Family Film Festival	Burbank	iffilmfest.org
Method Film Festival	Calabasas	methodfest.com
Danville International Children's Film Festival	Danville	caiff.org/Danville
Fallbrook Film Festival	Fallbrook	fallbrookfilmfestival.com
Fresno Film Festival	Fresno	fresnofilmfestival.com
168 Hour Project	Glendale	168project.com
Artivist Film Festival	Hollywood	festival.artivist.com
Famewalk International Film Festival	Hollywood	famewalkfilms.com
FirstGlance Film Fest	Hollywood	firstglancefilms.com
Hollyshorts Film Festival	Hollywood	hollyshorts.com
Hollywood Shorts	Hollywood	hollywoodshorts.com
Hollywood Film Festival	Hollywood	hollywoodawards.com
Hollywood Reel Independent Film Festival	Hollywood	hollywoodreelindependentfilmfestival.com
Los Angeles Cinema Festival of Hollywood	Hollywood	hollywoodcff.com
NewFilmmakers LA at Sunset Gower Studios	Hollywood	newfilmmakersla.com
Accolade Competition	La Jolla	accoladecompetition.org
Best Shorts	La Jolla	bestshorts.net
The Indie Fest	La Jolla	TheIndieFest.com
Lake Arrowhead Film Festival	Lake Arrowhead	lakearrowheadfilmfestival.com
AFI Fest: AFI Los Angeles Int'l Film Festival	Los Angeles	afi.com/afifest
Angelus Student Film Festival	Los Angeles	angelus.org
Awareness Festival	Los Angeles	awarenessfestival.healoneworld.com
Dance Camera West Dance Film Festival	Los Angeles	dancecamerawest.org
Dances With Films	Los Angeles	danceswithfilms.com
Downtown Film Festival Los Angeles	Los Angeles	dffla.com
Fusion: Los Angeles LGBT People of Color Film Festival	Los Angeles	outfest.org/fusion
Graphation Film Festival	Los Angeles	graphation.com
Indian Film Festival of Los Angeles	Los Angeles	indianfilmfestival.org
L.A. Comedy Shorts Film Festival	Los Angeles	lacomedyshorts.com
Los Angeles Asian Pacific Film Festival	Los Angeles	asianfilmfestla.org
Los Angeles Movie Awards	Los Angeles	thelamovieawards.com
Los Angeles Music Video Festival	Los Angeles	lamvf.com
Los Angeles Women's International Film Festival	Los Angeles	lawomensfest.com
New Media Film Festival	Los Angeles	newmediafilmfestival.com
Outfest: Los Angeles Gay & Lesbian Film Festival	Los Angeles	outfest.org
Singafest Asian Film Festival	Los Angeles	singafest.com
Southern California Business Film Festival	Los Angeles	scbff.com
United Film Festival Los Angeles	Los Angeles	theunitedfest.com
Malibu Film Festival	Malibu	malibufilmfestival.org
Mendocino Film Festival	Mendocino	mendocinofilmfestival.org

REGION	CITY	WEBSITE
California Independent Film Festival	Moraga	caiff.org
Poppy Jasper Short Film Festival	Morgan Hill	poppyjasperfilmfest.org
Napa Valley Film Festival	Napa Valley	napavalleyfilmfest.org
Newport Beach Film Festival	Newport Beach	newportbeachfilmfest.com
Harvard-Westlake Film Festival	North Hollywood	hw.com/filmfestival
Ojai Film Festival	Ojai	ojaifilmfestival.com
Pacific Palisades Film Fest	Palisades	friendsoffilm.com
Palm Springs International Film Festival	Palm Springs	psfilmfest.org
Palm Springs International ShortFest & Film Market	Palm Springs	psfilmfest.org
Action Film Festival	Pasadena	aoffest.com
Petaluma International Film Festival	Petaluma	petalumafilmfestival.org
Geography of Hope Film Festival	Point Reyes	ptreyesbooks.com/goh/film-festival
Sundial Film Festival	Redding	sundialfilmfestival.com
U.S. International Film & Video Festival	Redondo Beach	filmfestawards.com
Riverside International Film Festival	Riverside	riversidefilmfest.org
Sacramento Film and Music Festival	Sacramento	sacfilm.com
Sacramento International Film Festival	Sacramento	sacramentofilmfestival.com
Comic Con International Independent Film Festival	San Diego	comic-con.org
San Diego Black Film Festival	San Diego	sdbff.com
San Diego Film Festival	San Diego	sdff.org
San Diego Indie Fest	San Diego	sandiegoindiefest.com
American Indian Film Festival	San Francisco	aifisf.com
Madcat Women's Int'l Film Festival	San Francisco	madcatfilmfestival.org
San Francisco Int'l Festival of Short Films	San Francisco	sfshorts.com
San Francisco Jewish Film Festival	San Francisco	sfjff.org
San Jose Short Film Festival	San Jose	sjshortfest.com
Third World Indie Film Festival	San Jose	thirdworldindiefilmfest.com
San Luis Obispo Int'l Film Festival	San Luis Obispo	slofilmfest.org
Mill Valley Film Festival	San Rafael	mvff.com
Santa Catalina Film Festival	Santa Catalina Island	catalinaff.org
Santa Cruz Film Festival	Santa Cruz	santacruzfilmfestival.org
Sonoma International Film Festival	Sonoma	sonomafilmfest.org
Action/Cut Short Film Competition	Studio City	actioncut.com
Temecula Valley Intl Film & Music Festival	Temecula	tviff.com
Valley Film Festival	Toluca Lake	valleyfilmfest.com
Other Venice Film Festival	Venice	othervenicefilmfestival.com

Colorado

*Aspen Shortsfest	Aspen	aspenfilm.org
Aspen Film Festival	Aspen	aspenfilm.org
Breckenridge Festival of Film	Breckenridge	breckfilmfest.com
Boulder Adventure Film Festival	Boulder	adventurefilm.org
Boulder International Film Festival	Boulder	biff1.com
Moondance International Film Festival	Boulder	moondancefilmfestival.com
Castle Rock Film Festival	Castle Rock	castlerockfilmfestival.com
Indie Spirit Film Festival	Colorado Springs	indiespiritfilmfestival.org
Rocky Mountain Women's Film Festival	Colorado Springs	rmwfilmfest.org
Festivus Film Festival	Denver	festivusfilmfestival.com
The Film Festival of Colorado	Denver	thefilmfestivalofcolorado.org
Starz Denver Film Festival	Denver	denverfilm.org/festival
Durango Film Festival	Durango	durangofilm.org
Estes Park Film Festival	Estes Park	estesparkfilm.com
Telluride Film Festival	Telluride	telluridefilmfestival.com
Mountainfilm in Telluride	Telluride	mountainfilm.org
Vail Film Festival	Vail	vailfilmfest.com

Connecticut

New England Underground Film Festival	Hartford	newenglanduff.webs.com
Litchfield Hills Film Festival	New Milford	hillsfilmfestival.org
Connecticut Film Festival	Old Saybrook	ctfilmfest.com

REGION	CITY	WEBSITE
Delaware		
Newark Film Festival	Newark	newarkfilm.com
Rehoboth Beach Independent Film Festival	Rehoboth Beach	rehobothfilm.com
Hearts and Minds Film	Wilmington	heartsandmindsfilm.org
Florida		
*Florida Film Festival	Maitland	floridafilmfestival.com
Clearwater Film Festival	Clearwater	theclearwaterfilmfestival.com
Daytona Beach Film Festival	Daytona Beach	dbff.org
Downtown Boca Film Festival	Delray Beach	dbff.us
Fort Lauderdale International Film Festival	Fort Lauderdale	fliff.com
Fort Myers Film Festival	Fort Myers	fortmyersfilmfestival.com
Citrus Cel Animation Film Festival	Jacksonville	citruscel.com
Jacksonville Film Festival	Jacksonville	jacksonvillefilmfestival.com
DocMiami International Film Festival	Miami	docmiami.org
Italian Film Festival	Miami	cinemaitaly.org
Miami Gay & Lesbian Film Festival	Miami	mglff.com
Central Florida Film Festival	Ocoee	centralfloridafilmfestival.com
Global Peace Film Festival	Orlando	peacefilmfest.org
15 Minutes of Fame	Palm Bay	15minutefilmfest.com
Palm Beach Women's Int'l Film Festival	Palm Beach	pbwiff.com
Palm Beach International Film Festival	Palm Beach	pbifilmfest.org
Love Your Shorts Film Festival	Sanford	loveyourshorts.com
Sarasota Film Festival	Sarasota	sarasotafilmfestival.com
Tallahassee Film Festival	Tallahassee	tallahasseefilmfestival.com
Conga Caliente International Film Festival	Tampa	congacalienteiff.com
Gasparilla International Film Festival	Tampa	gasparillafilmfestival.com
India Int'l Film Festival of Tampa Bay	Tampa	iifftampa.com
Tampa Int'l Gay & Lesbian Film Festival	Tampa	tiglff.com
Georgia		
*Atlanta Film Festival	Atlanta	atlantafilmfestival.com
Atlanta Underground Film Festival	Atlanta	auff.org
BronzLens Film Festival	Atlanta	bronzelensfilmfestival.com
Docufest Atlanta	Atlanta	docufest.com
DragonCon Independent Short Film Festival	Atlanta	filmfest.dragoncon.org
Macon Film Festival	Macon	maconfilmfestival.com
Rome International Film Festival	Rome	riff.tv
Savannah Film Festival	Savannah	scad.edu/experience/filmfest
Hawaii		
Hawaii International Film Festival	Honolulu	hiff.org
Honolulu Film Awards	Honolulu	honolulufilmawards.com
Maui Film Festival	Maui	mauifilmfestival.com
Big Island Film Festival	Mauni Lani	bigislandfilmfestival.com
Idaho		
Sand Point Film Festival	Sand Point	sandpointfilmsfestival.com
Sun Valley Spiritual Film Festival	Sun Valley	svspiritualfilmfestival.org
LunaFest Short Films	Traveling Film Festival	lunafest.org
Illinois		
*Chicago Int'l Children's Film Festival	Chicago	cicff.org
Roger Ebert's Overlooked Film Festival	Champaign	ebertfest.com
Chicago Latino Film Festival	Chicago	chicagolatinofilmfestival.org
Chicago International Film Festival	Chicago	chicagofilmfestival.com
Chicago Comedy Film Festival	Chicago	chicagocomedyff.com
Chicago Int'l Movies and Music Festival	Chicago	cimmfest.org
Chicago Underground Film Festival	Chicago	cuff.org
Reality Bytes Independent Student Film Festival	DeKalb	realitybytes.niu.edu
Imago Film Festival	Elgin	imagofilmfestival.com
Talking Pictures Festival	Evanston	talkingpicturesfestival.org

REGION	CITY	WEBSITE
Geneva Film Festival	Geneva	genevafilmfestival.org
Naperville Independent Film Festival	Naperville	naperfilmfest.org
Route 66 Film Festival	Springfield	route66filmfestival.net
Illinois International Film Festival	Westmont	illinoisinternationalfilmfestival.com
Indiana		
Heartland Film Festival	Indianapolis	trulymovingpictures.org
Indianapolis International Film Festival	Indianapolis	indyfilmfest.org
River Bend Film Festival	South Bend	riverbendfilmfest.org
Iowa		
Iowa City Int'l Documentary Film Festival	Iowa City	icdocfest.com
Cedar Rapids Independent Film Festival	Marion	crifm.org
Kansas		
Kansas International Film Festival	Overland Park	kansasfilm.com
Kansas Silent Film Festival	Topeka	kssilentfilmfest.org
Tallgrass Film Festival	Wichita	tallgrassfilmfest.com
Kentucky		
Western Film Festival	Bowling Green	westernfilmfest.com
Danville Lawn Chair Film Festival	Danville	betterindanville.com/Visiting-Here-Film-Festival.aspx
One World Film Festival	Lexington	oneworldfilmfestival.org
Derby City Film Festival	Louisville	derbycityfilmfest.com
Fright Night Film Fest	Louisville	frightnightfilmfest.com
Louisville International Festival of Film	Louisville	louisvillefilm.net
River's Edge International Film Festival	Paducah	riversedgefilmfestival.com
Louisiana		
Red Stick International Animation Festival	Baton Rouge	redstickfestival.org
JamFest Indie Film Festival	Hammond	strawberryjam.org
New Orleans Film Festival	New Orleans	neworleansfilmsociety.com
The Louisiana Film Festival Student Division	Shreveport	lafilmfest.org
Maine		
KahBang Film Festival	Bangor	kahbang.com/film
Camden International Film Festival	Camden	camdenfilmfest.org
Lewiston Auburn Film Festival	Lewiston/Auburn	lafilmfestival.org
Maine Jewish Film Festival	Portland	mjff.org
Portland Maine Film Festival	Portland	portlandmainefilmfestival.com
Maine International Film Festival	Waterville	miff.org
Maryland		
Maryland Film Festival	Baltimore	mdfilmfest.com
Chesapeake Film Festival	Eaton	chesapeakefilmfestival.com
Frederick Film Festival	Frederick	frederickfilmfest.com
Maryland International Kid Film Festival	Frederick	mikff.com
Silverdocs Documentary Festival	Silver Spring	silverdocs.com
Massachusetts		
Boston Film Festival	Boston	bostonfilmfestival.org
Boston Underground Film Festival	Boston	bostonunderground.org
Boston LGBT Film Festival	Boston	bostonlgbtfilmfest.org
Independent Film Festival Boston	Boston	iffboston.org
Boston Cinema Census	Cambridge	bostoncinemacensus.org
European Short Film Festival	Cambridge	esff.mit.edu
Berkshire Int'l Film Festival	Great Barrington	biffma.com
Martha's Vineyard International Film Festival	Martha's Vineyard	mvfilmfest.com
Nantucket Film Festival	Nantucket	nantucketfilmfestival.org
Newburyport Documentary Film Festival	Newburyport	newburyportfilmfestival.org
Provincetown International Film Festival	Provincetown	ptownfilmfest.org

REGION	CITY	WEBSITE
Michigan		
*Ann Arbor Film Festival	Ann Arbor	aafilmfest.org
Detroit Independent Film Festival	Detroit	detroitiff.com
Detroit Windsor International Film Festival	Detroit	dwiff.org
East Lansing Film Festival	East Lansing	elff.com
Flint Film Festival	Flint	theflintfilmfestival.com
Michigan Film Festival	Grand Rapids	michiganfilmfest.org
Northern Lights Film Festival	Houghton	northernlights.smitherin.net
Capital City Film Festival	Lansing	capitalcityfilmfest.com
Riverside Saginaw Film Festival	Saginaw	riversidesaginawfilmfestival.org
Waterfront Film Festival	Saugatuck	waterfrontfilm.com
Traverse City Film Festival	Traverse City	traversecityfilmfest.org
Minnesota		
EDU Film Festival	Minneapolis	edufilmfest.org
Minneapolis St. Paul International Film Festival	Minneapolis/St. Paul	mspfilmfest.org
Solstice Film Festival	St. Paul	solsticefilmfest.org
Mississippi		
The Delta Int'l Film and Video Festival	Cleveland	difvf.com
Crossroads Film Festival	Jackson	crossroadsfilmfestival.com
Mississippi International Film Festival	Jackson	mississippifilmfest.com
Oxford Film Festival	Oxford	oxfordfilmfest.com
Magnolia Independent Film Festival	Starkville	magfilmfest.com
Tupelo Film Festival	Tupelo	tupelo.net/film-festival
Frozen River Film Festival	Winona	frff.org
Missouri		
*St. Louis Int'l Film Festival	St. Louis	cinemastlouis.org
Fault-Line Film Festival	Cape Girardeau	semo.edu/cie/faultline.htm
Silver Screen Film Festival	Columbia	silverscreen.missouri.edu
True/False Film Festival	Columbia	truefalse.org
Kansas City Filmmakers Jubilee	Kansas City	kcjubilee.org
Montana		
HATCHfest	Bozeman	hatchfest.org
International Wildlife Film Festival	Missoula	wildlifefilms.org
Montana CINE International Film Festival	Missoula	wildlifefilms.org
Griffon International Film Festival	St. Joseph	missouriwestern.edu/griff
Nebraska		
Omaha Film Festival	Omaha	omahafilmfestival.org
Nevada		
Dam Short Film Festival	Boulder City	damshortfilm.org
Cinevegas Film Festival	Las Vegas	cinevegas.com
Nevada Film Festival	Las Vegas	nevadafilmfestival.com
High Desert Shorts Int'l Film Festival	Pahrump	highdesertshortsiff.com
New Hampshire		
New Hampshire Film Festival	Portsmouth	nhfilmfestival.com
New Jersey		
Garden State Film Festival	Asbury Park	gsff.org
Cape May New Jersey Film Festival	Cape May	njstatefilmfestival.com
Hoboken International Film Festival	Hawthorne	hobokeninternationalfilmfestival.com
Black Maria Film + Video Festival	Jersey City	blackmariafilmfestival.org
Lighthouse International Film Festival	Long Beach Island	lighthousefilmfestival.org
Montclair International Film Festival	Montclair	montclairnjfilmfestival.org
New Jersey International Film Festival	New Brunswick	njfilmfest.com
Trenton Film Festival	Trenton	trentonfilmfestival.org

REGION	CITY	WEBSITE
New Mexico		
Albuquerque Film Festival	Albuquerque	abqfilmfestival.com
New Mexico International Film Festival	Jemez Springs	newmexicointernationalfilmfestival.com
Santa Fe 3-Minute Film Fest	Santa Fe	3mff.com
Santa Fe Film Festival	Santa Fe	santafefilmfestival.com
Taos Mountain Film Festival	Taos	mountainfilm.net
Taos Shortz Film Festival	Taos	taosshortz.com
New York		
*Hamptons International Film Festival	East Hamptons	hamptonsfilmfest.org
*New York International Children's Film Festival	New York	www.gkids.com
*Tribeca Film Festival	New York	tribecafilmfestival.org
Brooklyn Film Festival	Brooklyn	brooklynfilmfestival.org
Brooklyn Short Film Festival	Brooklyn	brooklynshorts.com
Coney Island Film Festival	Brooklyn	coneyislandfilmfestival.com
New York No Limits Film Series	Brooklyn	newyorknolimits.com
New York United Film Festival	Brooklyn	theunitedfest.com
Scene: Brooklyn Independent Film & Media Arts	Brooklyn	brooklynartcouncil.org
Williamsburg Independent Film Festival	Brooklyn	willfilm.org
Buffalo International Film Festival	Buffalo	buffalofilmfestival.com
New Paltz Climbing Film Festivals	New Paltz	chestnutmtnproductions.com
Astoria/LIC International Film Festival	New York	astorialicff.com
Athena Film Festival	New York	athenafilmfestival.com
Asian American International Film Festival	New York	asiancinevision.org
Bicycle Film Festival	New York	bicyclefilmfestival.com
Big Apple Film Festival	New York	bigapplefilmfestival.com
Columbia University Film Festival	New York	cufilmfest.com
Harlem International Film Festival	New York	harlemfilmfestival.com
Havana Film Festival New York	New York	hffny.com
HDFest	New York	hdfest.com
The Iron Mule Short Comedy Screening Series	New York	ironmulenyc.com
Manhattan Film Festival	New York	manhattanfilmfestival.org
Metropolitan Film Festival of New York	New York	metrofilmfest.com
NYC Downtown Short Film & Feature Festival	New York	duotheater.org/film.php
New York Film Festival	New York	filmlinc.com
New York Indian Film Festival	New York	iaac.us/nyiff2011
Soho International Film Festival	New York	site.siffnyc.net
360	365 George Eastman House Film Festival	Rochester	film360365.com
Rochester International Film Festival	Rochester	rochesterfilmfest.org
Staten Island Film Festival	Staten Island	sifilmfestival.org
Syracuse International Film Festival	Syracuse	syrfilmfest.com
Woodstock Film Festival	Woodstock	woodstockfilmfestival.com
North Carolina		
Full Frame Documentary Film Festival	Durham	fullframefest.org
North Carolina Gay & Lesbian Film Festival	Durham	ncglff.org
Carolina Film & Video Festival	Greensboro	cfvfestival.org
Real to Reel International Film Festival	Kings Mountain	ccartscouncil.org/realtoreel
Cucalorus Film Festival	Wilmington	cucalorus.org
RiverRun International Film Festival	Winston-Salem	riverrunfilm.com
North Dakota		
Fargo Film Festival	Fargo	fargofilmfestival.org
Ohio		
*Athens Int'l Film & Video Festival	Athens	athensfest.org
*Cleveland International Film Festival	Cleveland	clevelandfilm.org
Cincinnati Film Festival	Cincinnati	cincyfilmfest.com
Arnold Sports Film Festival	Columbus	arnoldsfilmfestival.com
Columbus International Film & Video Festival	Columbus	chrisawards.org
Standing Rock Int'l Short Film Festival	Kent	standingrock.net/FilmEvents.htm

REGION	CITY	WEBSITE
Oklahoma		
Trail Dance Film Festival	Duncan	traildancefilmfestival.com
Bare Bones International Film Festival	Muskogee	barebonesfilmfestivals.org
deadCENTER Film Festival	Oklahoma City	deadcenterfilm.org
Bare Bones Script 2 Screen Film Festival	Tulsa	script2screenfilmfestival.com
Tulsa International Film Festival	Tulsa	tulsafilmfestival.org
Oklahoma Horror Film Festival & Convention	Tulsa	tulsafilmfestival.org/ohff
Oregon		
Ashland Independent Film Festival	Ashland	ashlandfilm.org
Bend Film Festival	Bend	bendfilm.org
da Vinci Film Festival	Corvallis	davincidays.org
Eugene Celebration Film Festival	Eugene	eugenecelebration.com
Eugene International Film Festival	Eugene	eugenefilmfest.org
Love Unlimited Film Festival	Portland	lovefilmandart.org
Northwest Film & Video Festival	Portland	nwfilm.org
Portland International Film Festival	Portland	festivals.nwfilm.org/piff34/
Oregon Film Awards	Wilsonville	oregonfilmfestival.com
Pennsylvania		
SouthSide Film Festival	Bethlehem	ssff.org
Great Lakes Independent Film Festival	Erie	greatlakesfilmfest.com
Lancaster Area Film Festival	Lititz	lancasterareafilmfestival.com
Black Bear Film Festival	Milford	blackbearfilm.com
First Glance Philadelphia Film Festival	Philadelphia	firstglancefilms.com
Lost Film Festival	Philadelphia	lostfilmfest.com
Philadelphia Asian American Film Festival	Philadelphia	phillyasianfilmfest.org
Philadelphia Film & Animation Festival	Philadelphia	projecttwenty1.com
Philadelphia Film Festival	Philadelphia	filmadelphia.org
Philadelphia Independent Film Festival	Philadelphia	philadelphiaindependentfilmfestival.com
Philafilm - Film Festival and Market	Philadelphia	philafilm.org
Urban Suburban Film Festival	Philadelphia	urbansuburbanfilmfestival.com
The Boonies International	Warren	thebooniesinternational.com
West Chester Int'l Short Film Festival	West Chester	westchesterfilmfestival.com
Rhode Island		
*Rhode Island International Film Festival	Providence	film-festival.org
South Carolina		
Beaufort International Film Festival	Beaufort	beaufortfilmfestival.com
Charleston International Film Festival	Charleston	charlestoniff.com
Indie Grits Film Festival	Columbia	indiegrits.com
South Dakota		
South Dakota Film Festival	Aberdeen	southdakotafilmfest.org
Tennessee		
*Nashville Film Festival	Nashville	nashvillefilmfestival.org
Mountain Madness Film Festival	Gatlinburg	mmfilmfestival.com
International Black Film Festival of Nashville	Nashville	ibffnashville.com
Doorpost Film Project	Nashville	thedoorpost.com
Indie Memphis Film Festival	Memphis	indiememphis.com
Texas		
*Austin Film Festival	Austin	austinfilmfestival.com
*South By Southwest (SXSW)	Austin	sxsw.com
*USA Film Festival	Dallas	usafilmfestival.com
Cine Las Americas International Film Festival	Austin	cinelasamericas.org
Fantastic Fest	Austin	fantasticfest.com
Asian Film Festival of Dallas	Dallas	affd.org
Dallas International Film Festival	Dallas	dallasfilm.org
Dallas Video Festival	Dallas	videofest.org

REGION	CITY	WEBSITE
Texas Black Film Festival	Dallas	texasblackfilmfestival.com
Thin Line Film Fest	Denton	thinlinefilmfest.com
Lone Star International Film Festivals	Fort Worth	lsiff.com
Hill Country Film Festival	Fredericksburg	hillcountryff.com
Worldfest Houston International Film Festival	Houston	worldfest.org
Houston Comedy Film Festival	Houston	houstoncomedyfilmfestival.com
Texas International Film Festival	Kennedale	texasfilmfest.com
Flatland Film Festival	Lubbock	flatlandfilmfestival.com
Gulf Coast Film & Video Festival	Nassau Bay	gulfcoastfilmfest.com
Rockport Film Festival	Rockport	rockportfilmfest.com
SAFILM - San Antonio Film Festival	San Antonio	safilm.com

Utah

*Sundance Film Festival	Park City	sundance.org
*Slamdance Film Festival	Park City	slamdance.com
Thunderbird Film Festival	Cedar City	thunderbirdfilmfestival.suu.edu
Foursite Film Festival	Farmington	foursitefilmfest.com
Docutah International Documentary Film Festival	St. George	docutah.com
Red Rock Film Festival of Zion Canyon	St. George	redrockfilmfestival.com

Vermont

Women's Film Festival	Brattleboro	womensfilmfestival.org
Vermont International Film Festival	Burlington	vtiff.org
Green Mountain Film Festival	Montpelier	greenmountainfilmfestival.org

Virginia

Alexandria Film Festival	Alexandria	alexandriafilm.org
Rosebud Film and Video Festival	Arlington	rosebudfestival.org
Virginia Film Festival	Charlottesville	vafilm.com
Virginia Student Film Festival	Charlottesville	vasfilm.com
Appalachian Film Festival	Huntington	appyfilmfest.com
Williamsburg Independent Film Festival	Williamsburg	willifest.com

Washington

*Seattle International Film Festival	Seattle	siff.net
Ellensburg Film Festival	Ellensburg	ellensburgfilmfestival.com
Gig Harbor Film Festival	Gig Harbor	gigharborfilmfestival.org
Tumbleweed Film Festival	Okanogan County	tumbleweedfilmfest.com
Olympia Film Festival	Olympia	olympiafilmsociety.org
Port Townsend Film Festival	Port Townsend	ptfilmfest.com
'2D OR NOT 2D' Animation Festival	Seattle	2dornot2d.org
Children's Film Festival Seattle	Seattle	nwfilmforum.org/go/childrensfilmfest/
Maelstrom International Fantastic Film Festival	Seattle	mifff.org
National Film Festival For Talented Youth	Seattle	nffty.org
Official Best of Fest Awards	Seattle	officialbestoffest.com
Seattle Jewish Film Festival	Seattle	seattlejewishfilmfestival.org
Seattle Latino Film Festival	Seattle	slff.org
Seattle Lesbian & Gay Film Festival	Seattle	seattlequeerfilm.com
Seattle Polish Film Festival	Seattle	polishfilms.org
Seattle True Independent Film Festival	Seattle	trueindependent.org
Spokane International Film Festival	Spokane	spokanefilmfestival.org
Spokane's GLBT Film Festival	Spokane	spokanefilmfest.org
Tacoma Film Festival	Tacoma	grandcinema.com

Washington D.C.

Capital Irish Film Festival	Washington, DC	irishfilmdc.org
DC Independent Film Festival	Washington, DC	dciff.org
DC Shorts Film Festival	Washington, DC	dcshorts.com
CINE Golden Eagle Film & Video Competitions	Washington, DC	cine.org
Film/Neu Festival	Washington, DC	filmneu.org
GI Film Festival	Washington, DC	gifilmfestival.com

REGION	CITY	WEBSITE
Politics on Film	Washington, DC	politicsonfilm.com
ThrillSpy International Thriller & Spy Film Festival	Washington, DC	thrillspy.org
Washington Jewish Film Festival	Washington, DC	wjff.org
Washington, DC International Film Festival	Washington, DC	filmfestdc.org
West Virginia		
West Virginia International Film Festival	Charleston	wviff.org
Appalachian Film Festival	Huntington	appyfilmfest.com
West Virginia Filmmakers Festival	Sutton	wvfilmmakersfestival.org
Wisconsin		
Wildwood Film Festival	Appleton	wildwoodfilmfest.com
Beloit International Film Festival	Beloit	beloitfilmfest.org
Wisconsin Film Festival	Madison	wifilmfest.org
Flyway Film Festival	Stockholm	flywayfilmfestival.org
Wyoming		
Cheyenne International Film Festival	Cheyenne	cheyenneinternationalfilmfestival.com
Wyoming Short Film Contest	Cheyenne	wyomingshortfilmcontest.com
Jackson Hole Wildlife Film Festival	Jackson	jhfestival.org
Wyoming Film Festival	Saratoga	wyomingfilmfestival.org

Check out **www.ManeuveringFilmFestivals.com** for a free downloadable version of our comprehensive **film festival listings**.

ABOUT THE AUTHORS

MONIKA SKERBELIS

Monika Skerbelis started her industry career with the studios as an assistant in the Story Department for Paramount Pictures, then moved over to 20th Century Fox as an assistant story editor, later promoted to story editor. At the same time, Universal Pictures offered her the opportunity to run their story department where she worked for ten years and was promoted from an executive story editor to a vice president. She developed a number of screenplays including *Black Dog* starring Patrick Swayze. In addition to her story department duties at Universal, she scoured film festivals, student film screenings, and screenwriting competitions in search of new filmmakers.

Monika co-produced the feature-length mockumentary *Quest for the Yeti*, directed by Victoria Arch, and she directed the short film *Reel Footage: The Secret Lives of Shoes* that screened at the 2008 Short Film Corner at the Cannes Film Festival. She was associate producer on two movies, *Killer Hair* and *Hostile Makeover* based on the "Crimes of Fashion" novels by Ellen Byerrum for the Lifetime Movie Network.

Since its inception in 2000, Monika has been programming films for the Big Bear Lake International Film Festival in addition to helping turn a mom and pop festival into a profitable venture. She has met many filmmakers from around the world and introduced them to the appropriate industry insiders. In addition to being the Artistic & Programming Director, she is a member of the dedicated board of directors. In 2006 she was president of the festival and in 2011 became co-president with writer Sandy Steers, whom she has been working alongside for over ten years. In 2009, Monika received the festival's President's Volunteer Appreciation Award (a lovely bear statuette) for a decade of volunteer service to the festival.

Monika has been the director of The American Pavilion Emerging Filmmaker Showcase at the Cannes Film Festival since 2008, where she watches hundreds of short films in order to create a showcase at The American Pavilion during the Cannes Film Festival, allowing her the opportunity to experience one of the largest film festivals in the world. She is a member of the Producers Guild of America.

RONA EDWARDS

Graduating from California Institute of the Arts, Rona Edwards became Vice President of Creative Affairs for multiple Emmy-winner John Larroquette (*Night Court*), Academy Award Winner Michael Phillips Productions (*The Sting, Close Encounters Of The Third Kind, Taxi Driver*), and Emmy-winning and Oscar-nominated Producer, Fern Field (*Monk, Heartsounds*), before she was dragged kicking and screaming into the world of independent producing. As a producer, she co-produced and/or executive produced *One Special Victory* (NBC) starring John Larroquette, *The Companion* (USA/SYFY) directed by Gary Fleder, *I Know What You Did* (ABC) starring Rosanna Arquette, *Out Of Sync* (VH1) starring Gail O'Grady, and *Der Morder Meiner Mutter* (Sat.1/Studio Hamburg) for German television. She's had features set up at Warner Bros., Phoenix, and Ed Pressman, to name a few, and developed from scratch the film *Blind Trust*, which aired in 2007 on Lifetime television. Recently, she produced a series of movies for Lifetime based upon a book series she optioned, subtitled "Crimes of Fashion" by Ellen Byerrum. The first two books, *Killer Hair* and *Hostile Makeover*, aired on the Lifetime Movie Network in 2009. She's also produced and/or executive produced a few documentaries including the award-winning *Unforgettable* written and directed by Eric Williams (*Mad City, Out Of Sync*) and *Selling Sex In Heaven* directed by Canadian filmmaker Meredith Ralston, which won the Beyond Borders Award for documentary film, the juror's award at the Big Bear International Lake Film Festival, and aired on the Canadian Broadcasting Company (CBC). As a contributing writer to the *Beachwood Voice*, Edwards was also the newspaper's restaurant reviewer and feature writer.

Rona is also a lifestyle columnist for the *Los Feliz Ledger* and a contributing writer to *Produced By* magazine, the official magazine of the Producers Guild of America. In addition, her column, "Rona's Reel Take," appears in the New York quarterly newspaper, *The Neworld Review*, where she rants and raves about the film business. Edwards teaches screenwriting and visual storytelling at Chapman University's Dodge College of Film and Media Arts. More recently, she teaches creative producing at Chapman University in Singapore, splitting her time between there and Los Angeles.

EDWARDS & SKERBELIS

Together, Edwards and Skerbelis have taught "Introduction to Feature Film Development" for UCLA's Entertainment Studies Program (both on campus and online) for more than ten years, as well as "Story Development Process" at Riverside Community College's Open Campus online, and "Basic Fundamentals of Screenwriting" at Chapman University's Dodge College of Film and Media Arts. Their first book collaboration was the critically acclaimed book, *I Liked It, Didn't Love It: Screenplay Development From The Inside Out*, now in its 2nd edition. Edwards and Skerbelis are also the co-founders of ESE Film Workshops Online; global online classes that teach the ins and outs of the film industry. Classes include "Creating a Production Company," "Maneuvering Film Festivals," "Screenplay Development from the Inside Out," "Finding & Developing New Ideas," and "Basic Screenwriting from the Inside Out." *The Complete Filmmaker's Guide to Film Festivals: Your All-Access Pass to Launching Your Film on the Festival Circuit* is their second book collaboration.

You can contact them at:
Website: www.ESEFilmWorkshopsOnline.com
Twitter: @ESEFILM
Facebook: facebook.com/esefilm

SELLING YOUR STORY IN 60 SECONDS

THE GUARANTEED WAY TO GET YOUR SCREENPLAY OR NOVEL READ

MICHAEL HAUGE

Best-selling author Michael Hauge reveals:

- How to Design, Practice and Present the 60-Second Pitch
- The Cardinal Rule of Pitching
- The 10 Key Components of a Commercial Story
- The 8 Steps to a Powerful Pitch
- Targeting Your Buyers
- Securing Opportunities to Pitch
- Pitching Templates
- And much more, including "The Best Pitch I Ever Heard," an exclusive collection from major film executives

"Michael Hauge's principles and methods are so well argued that the mysteries of effective screenwriting can be understood — even by directors."
> – Phillip Noyce, Director, *Patriot Games, Clear and Present Danger, The Quiet American, Rabbit Proof Fence*

"... one of the few authentically good teachers out there. Every time I revisit my notes, I learn something new or reinforce something that I need to remember."
> – Jeff Arch, Screenwriter, *Sleepless in Seattle, Iron Will*

"Michael Hauge's method is magic — but unlike most magicians, he shows you how the trick is done."
> – William Link, Screenwriter & Co-Creator, *Columbo; Murder, She Wrote*

"By following the formula we learned in Michael Hauge's seminar, we got an agent, optioned our script, and now have a three picture deal at Disney."
> – Paul Hoppe and David Henry, Screenwriters

MICHAEL HAUGE, is the author of *Writing Screenplays That Sell*, now in its 30th printing, and has presented his seminars and lectures to more than 30,000 writers and filmmakers. He has coached hundreds of screenwriters and producers on their screenplays and pitches, and has consulted on projects for Warner Brothers, Disney, New Line, CBS, Lifetime, Julia Roberts, Jennifer Lopez, Kirsten Dunst, and Morgan Freeman.

$12.95 · 150 PAGES · ORDER NUMBER 64RLS · ISBN: 1932907203

THE SCRIPT-SELLNG GAME - 2ND ED.
A HOLLYWOOD INSIDER'S LOOK AT GETTING YOUR SCRIPT SOLD AND PRODUCED

KATHIE FONG YONEDA

The Script-Selling Game is about what they never taught you in film school. This is a look at screenwriting from the other side of the desk — from a buyer who wants to give writers the guidance and advice that will help them to not only elevate their craft but to also provide them with the down-in-the-trenches information of what is expected of them in the script selling marketplace.

It's like having a mentor in the business who answers your questions and provides you with not only valuable information, but real-life examples on how to maneuver your way through the Hollywood labyrinth. While the first edition focused mostly on film and television movies, the second edition includes a new chapter on animation and another on utilizing the Internet to market yourself and find new opportunities, plus an expansive section on submitting for television and cable.

"I've been writing screenplays for over 20 years. I thought I knew it all — until I read The Script-Selling Game. *The information in Kathie Fong Yoneda's fluid and fun book really enlightened me. It's an invaluable resource for any serious screenwriter."*

> — Michael Ajakwe Jr., Emmy-winning TV producer, *Talk Soup*; Executive Director of Los Angeles Web Series Festival (LAWEBFEST); and creator/writer/director of *Who...* and *Africabby* (AjakweTV.com)

"Kathie Fong Yoneda knows the business of show from every angle and she generously shares her truly comprehensive knowledge — her chapter on the Web and new media is what people need to know! She speaks with the authority of one who's been there, done that, and gone on to put it all down on paper. A true insider's view."

> — Ellen Sandler, former co-executive producer of *Everybody Loves Raymond* and author of *The TV Writer's Workbook*

KATHIE FONG YONEDA has worked in film and television for more than 30 years. She has held executive positions at Disney, Touchstone, Disney TV Animation, Paramount Pictures Television, and Island Pictures, specializing in development and story analysis of both live-action and animation projects. Kathie is an internationally known seminar leader on screenwriting and development and has conducted workshops in France, Germany, Austria, Spain, Ireland, Great Britain, Australia, Indonesia, Thailand, Singapore, and throughout the U.S. and Canada.

$19.95 · 248 PAGES · ORDER NUMBER 161RLS · ISBN 13: 9781932907919

THE MYTH OF MWP

In a dark time, a light bringer came along, leading the curious and the frustrated to clarity and empowerment. It took the well-guarded secrets out of the hands of the few and made them available to all. It spread a spirit of openness and creative freedom, and built a storehouse of knowledge dedicated to the betterment of the arts.

The essence of the Michael Wiese Productions (MWP) is empowering people who have the burning desire to express themselves creatively. We help them realize their dreams by putting the tools in their hands. We demystify the sometimes secretive worlds of screenwriting, directing, acting, producing, film financing, and other media crafts.

By doing so, we hope to bring forth a realization of 'conscious media' which we define as being positively charged, emphasizing hope and affirming positive values like trust, cooperation, self-empowerment, freedom, and love. Grounded in the deep roots of myth, it aims to be healing both for those who make the art and those who encounter it. It hopes to be transformative for people, opening doors to new possibilities and pulling back veils to reveal hidden worlds.

MWP has built a storehouse of knowledge unequaled in the world, for no other publisher has so many titles on the media arts. Please visit www.mwp.com where you will find many free resources and a 25% discount on our books. Sign up and become part of the wider creative community!

Onward and upward,

Michael Wiese
Publisher/Filmmaker